RESURRECTION

RESURRECTION

Salvaging the Battle Fleet at Pearl Harbor

Daniel Madsen

Naval Institute Press
Annapolis, Maryland

This book has been brought to publication
with the generous assistance of Edward S. and Joyce I. Miller.

Naval Institute Press
291 Wood Road
Annapolis, MD 21402

First Naval Institute Press paperback edition published in 2013.
ISBN: 978-1-59114-540-0

The Library of Congress has cataloged the hardcover edition as follows:
Madsen, Daniel
  Resurrection : salvaging the battle fleet at Pearl Harbor / Daniel Madsen.
      p. cm.
  Includes bibliographical references and index.
  ISBN 1-55750-488-1 (hard : alk. paper)
  1. Pearl Harbor (Hawaii), Attack on, 1941. 2. Damage control (Warships). I. Title.
D767.92 .M33 2003
940.54'25—dc21

                                                                              2002153479

♾ This paper meets the requirements of ANSI/NISO z39.48-1992 (Permanence of Paper).
Printed in the United States of America.

25 24 23 22 21   12 11 10 9 8

To my mom and dad

And to Radarman Second-Class George Schoen,
United States Navy, 1924–2001

CONTENTS

Acknowledgments

It is gratifying to publicly thank the people who helped bring this book to fruition. Paul Wilderson, executive editor at the Naval Institute Press, again gave me the chance to tell a story. The advice, questions, comments, and input of manuscript editor Mary Yates were most welcome and always helpful. The book is a better one because of her. Craig Triplett was the production editor at the press and was both knowledgeable and a pleasure to work with, as was photo editor Jennifer Till. Anne Boston designed the striking book jacket.

I am grateful to Dave Genereaux, who shared photographs and articles about his uncle, Emile Genereaux. Lebbeus Curtis VII also contributed a photograph and memories of his grandfather, Lebbeus Curtis V. Tom Gillette sent me helpful information about his father, Claude Gillette, as did Vice Adm. George P. Steele, USN (Ret.), about his father, James Steele. And I had a most pleasant visit with Norm Wallin as he shared memories, photographs, tapes, and documents about his father, Homer Wallin.

The staff at the National Archives was as helpful as always. Thanks to Kathy O'Connor, Lisa Miller, and Bob Glass in San Bruno, California; and Barry Zerby and Annette Williams in College Park, Maryland.

Ken Johnson at the Naval Historical Center provided the papers of Vice Adm. Homer N. Wallin, and Ed Finney researched photographs of the attack and salvage.

I'm also grateful to Susan Evans of the Society of Naval Architects and Marine Engineers for permission to use illustrations from the 1944 article in *Transactions* on the *Oklahoma* salvage. Thanks also to Helen Weltin of the Schenectady Museum Archives for information from *Men and Volts at War,* and to Mairi Decalvo of the Petaluma Library for tracking down volumes of the congressional hearings on the attack for my extended use at home.

I had the encouragement of friends every step of the way. Kari Holmes gave me a most interesting book on marine salvage, while Gary Delagnes read parts of the manuscript for me. To them, and to all of my friends, I say thank you. Your support meant more than you could know.

Acknowledgments

My thanks and love to my mom and dad and sister for their unending support. And to my brother Scott, who also read parts of the manuscript with a helpful eye for detail.

Finally, my thanks and love to my sons Robert and Matthew and to my wife Lorrinda, who once again kept me on track and always knew I could. The book would not have been possible without her.

Introduction

The attack on Pearl Harbor on 7 December 1941 was perhaps the defining moment of the past century for the United States. In less than two hours the country was transformed from a divided, isolationist nation still in the grip of the Great Depression into a single-minded juggernaut that developed the industrial, economic, and military might to lead the Allies to victory over the combined armed forces of Germany, Italy, and Japan.

More than six decades later, the subject of the Japanese sneak attack on Hawaii that December morning is still a seemingly inexhaustible source of debate, discussion, research, and interest. This book is concerned with one aspect of the Pearl Harbor saga: the aftermath of the attack and the salvage of the ships. Surprisingly little has been written about the salvage operation in book form. Captain (later Vice Admiral) Homer Wallin, in charge of the effort from early January to mid-July 1942, wrote an account more than twenty years later based on his official salvage report. There have been some memoirs that dealt with the aftermath. But in most works on Pearl Harbor the account of the salvage operation is little more than a postscript.

As important as it is to tell what this book is, it may be equally important to tell what it is not. It is not an examination of the events that led to the attack, or of the attack itself. That story has been told and told well. It is not a definitive summary of the damage inflicted. The salvage officers were less concerned with the number of torpedo and bomb hits than they were with the resulting damage, and then only as it pertained to the problem of salvage, so that subsequent damage analysis unknown to the salvage teams at the time has been avoided. It is not a technical report filled with weight and buoyancy calculations, engineering minutiae, and construction details.

The goal of the Salvage Organization formed in the days after the attack was simply stated in the first of the daily memoranda issued by its commanding officer: "to deliver ships and equipment to the Navy Yard for disposition." The goal of this book is equally simple: to tell that story. History is, after all, a series of stories. This book is one of them, that of the officers and men at Pearl Harbor trying to bring order out of chaos in the days after the attack; prioritizing the use of scarce equipment, supplies, and men; learning what they could about what had happened; and recovering from the blow. With the benefit of time it is easy to lose sight of the fact that the outcome of the war was far from a foregone conclusion in early 1942. The very real possibility existed that America could lose the war. It was against this backdrop that the salvage team got down to work getting the damaged fleet back into the fight.

RESURRECTION

Prologue

Saturday, 6 December 1941, was a typical late autumn day in Hawaii: sunny and breezy with high white clouds and bright blue skies. Pearl Harbor, on the island of Oahu, was the home port of the United States Pacific Fleet, and over one hundred warships and auxiliary vessels, along with scores of yard craft, barges, tugs, and derricks, crowded the small anchorage on this quiet eighteenth day before Christmas. The warm wind fluttered the Stars and Stripes on the ships and snapped the signal flags strung along the halyards. Small boats plied the waters carrying liberty parties and work crews to and from the ships.

The sloping hills surrounding the harbor were green with lush tropical vegetation and sugarcane fields, and the mountain range to the north was topped with the ubiquitous white and gray clouds. The harbor water was calm, the surface disturbed only by the wind and by the occasional small boat. The glare of the tropical midday sun was gradually replaced by the sharpened features and raised relief brought out by the late-afternoon light, and before long the setting sun cast long shadows, darkening the stately gray battlewagons tied up in the center of the harbor alongside Ford Island at Battleship Row. Eight of the Pacific Fleet's nine battleships were in port this weekend, one of them in dry dock.

Three had entered the harbor yesterday, the other five the Friday before. The procession of the Battle Line, or even a part of it, was an event worth a glance even from the seasoned old chiefs who were the backbone of the Navy. The dark gray shapes emerged from the narrow sea channel and swung to port, moving slowly in the confined harbor, wakes and bow waves rippling the water. One after another they entered the North Channel above Ford Island and steamed clockwise around the Naval Air Station, wisps of smoke from single or twin funnels blowing away in the stiff breeze. As they approached their assigned berths, tugs nosed into the port side of each one, easing them the last few yards to the quay or the hull of an inboard ship. Line handlers on deck and on the quays stood in small groups to gather in the thick moor-

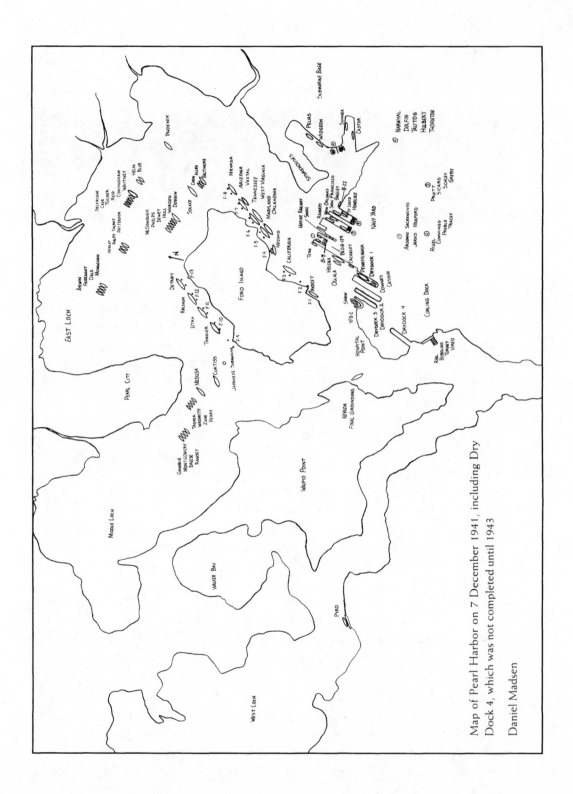

Map of Pearl Harbor on 7 December 1941, including Dry Dock 4, which was not completed until 1943

Daniel Madsen

(2)

ing ropes and wires. Anxious captains took in every detail, computing speed, distance, and wind and tide effects on the big ships as they were guided home. The battleships were painted dark gray to the tops of the funnels, with the upper portion of the tripod masts or symmetrical cage masts a light gray. The symmetry was soon to disappear; the cage mainmasts were to be removed; but for now they gleamed like pillars in the fading light.

Aboard ship, men went on watch or prepared to go ashore on liberty. Many wrote letters home, for since the relocation of the fleet from San Pedro, California, to Hawaii in May 1940, most had seen little of their families. Regular liberty had been granted to three-quarters of the officers and half of the men. It was a welcome break from their rigorous training for the war with Japan that most believed was only a matter of time. Some planned a quiet Saturday night aboard. The gun crews looked forward to the end of their watch, when they could go below deck and get some sleep, plan for Sunday-morning church services and a day at the beach. Officers prepared for upcoming inspections.

As night fell on the ships of the Pacific Fleet, nestled together at their anchorage under the protection of the Army's Hawaiian Detachment, another fleet was bearing down undetected on the Hawaiian Islands. Its purpose was to smash the American fleet in a surprise dawn raid, paving the way for a series of invasions on the other side of the Pacific.

ONE

8 December 1941

It was raining when dawn broke over Pearl Harbor on Monday, 8 December 1941. The fires that had been burning along Battleship Row for nearly twenty-four hours had prevented complete darkness from enveloping the harbor the previous night. The flames flickered and crackled in the warm Hawaiian air from the port side of the battleship *West Virginia* and from the forecastle of the battleship *Arizona* as they lay on the bottom in the shallow water, only their upper works above the waves. The *West Virginia* had been torn open by torpedoes, and the *Arizona* had been pounded by bombs until her forward magazines exploded with volcanic fury. The twin columns of smoke that churned skyward from these ships were just a part of the destruction that was being illuminated by the climbing tropical sun. All around the anchorage lay sunken, beached, capsized, and damaged ships, the aftermath of a stunningly successful Japanese aerial assault the previous morning.

Japan and the United States had been on a collision course throughout the 1930s, a course that continued to converge into 1940 and 1941. Japan lacked the natural resources that would enable it to become the great power its leaders envisioned as their destiny, and nationalists demanded the establishment of a Greater East Asia Co-Prosperity Sphere, a euphemism for Japanese hegemony over the resource-rich lands of China and Southeast Asia. The coal, oil, and rubber of Dutch Borneo and Java, the tin of British Malaya, and the rice paddies of French Indochina were the keys to empire. Expansionism at the expense of the Chinese and the European colonies was unacceptable to the United States and its allies, which had close economic, social, and political ties to the region.

Japan's desire to become a world power had not been damped by a punitive U.S. embargo on scrap metal and oil, or by the transfer of the Pacific Fleet from California to Hawaii as a demonstration of American resolve to halt Japanese aggression. While ambassadors spoke of peace and continued to pursue fruitless negotiations with the

Roosevelt administration, the government and military planned for war. The Imperial Navy would seize the sea lanes into Southeast Asia, brushing aside opposition from the weak American, British, and Dutch naval forces in the area, and land invasion forces with relative impunity in Malaya and the Dutch East Indies. Yet Japan's leaders knew that America would not stand idly by while Japanese forces ran rampant and that the Pacific Fleet would sortie from Pearl against the left flank of the advance. Success therefore depended on paralyzing the American navy at the outset. Adm. Isoruku Yamamoto, the commander in chief of the Combined Fleet, developed a plan daring in concept, requiring precise execution: cripple the Pacific Fleet at Pearl Harbor with a surprise attack at dawn on a Sunday morning, using carrier aircraft of the First Air Fleet to strike the blow.

Throughout late 1941 Yamamoto's forces trained for the attack while negotiations between Japan and the United States dragged on and relations worsened. There was no common ground for compromise. Japan was determined to fulfill its quest for empire at the expense of European powers hamstrung by war with Nazi Germany. America was equally determined that Japan would not. In late November a six-carrier task force set sail from the Kuriles in northern Japan and in silence transited the lonely, foggy northern Pacific, bound for Hawaii. The die was cast: Japan would make war on the United States, cripple its fleet, seize the land Japan needed for empire, then fortify and defend it.

Meanwhile, the United States Navy continued to train for the war few in the American military believed could be avoided but all hoped could be delayed while the fleet was strengthened. The Pacific Fleet commander, Adm. Husband E. Kimmel, divided his warships into three task forces and rotated them in and out of Pearl Harbor on an intensive training schedule. Task Force 1 was the main battle force and had six of the fleet's nine battleships assigned to it, along with the carrier *Saratoga* and a light cruiser division. Task Force 2 was a raiding force, with the carrier *Enterprise*, three battleships, and a heavy cruiser division. Task Force 3 was the landing force, the precursor of the great amphibious armadas to be formed a few years later. It had the fleet's third carrier, the *Lexington*, eight heavy cruisers, a minesweeping squadron, and attack transports to land the 2d Marine Division. These groups were complemented by the submarines of Task Force 7, the patrol planes of Task Force 9, and the vital oilers, tenders, and repair and supply ships of Task Force 4, the Base Force.

Task Forces 1, 2, and 3 operated out of Pearl Harbor according to the Employment Schedule, the fleet's quarterly training calendar. When not at sea, the ships returned to Hawaii for upkeep periods. This first weekend in December found most of the ships of Task Forces 1 and 2 in port, with Task Force 3 at sea for training. A provisional task force of cruisers, destroyers, and the *Enterprise* was returning from delivering fighters to Wake. Another force built around the *Lexington* was on the way to Midway and had been drawn from Task Force 3, the rest of which was now in the fleet training area to the south of Oahu.

While at Pearl the fleet was under the protection of the United States Army and Lt. Gen. Walter Short's Hawaiian Detachment. It was a logical arrangement, since the

Navy could hardly be expected to protect itself while in port for rest and refit. The Army's role on Oahu was to protect the fleet and its base from attack, though Short focused more on sabotage threats than attack by air. He was not alone in underestimating the threat to Oahu from the Japanese. The best naval intelligence estimates placed the likely initial attacks in the Far East.

So it came to be that on the first Sunday in December, while battleships, cruisers, destroyers, and auxiliaries lay in Pearl Harbor for upkeep, Japanese planes roared over Oahu. The raid was an overwhelming success. The Japanese had been prepared to be discovered, prepared to fight their way in to the target if necessary. But despite the fact that the incoming planes had been detected on radar, despite the fact that a midget submarine had been sunk by a destroyer off the harbor entrance a few hours before the attack, despite the heightened tensions in the Pacific and a vague war-warning message sent to the islands from Washington a week before, the Japanese had achieved complete surprise. Torpedo planes, dive and high-level bombers, and fighters converged on Kaneohe Naval Air Station, on the Army's Wheeler and Hickam Fields, on the Marine base at Ewa, and on Battleship Row, and had laid waste to them all.

The carriers of the First Air Fleet were now retiring to the west, though there were those who would say they had left the job half done. Repeated attacks could have been made against the repair shops and dry docks of the Navy Yard, against the fuel tank farm, against the ships already crippled in the harbor, to pummel them into

War begins in the Pacific as Japanese planes attack Pearl Harbor. The first torpedoes have already struck the *West Virginia* and *Oklahoma* along Battleship Row.
U.S. Naval Institute

Battleship Row on fire. Columns of smoke erupt from the *West Virginia* and *Arizona*. The hull of the capsized *Oklahoma* is visible outboard of the *Maryland*.
Naval Historical Center 80 G 32691

wrecks beyond repair. What the raiders left behind, however, was, in the minds of those who had endured it, a catastrophe of the first order.

Oil was everywhere, thick, black, and foul-smelling. It floated on the water, flowing down the channel to the sea, coating the shoreline along the way. It had come mainly from the ruptured fuel tanks of the battleships, by the tens of thousands of gallons. Some of it had caught fire and burned on the surface; most had simply gushed out of the torn sides of the big ships, bubbled to the surface, and floated away with the wind and the tide. The smell of it, mixed with smoke and gunpowder and burned flesh, was everywhere.

Small boats darted across the harbor all day on Monday, carrying ammunition and pumps and diving equipment. They dodged oil slicks and pieces of wood, life vests and mattresses, canvas awnings and clothing. Occasionally a boat could be seen stopped off Battleship Row, its crew struggling to retrieve a large, inert form from the water. Sometimes they merely attached a line to the object that bobbed in the oil and towed it slowly toward shore. More motionless shapes washed ashore on Ford Island or drifted uncollected down the channel with the tide. They were the bodies of American sailors and Marines who had been blown clear of their ships and floated until someone had a moment to retrieve them from the warm water.

The minesweeper *Tern* fights fires on the *West Virginia* on 7 December 1941.
U.S. Naval Institute

Many of the bodies had come from the *West Virginia*. The minesweeper *Tern*, small and unimposing, lay alongside the port side of the great battleship. The day before, the weather decks of the *West Virginia* would have towered over the little vessel. Now, on Monday, the situation had been reversed. The "Weevee" sat on the hard coral bottom, her hull filling with seawater. The *Tern* played streams of water onto her fires while the engines kept the minesweeper's stern pointed into the wind that blew down the channel. The *Tern* had joined a garbage lighter that had driven its bow into the smoke and fire on the water to get close enough to the stricken battleship to hose down the flames. The fires that had begun on, in, and around the *West Virginia* nearly twenty-four hours before would continue to burn until early Monday afternoon. The dark smoke that rose over her bow covered the conning tower and foremast with soot. The superstructure deck on her port side tilted steeply down, the supporting beams and bulkheads below mangled and unable to support the weight of the decks above (no one had yet pieced together the sequence of events, though it was believed that she had been hit by four torpedoes and a bomb).[1] The sailors who walked her decks— fighting fires, removing dead friends and parts of unidentified shipmates—occasionally looked around them, around the harbor, at a scene that in some way defied immediate understanding. Their ship was "uninhabitable," a "total loss, [so] wrecked and gutted by fire and flooded that repair appears impractical."[2]

After getting under way from Ten Ten Dock, the *Tern* had been alongside since 1050 Sunday, dousing the fires that burned on deck and in the water with five separate streams of water. By 1520 on the seventh, the weather decks of the battleship had cooled enough that the *Tern*'s crew could put hoses aboard to fight the fires in the casemates and below deck. When the fires aboard the *West Virginia* had finally been extinguished, at about 1400 on the eighth, the *Tern* moved aft to the *Arizona* to fight a blaze that would continue to burn for another twenty-four hours.

There was no doubt that the *Arizona* was wrecked, and little doubt that her captain and Adm. Isaac Kidd, the commander of Battleship Division 1, had died aboard her. Details of the exact nature of her damage were vague: possibly three bomb hits, a torpedo hit reported by the *Vestal*, a bomb seen to go down the stack. The forward part of the ship was completely obscured by smoke, as if it were no longer there. The Navy Yard's Planning Section was notified that she was "broken in half and burning. Completely submerged except for two after turrets and tripod mast. No job orders issued."[3] By "no job orders issued" the Navy Yard meant that there were no requests for work on the ship. There was nothing that could be done for her. By the afternoon of the seventh she had already been declared a total loss,[4] and by Monday the main concern was not the damage but the smoke still pouring from her. Not only was it "exceedingly unpleasant and unhealthy for the *Tennessee* with a certain degree of menace in it, but it constitutes a highly undesirable marker both day and night which would assist attacking planes."[5]

A few hundred yards down Battleship Row the crew of the *Maryland* were trying to stop the flooding caused by a bomb hit below the waterline at the bow. It had exploded within the ship and caused enough flooding to put her 5 feet down by the head. Another bomb had slammed into her forecastle deck but had done little damage. Her captain, D. C. Godwin, reported only four casualties, two dead and two wounded. She was the most lightly damaged of the battleships and was ready for a fight—if, that is, she could be maneuvered out from behind the hull of the capsized battleship *Oklahoma* next to her.

Tied to mooring quays on the opposite side of Ford Island from the battleships was the light cruiser *Raleigh*, her crew struggling to keep her from capsizing. She had been hit between the firerooms by a torpedo, flooding both compartments and the adjacent forward engine room, and a bomb had gone through her port side to explode on the harbor bottom. Despite the closure of all watertight doors and hatches with the setting of Condition Zed, many of them had apparently failed.[6] The *Raleigh* had listed immediately to port, and to keep her from capsizing, any and all removable weight, including her scout planes, had been lowered over the side or simply tossed overboard, the positions of the equipment being noted for later recovery. The stanchions, boat skids, life rafts, anchors, chains, gangways, and booms were cast off. Torpedoes, without warheads, were taken by boat to Ford Island. In all, about 60 tons of material were sent overboard. Oil-soaked bedding and clothing were taken off to reduce the fire hazard. Pontoons and a lighter that were alongside the old retired cruiser *Baltimore* were brought to the *Raleigh* and were tied to the port quarter by riggers from the shipyard, to act as a stabilizing outrigger. Four 2-inch steel hawsers were run completely around the barge and ship, then wire straps were run about the top and bottom wires

The capsized USS *Utah*. Just ahead is the *Raleigh*, with pontoons lashed to the port side to prevent her from rolling over.
Naval Historical Center NH 97401

between the ship and barge and cinched up tight.[7] She was low in the water, with barely any freeboard, and extremely unstable because of the amount of free surface water on her main deck. The tug *Sunnadin* was alongside and had passed pumping hoses to the stricken cruiser in an effort to rid her of some of that water. A significant shift in this weight from one side of the ship to the other, and she would roll over, just as the target and gunnery training ship *Utah* had done, astern of her.

The *Utah*, a former battleship launched two days before Christmas in 1909, belonged to the Base Force, the collection of repair ships, tankers, auxiliary vessels, tenders, and supply ships that kept the warships ready to fight. She had come into port late Friday afternoon, about a half-hour behind the *Sunnadin*. She was maneuvered to the quays on the north side of Ford Island, where she moored at berth Fox 11 (F-11). The *Utah* had been serving most recently as a target ship. The weapons she carried for training, the 5-inch dual-purpose and 1.1-inch machine guns, had been covered with steel sheds known as doghouses, and the .50-caliber machine guns were stowed below. Her weather decks were covered with a double layer of 6-by-12-inch timbers to shield her from practice bombs. On Saturday her crew had been busy untying those planks so that they could be removed when she went into the yard the following Monday for maintenance. Minutes after the attack began she became a target, along with the *Raleigh* and *Detroit* just ahead of her, of the torpedo bombers that came in low over Pearl City. Two torpedoes struck the *Utah*, and she rolled over almost immediately, timbers splashing into the water, mooring lines parting with a crack as her frail cage foremast disappeared under the water. Not all of her crew escaped; some were trapped below, and the *Raleigh*'s crew had cut one man out of the bottom. For now, the ship was still and silent, the only sound the floating timbers knocking against the hull.

A few hundred yards ahead of the funeral pyre that was now the *Arizona* was a claustrophobic nightmare of darkness, of death by drowning or asphyxiation: the upturned hull of the *Oklahoma*. She had been overwhelmed by a barrage of torpedoes and had capsized over 150 degrees to port, stopped only by her masts and superstructure hitting firm layers of sediment beneath the soft mud bottom at berth F-5.

No one knew precisely how many times she had been hit. Some survivors estimated three torpedoes striking within a minute and ten seconds. Others thought five, a few as many as seven, all hitting her portside between frames 25 and 120.[8] The first few had torn open her side, filling voids and fuel spaces with water and causing her to list rapidly to port. The final pair, it was thought, had struck on or above the armor belt as she listed 40 degrees, caving in her shell and sealing her fate.[9]

Exact details of the damage were sketchy. Most of the men who could have provided a look at the sequence of flooding below decks either had drowned or were about to drown in the pitch blackness of the ship's interior. Over four hundred of the

Lt. Cdr. William Hobby directs rescue operations on the *Oklahoma* on 8 December 1941. These men are cutting a hole near frame 22, one of four locations where survivors were thought to be located.
U.S. Naval Institute

crew were unaccounted for, most probably trapped inside, but some of them, at least, were still alive. Sailors and civilians from the Navy Yard were perched on top of the hull like birds, trying to cut them out, guided by the persistent and sometimes frantic tapping that signaled the presence of men who had made their way through the black upside-down maze of hatches and passageways to compartments nearer the bottom of the hull—men whose time was rapidly running out.

The rescue efforts had begun while Japanese planes still roared overhead. Lt. Cdr. William M. Hobby, the *Oklahoma*'s first lieutenant and damage control officer, was atop her hull by 0915 to coordinate the attempt to extricate as many men as possible. Some of the crew had survived the capsizing, swimming downward to the nearly inverted main deck, feeling their way along the deck until they reached the edge, and then frantically kicking their way to the oil-covered surface. One had reached the surface after emerging from a hatch just aft of turret 4, swimming across the deck and up the starboard side. He reported that men were alive in the area of frame 117. The trip was at the very limit of endurance.

Hobby was soon joined by Cdr. Edgar Kranzfelder, the Battle Force material officer. Kranzfelder had brought a set of *Oklahoma* plans and stayed just long enough to get an assessment of the situation from Hobby before heading to the *Maryland* to arrange for diving and cutting equipment to be sent. He was joined on the *Maryland* by Lt. Cdr. Herbert Pfingstang, the Navy Yard's hull planning officer, and together they discussed what would be needed. A *Maryland* boat was sent to the yard for air-driven cutters and drills and any pumps that could be spared. Crewmen ran a sound-powered phone line to the hull so that Hobby could be in touch with the Battle Fleet staff.

A boat from the *Rigel* was sent with an oxygen-acetylene torch, and one came from the *Solace* with medical personnel. The Submarine Base sent a diving boat and a diver to release a buoy into the hatch at frame 117, but there was no indication that anyone inside the ship saw it. The deck hatch was too small for the diver with his equipment, and he returned to the surface.

Hobby ordered men to tap on the hull and listen for replies, and soon four areas, at frames 22, 78, 116, and 131, had been pinpointed as having survivors somewhere nearby. Strainers were removed from the main injection and overboard discharge lines so that they could be used for entry into the hull, and the plans were studied for the best place to cut into the blister. But the oxygen-acetylene torches could not cut into an oil-laden fuel tank, and most of the ship's tanks were 95 percent full. Three initial entry locations were decided upon: one forward, one amidships, and one aft. The one amidships was burned through the ship's shell into a void, then into a feedwater tank and into a fireroom. Two men were trapped in the evaporator pump room nearby, and food and water were passed to them through a discharge line. At 2300 on Sunday a hole was finally burned into the pump room, where rescuers found to their horror that the two men, both machinist's mates, were dead. They had apparently been suffocated by fumes and by the torches using up their oxygen. The pair were carried topside and taken to the Naval Hospital, while Hobby and his crew debated how to proceed next.

Two hours later, as flames from the *West Virginia* and *Arizona* illuminated the scene, a barge from the shipyard came alongside the *Oklahoma* with air compressors, blowers, and pneumatic cutting tools. Throughout the night, yard civilians cut into the hull. A 2-foot-square hole was burned into the lower blister nearly abeam of turret 4 and from there into a feedwater tank. An adjoining void was entered via a manhole, then a hatch was removed to the emergency radio compartment, where six men were trapped. They were freed at 0800 Monday morning. Another hole was cut into the "Lucky Bag," the ship's clothing lost and found, and eleven more tired and frightened men were led topside. It had been a close call, for the compartment was far below the surface of the water and flooded rapidly as the air in it was released.

At about 1400 on Monday afternoon, five more men were freed from a 5-inch/.25 (5-inch .25-caliber gun) ammunition-handling room after a hole was cut into the adjoining shaft alley. Several hours later, seven more emerged from the steering room aft. The men in the radio room and the Lucky Bag had been in touch with them through Morse code, and the rescue teams used the same entry through the blister and feedwater tank. They moved aft, chipping a hole in an empty oil tank and then into the steering room. The water rose so fast that three pumps had to be used to keep the level down so that the chippers could continue, and the trapped men were in water up to their necks when the hole was finally cut to free them. Finally, at 0230 on the ninth, two more men were plucked from a linen storeroom near the forward air compressor compartment. How many more men waited for rescue in the silence and darkness no one knew. But there would be no more survivors.[10]

The activity aboard the *Oklahoma* was visible from the maintop of the Pacific Fleet flagship *Pennsylvania*. She shared Dry Dock 1 with the mangled wrecks that were the *Mahan*-class destroyers *Downes* and *Cassin*. Bombs, burning fuel, and exploding torpedo warheads and ammunition had punched both ships full of holes, demolished the topside of the *Downes*, and rolled the *Cassin* over so that her starboard side lay against the *Downes*. The flooded dock was full of wreckage. Ladders, scaffolding lumber, and oil coated the water. The *Pennsylvania* had been in the dock for repairs, and three of her four screws and tail shafts had been removed. A bomb had struck her on the superstructure deck, next to 5-inch/.25 antiaircraft gun 7, abreast of the motor launch. The bomb plunged through the deck and into the casemate of 5-inch/.51 broadside gun 9 one deck below and slightly aft. It bounced inboard, toward the galley, repelled by the heavy framing and stanchions that supported the gun, and exploded, riddling with splinters the galley and the crew spaces one deck down. The meat slicer, the dough mixer, and a pair of steam kettles were wrecked in the galley, and other fragments pierced the motor launch above and destroyed several life rafts. The fire that broke out was quickly extinguished.[11] Two officers and fourteen men had been killed by the bomb; another forty-eight were wounded. The dock had been flooded enough to lift the *Pennsylvania* off her keel blocks in case the caisson had been ruptured by a bomb or torpedo, but this precautionary step also meant that the repairs to the shaft bearings would be delayed. Nevertheless, repairs had already begun aboard to get her ready for sea, to get her into the fight.

Ten Ten Dock and the dry docks under attack. Nearest the camera is the *Oglala*. Just ahead of her is the *Helena*, and the smoke beyond the cruiser is coming from the *Cassin* and *Downes* in Dry Dock 1. The *Shaw* burns in YFD-2 to the right, and the beached *Nevada* can be seen at far right. Between Dry Dock 1 and YFD-2 is the incomplete Dry Dock 2.
U.S. Naval Institute

Along Ten Ten Dock, the flagship's normal berth, the crew of the light cruiser *Helena* was shoring bulkheads adjacent to where a torpedo had torn open her starboard side and killed about twenty men. Her feedwater had been contaminated, limiting her to 10 knots and about eight hours of steaming, and she had stayed tied to the dock. Early Sunday afternoon her commanding officer recommended that all boiler fires be extinguished so that repairs could be made to her propulsion plant.[12] Behind her, further down the dock, only a bit of hull, superstructure, and masts resting against the dock showed the location of the *Oglala*, a thirty-four-year-old minelayer and flagship of the Mine Force, now a derelict obstructing one of the most valuable piers in the harbor.

To the west, on the far side of the two dry docks still under construction and near the channel entrance, floated three-quarters of the destroyer *Shaw*, sister to the *Cassin* and *Downes*. Her bow was gone, torn loose by a magazine explosion, and lay at the bottom of the floating dry dock where she had been when the attack began. The dock itself rested on the bottom, listing heavily to port. It had been flooded and submerged to prevent severe damage to it, but even so had been peppered with holes before going down. What was left of the *Shaw* had stayed afloat, her watertight bulkheads holding for the present, her bridge structure reduced to melted metal. She had drifted partly out of the dock and over to the starboard side of it and was now lashed to what little of the dock's structure remained above water. Most of the *Shaw*'s depth charges had been removed Sunday, as well as the remains of her dead crewmen. Another forty or fifty of her crew had been sent over to the destroyer tender *Whitney* to be assigned to other ships, ships that could join the war.[13] They went without their records, since most of the ship's files and papers had been burned. Only a lonely watch of one officer and four men had remained aboard during the night, and in the morning a portable gasoline pump had been brought aboard. The destroyer was reported to be taking water in her number 2 fireroom.[14]

While crews struggled to keep their ships afloat or to put out fires, Americans all across the country were reading the latest accounts of the attack in their morning newspapers. Some accounts reported that the *Oklahoma* had been set afire, others that the *West Virginia* had been sunk. The *Lexington* was rumored to have been sent to the bottom. So was the *Pennsylvania*. Most newspapers carried maps of the Pacific, some of Hawaii and even Pearl Harbor itself. There were photographs of the fleet in peacetime maneuvers, and many papers carried a report from United Press's Francis McCarthy that the Pacific Fleet had steamed out of Pearl Harbor in strength and was engaging the Japanese fleet in a fierce gun battle off Oahu. The number of casualties continued to climb as each new edition of the newspapers hit the street. The War Department first announced that 104 servicemen had been killed and more than 300 wounded. By afternoon the White House was announcing the staggering news that the actual casualties were closer to three thousand, half of them fatalities. In countless restaurants, filling stations, office buildings, schools, and factories Americans read the stunning headlines on this Monday morning: "Japs Bomb U.S. Islands," "U.S. Declares War on Japan," "Japanese Open War on U.S. Fleets in Battle off Honolulu."[15] Most had heard the incredible news on the radio the day before. Now the public awaited each new edition, digested each new bit of information. For most, the news was difficult to grasp. There was nothing to relate it to in modern times, except perhaps the crash of the dirigible *Hindenburg*. The United States was at war, and the mighty United States Navy had been dealt a severe blow. It was fortunate that few in the country knew how bad it was.

At Waipio Point the battleship *Nevada* lay aground stern first. Her crew were still fighting fires, still trying to keep her afloat, still trying to clean up the damage done the day before. The ship had been flooding since a torpedo had opened up her port side between the two forward turrets. Bomb hits and near misses had burst seams and torn more holes in her bow. A losing battle was being fought to contain the spread of water and the fuel oil carried along with it into the interior of the ship. Actually, it was not much of a battle; it was, the war damage report would later state, a "losing fight against water spreading through boundaries and fittings which should have been watertight

Looking down the Pearl Harbor channel on 8 December 1941. The *Nevada* is at far right, beached on Waipio Point after first running aground at Hospital Point to the left.
NA 80 G 32504

but actually were not."[16] The *Nevada* was flooding slowly and inexorably, from bow to stern, and the water and its accompanying layer of oil rose deck by deck as the damage control parties retreated before it.

The single torpedo had hit at about 0810 between the second and first platform decks, about 15 feet below the waterline and 5 or 6 feet below the armor belt that was designed to protect her from the shallow-arcing shells of an enemy dreadnought. The torpedo defense of the old battleship consisted of a series of empty compartments, or voids, and adjacent fuel tanks surrounding most of the vessel next to and below the armor belt. These were supposed to absorb the impact of a torpedo, dissipating the explosion into those voids and fuel tanks while preventing the innermost bulkhead from being ruptured and flooding the interior of the ship.

The steel plating of the *Nevada*'s outer shell had burst open instantly, and water rushed into the exposed void spaces. The blast opened up the bulkheads to the first of the outer, or "wing," fuel tanks, and the bulkheads to the inner ring of fuel tanks gave way, too. In theory these three compartments and four bulkheads should have limited the damage to the outer layers of the ship, keeping the final bulkhead intact, beyond which lay the magazines, workshops, storerooms, and crew spaces. But they didn't.

An ordnance storeroom on the second platform deck directly in the path of the torpedo hit flooded immediately as the innermost bulkhead sprang leaks. The 5-inch powder magazine aft began to flood slowly, too. Above the storeroom on the first platform was a powder magazine for the 14-inch main battery guns. Here, several feet below the waterline, the innermost protective barrier was voids that rested atop the fuel tanks. Oil and water filled the void from the torn fuel tank below, and this mixture now began to enter the magazine. Again the inner skin of the ship had been pierced. Nor was that all. The first platform voids, and the smaller triangular voids just above them, were reached by manholes on the third deck above. The watertight covers to the manholes were either loose or had been sprung open by the hit, and the oil and water mixture spurted up through them. As the ship took on more water forward, the bow dipped lower and increased the water pressure being exerted against the leaking manholes. In the crew spaces between the turret barbettes along the centerline of the ship, oil was shooting up through the sounding tubes that led to the fuel tanks below. The caps to the tubes were sealed with gaskets, but they either had been damaged or were missing altogether.

So far, however, as the attack by torpedo and dive bombers continued unabated, the flooding was relatively minor. The steel "holding" bulkheads had been dished in about 2 feet in places, over an area of 400 square feet, and the gaps in the plating seams were several inches long. But the inner protective bulkheads had not been ruptured by the torpedo, instead having come apart at the seams. The ship heeled 5 degrees to port with the weight of the water flooding her, but by counterflooding several voids on the starboard side the *Nevada* was brought back upright. By now her bow was 3 feet lower in the water.

The battleship had had partial steam up before the attack, and by 0840 was backing away from her berth F-8. Once clear, she began moving slowly down Battleship Row, past the demolished *Arizona*, heading for the channel entrance. Then, by mistake, her after magazines were flooded. These were flooded by direct sea connections, rather than by more controllable sprinkler systems, and the magazines rapidly filled with water. The added weight brought her bow back out of the water several feet and sank her stern over 5 feet in a slow seesaw motion. She sailed past the burning ships on Battleship Row and was almost opposite the *California* when her situation changed rapidly and dramatically for the worse.

Orders were received from the signal tower not to leave the harbor, not to be caught in the narrow channel and sunk. The crew were preparing to drop anchor off Ten Ten Dock when the ship was pounced on by several flights of bombers, which scored a series of hits in a matter of minutes. At least three bombs hit her in the forecastle forward of turret 1. Another hit between the stack and superstructure, and a fifth exploded between the stack and the mainmast. Two of the forecastle hits opened more holes in her port and starboard bow. The real damage, though, was the fires they started, which began to burn out of control.

The *Nevada*'s forward magazine bulkheads grew hot from the forecastle fires, and the magazines were flooded as a precaution. This further increased her draft forward to more than 40 feet, and her keel was now skimming only a few feet above the bottom. More important, this put her second deck, and the exit hole made by one of the bombs, under water. The farther her hull dipped below the surface, the faster the water flooded in. Water flowed aft along the second deck and disappeared down drain and ventilation openings into the belly of the ship. With her anchor gear wrecked by the forecastle hits, she was run aground near the *Shaw* to keep her clear of the channel.[17]

The wind blew the *Nevada*'s stern out into the channel and in the way of other ships now trying to get clear of the harbor. When the magazines of the *Shaw* detonated, showering the *Nevada*'s deck with flaming debris, it was decided to get her out of the way by beaching her across the entrance channel. Tugs pushed her across, and her engines were backed at the last instant to run her aground stern first atop a coral ledge at about 1030.

All day Sunday, repair parties retreated in the face of the rising water on the third deck while water continued to flow beyond them on the second deck above. The watertight bulkhead just forward of turret 1 on the second deck had been blown out by one of the bomb hits, and water rushed past it and into the junior officers' messroom. It then flowed into warrant-officer country, surrounding the turret barbettes. When the water level rose high enough, it spilled over the 6-inch-high coamings of the ventilation trunks in the "bull ring," the area on the second deck that supplied air, through vents that reached up to the superstructure deck, to the dynamo rooms, the boiler rooms, and the forward part of the ship. The dynamo room now flooded and water backed up in the trunk, eventually as far up as the third deck. By this time, midafternoon Sunday, the crew spaces on the third deck, between and aft of the turrets, were under several feet of water. More water from the second deck, still pouring over the coamings and down the ventilation trunk, filled the trunk to the third-deck level and overflowed into the crew spaces through the ventilation openings, submerging the entire area. The damage control party abandoned the sloping deck, wading in the swirling water and dim emergency lighting all the way back to bulkhead 60 just forward of the stack uptakes.

By evening, the water was hip-deep on the *Nevada*'s second deck between the two forward turrets, and deep water extended as far back as the stack uptakes. The men on the third deck could hear the water pouring down the vent trunk in the bull ring above to flood the boiler rooms, while water cascaded down on top of them through leaks in the second deck. They continued their retreat, compartment by compartment, past the uptakes from the six boiler rooms below. The rising water was relentless. When the water had reached the air intakes in the bull ring on the second deck, the boilers began to be shut down as the water poured in.

Boilers 5 and 6, the two farthest aft and the last to flood, were the only two still supplying steam at midnight on Sunday, although they were beginning to salt up from contaminated feedwater.[18] They were still thought to be in good shape, but to reduce the load on the power, most of the interior lights and nearly all of the electricity were cut off at 0100 Monday morning. Only the antiaircraft batteries and some pumps were kept in operation. The number 5 boiler room flooded at daybreak, and so the entire engineering plant was secured. The weary firemen and water tenders climbed ladders out of the dark interior as the *Nevada* lay dead in the water, continuing to flood, continuing to sink.

Now, on Monday, the third deck had been abandoned entirely as the second-deck spaces continued to flood progressively aft. The printing office went under, then the issuing room, and by nightfall the repair crews were at the last holding bulkhead, at frame 115, just aft of the number 4 turret barbette. The bulkhead flange to this turret gave way under the pressure, and the second deck was given up as the last of the sailors retreated topside, surrendering the interior of the ship to the rising water and oil.

Some of the fires started by the bomb hits during the *Nevada*'s run for the sea continued to burn on Monday. They raged below the forecastle, on the main deck, and in the warrant officers' and junior officers' staterooms on the second deck, from the bow as far back as turret 1. The minesweepers *Rail* and *Turkey* were on either side of her bow hosing down the flames. Both had come alongside late Sunday afternoon after sweeping the waters outside the harbor for mines. The holes in the *Nevada*'s deck were covered with mattresses, and the *Turkey* ran a steam hose over to her in an effort to smother the fire. The rising water helped, but the flames continued to consume every-

The *Nevada* continues to burn at Waipio Point after the attack, despite assistance by the tug *Hoga* (foreground) and the seaplane tender *Avocet*.
Naval Historical Center 80 G 33020

thing in their path, fed by paint on the bulkhead walls, bedding, clothing, and papers in the officers' quarters. The upper deck was a mess of torn, buckled steel and splintered wood.

Through the smoke and steam on the forecastle could be seen what remained of the wardroom on the main deck below. Barely visible was another hole blasted into the main deck. As with the damage on the upper deck, the edges of this hole had been blown upward. An inspection by *Nevada* and yard officers on Monday revealed much more fire and bomb damage. The after section of the superstructure had been almost completely burned out. The chart house had been destroyed, the deck burned out of it. Below, all four compartments of the signal bridge had been burned completely out. The deckhouse on the signal bridge was demolished, signal flags and life jackets burned to a crisp. The decks of the signal bridge and chart house above contained brass to shield the magnetic compass from the steel, and the brass had disintegrated from the heat. Immediately below, the captain's bath, pantry, and cabin were gutted. The stack had been riddled with fragments from exploding antiaircraft ammunition that had cooked off in the fire.

A bomb had exploded on the roof of the galley, further showering the stack with fragments, damaging a nearby 5-inch/.25 antiaircraft gun and peppering the mast legs

Damage to the forecastle of the *Nevada*. Note the buckling of the deck caused by bombs and vapor explosions in this view taken on 12 December 1941.
Naval Historical Center NH 50104

and searchlight platform. The galley was wrecked, though fortunately the oil tanks that supplied the stoves and ovens had not caught fire. Just outboard of the galley, the casemate of 5-inch/.51 broadside gun 9 was in cinders, the ready bags of powder having been ignited by the blast.[19]

Flooding inside, burned and battered topside, the *Nevada* was a forlorn-looking ship on Monday afternoon. Only about three hundred of her crew were still aboard, the rest having been sent ashore to bring other ships to full war complement. Those who remained were divided into three watches and manned her antiaircraft battery. There were only 175 rounds of 5-inch ammunition left, but the ship was well supplied with .50-caliber machine-gun ammunition, and her gunners kept a close watch on the sky and the channel to the sea.[20] She was not completely on the steeply sloped bottom but soon would be. The water under her bow was 54 feet deep, and she was drawing 51 feet. Aft, the water just offshore was 15 feet deep, and the *Nevada* was drawing nearly 17 feet as her stern sank into the mud. A 20-ton derrick from the yard had been requested to assist the ship in laying stabilizing anchors astern.[21] Divers sounded the hull with hammers every 30 feet, searching for anyone caught in an unflooded compartment below the rising waterline. No one answered.[22]

Up the channel, another battlewagon was undergoing her own struggle to stay afloat. At berth F-3 in the small lagoon off Ford Island, the officers and men of the battleship *California* watched almost helplessly as their ship sank beneath them. A few thin

Surrounded by minesweepers, a submarine rescue ship, tugs, and floating derricks, the crew of the *California* struggle to keep their ship afloat on 8 December 1941.
U.S. Naval Institute

streams of water shooting over the side showed where pumps were trying to stay ahead of a rising tide inside her, but it was not enough, and the oil-covered water continued to climb up the sides of her hull.

Japanese torpedoes had punched holes in the *California* in two places on Sunday, just aft of turret 1 and slightly forward of turret 3. Many aboard thought that three torpedoes had struck the ship, one forward and two aft, just after dive bombers signaled the start of the war by pouncing on the seaplane ramp a short distance away on Ford Island.[23] Twenty minutes later the ship had been jolted again, whether by another torpedo or by a bomb no one was yet sure. Less than a half-hour after that she had been rocked by a bomb hit on her starboard side. The big ship was mortally wounded, her clipper bow low in the water. The heavy barrels of turrets 2 and 4 had been trained to starboard on Sunday to try to offset the list to port, which at one time had reached an alarming 16 degrees. Her stern had been blackened by fire, the paint scorched and peeling. Divers had gone down Sunday afternoon and reported two large holes, each 12 feet square.[24]

As the *California* wallowed with the gentle harbor swells this Monday morning, she was attended by a flotilla of smaller vessels that had come to her aid after the attack. The submarine rescue ship *Widgeon* had been alongside since 1125 Sunday, having steamed straight from the Submarine Base piers, and put divers over the side to look at the extent of the forward torpedo damage. A half-hour later the *Widgeon* was briefly joined by the seaplane tender *Avocet*. The tug *Nakomis* was already moored to the *California*'s starboard side, between the quays, trying to put out the fire caused by the bomb hit, and a fuel barge was alongside to port to pump out her undamaged fuel tanks.[25] Six hours later the minesweeper *Bobolink* tied up to *Widgeon*'s starboard side, ran hoses into the forward compartments of the *California*, and began pumping. The little ship had spent a busy day. At noon she had been ordered, with the *Turkey*, to sweep the harbor for mines. The orders were changed to have her sweep the approaches to Pearl and Honolulu Harbors, and she went alongside the coal docks to be outfitted with a wire that could be strung between her and the *Turkey*. Late in the afternoon she was then ordered back into the harbor, to Ten Ten Dock. The *Nevada* was to be her next stop, but before she left Ten Ten Dock she was told to proceed to the aid of the *California*. By 1740 she had pump hoses run over to the battleship. Less than fifteen minutes later the *Swan*, a seaplane tender, tied up to the *California*'s port quarter. She had been on the marine railway for upkeep when the attack started. The railway, a dry dock that could be pulled out of the water by chains with a ship cradled inside, was located in the Navy Yard. A yard tug, YT-130, tied up to her stern and pulled her clear of the dock, and she headed for F-3. Another minesweeper, the *Vireo*, moored portside to the *California*'s starboard quarter at about 2100 after shuttling ammunition from the West Loch ammunition depot. Throughout the night the four ships pumped water, starting and stopping frequently, and were joined in the middle of the night by the tug *Navajo*. They were still at it Monday when a few gasoline-driven centrifugal pumps were brought aboard. More pumps might have been able to stay even with the flooding, or even gain on it, but none were available. The fight to keep the *California* from sinking would be made with what was on hand while seawater continued to pour unabated into her hull.

As on the *Nevada*, the torpedo protection of the *California* consisted of a series of parallel compartments below the waterline, extending outboard from the innermost bulkhead that protected the interior of the ship. The *California*'s protective system was more extensive than that of the older ship. Next to the inner bulkhead was a 4½-foot-wide void. Then came three separate 3-foot-wide fuel tanks, abreast of each other, and an outer 4-foot void that was the shell of the hull. Altogether there were 17½ feet of empty space and fuel tanks between the skin of the ship and the interior.

The blast and shock wave of the forward torpedo had been easily absorbed by this defense. The shell and first bulkhead had ruptured, and the second bulkhead was deeply caved in, with two large holes punched through it. The third and fourth bulkheads were dished in by the impact but had held, while the fifth bulkhead, the last one, was nearly undamaged. The same situation existed at the torpedo hit aft, at frame 101. Oil gushed out, rose to the surface, and spread out in two widening pools as the ship took a list to port. Neither hit nor the combination was fatal or even particularly serious. The system had performed as designed, and the builders at the Mare Island Naval Shipyard two decades before had done their job well. "Workmanship . . . of the highest order," the *California*'s war damage report would say months later.

Unfortunately, the water did not stop once it had penetrated the first few layers of defense. As on the *Nevada*, the voids were reached below the waterline for maintenance and inspection by manholes atop them. On Sunday morning the voids were to have been inspected for possible leakage from the adjacent fuel tanks, which had been filled to 95 percent capacity when the ship was fueled.[26] The covers to five or six on the port side, and an equal number starboard, had been removed. As many as a dozen others had the securing nuts loosened.[27] The rectangular manholes, 15 inches wide and 23 inches long, were watertight when they were dogged down, which was precisely what should have occurred once Condition Zed was ordered. The crew managed to secure the ones on the starboard side, but there had been no time to reach those on the port side.

Two of the open manholes were in the brig, directly above the forward hit, and water and fuel oil shot up through the openings. The bulkheads to the cobbler shop next door had been lifted several inches off the deck by the blast, and that compartment flooded next. Similarly, the bulkhead between the cobbler shop and the clothing and small-stores compartment had also been lifted clear of the deck by the explosion, and within seconds that compartment swirled with rising water and noxious fuel oil. The third deck was 8 feet below the surface, rapidly filling with water, and the ship took a 6-degree list to port.

The crew berthing on the third deck behind the turrets and the passageways between and around them began to take water, probably through doors left open to the flooding compartments. Water and oil splashed in and around lockers and bedding and sent the few remaining crewmen there scrambling up ladders. The ammunition passage just inboard of the cobbler shop and aft of the crew spaces flooded, too. A pair of electrical storerooms forward of the brig also flooded as the water spread around the turret barbettes. There were several ventilation systems leading from the third deck to the first and second platforms below, and the water poured down them into the magazines, Central Station, and the plotting room. Within twenty minutes the main radio room on the first platform, underneath the crew space on the port side, was flooded and abandoned. The room was directly in the path of the torpedo, which had exploded some 18 feet away, yet it was undamaged, protected by the outboard voids and tanks as intended. Nevertheless, the interior of the ship had been compromised by the missing or sprung manhole covers, by open doorways and hatches, and by a lack of time to seal up the ship.

The situation was the same aft. The torpedo immediately flooded the outer voids and the first of the fuel tanks. There were loose manhole covers over those voids, and others may have been ruptured or severely distorted by the blast. Water burst through one cover like a fountain into the shipfitter and plumber shop. The fuel oil tank relay room, just forward, flooded from under the bulkhead between it and the shipfitter room. The innermost bulkhead, number 5, was fractured when the 8-inch fuel oil relay line, running through and perpendicular to it, was forced inward by the explosion. Open doorways from the shipfitter and plumber shop to the crew quarters surrounding the barbettes of turrets 3 and 4 led to those spaces flooding at once. As the California's war damage report put it, "The flooding of D-501-L [the after crew spaces] was as disastrous to the after portion of the California as was the flooding of A-518-L [the forward crew spaces] and A-509-T [the passageway around the barbettes of turrets 1 and 2] forward. Four large ventilation fans are located in this compartment and supply air for the first and second platforms and hold from bulkhead 103 aft. With many watertight fittings open [the] spread of liquid down must have been quite rapid."

The shortage of antiaircraft ammunition quickly became acute, and the turret crews as well as the 5-inch/.51 broadside gun crews were ordered to bring more up from the magazines. But flooding and oil fumes severely hampered their efforts.[28] Almost immediately after the torpedoes struck, the ship lost lights and power. Water, through broken fuel lines in the area of the hits, had gotten into the oil supplying the boilers, and the fires beneath them were going out. Steam pressure dropped, and the ship was plunged into near darkness below decks. Oil fumes choked the men trying to pass ammunition and seal hatches against the rising water in the gloom of inadequate auxiliary lights. The effort was soon abandoned, the men clambering up ladders to the second deck and to the daylight and fresh air of the weather decks. Below in the boiler room, crews fought to get steam pressure up, to get the generators going, to get electricity flowing back into the ship. They also sought to isolate the contaminated fuel source and find intact lines and tanks while the California's list increased.

The ship was soon rocked by another hit near the bow, which her crew assumed was either a fourth torpedo or a bomb. Compartments that had previously been dry were opened to the sea, the California's bow sank 3½ feet, and her list grew steeper. At about 0845 she was hit on the starboard side of her upper deck by a bomb that pierced the deck next to 5-inch/.51 gun 3 at frame 59, went through the main deck below, bounced inboard off the second deck, and exploded in the crew spaces. The bomb killed about fifty men, riddled the crew spaces with fragments, destroyed the junior officers' bunk room, and started a fire. The flames leaped up through the hole in the main deck above and spread forward and aft. There was no power for the fire mains, and even if there had been, the closest riser had been destroyed by the blast. Soon the forward engine room bulkheads were hot to the touch, and smoke was pouring in through the ventilation system. Worse, the fire and smoke severely hampered the effort to close off the second and third decks and slow the spread of water.

Despite the lack of lighting and the danger of being drowned, roasted alive, or asphyxiated by smoke, the *California*'s engine room crew restored power to her at 0855. The four after boilers were lit off with cold oil and natural draft, and this plant was isolated and ready to get the ship under way within a few minutes.[29] But it seemed folly to move in her condition. There was nowhere to go. The channel was too dangerous. Dry Dock 1 was occupied, Dry Dock 2 not yet completed. So she stayed where she was.

Throughout the morning the ship continued to settle at F-3. Lights came back on, and pressure on the fire main rose, but since the riser near the fire had been destroyed, the three plugs that could have battled the blaze were useless, and the fire raged on. To the northeast, thick black smoke had been erupting from Battleship Row for nearly an hour and forty-five minutes, and it was getting closer. The oil fire on the water was being blown down the channel, past the upturned *Oklahoma*, past the gasoline dock, toward the *California*. Just before 1000 the stern was engulfed in the burning oil, and within minutes came the order to abandon ship. The wind quickly shifted, blowing the fire clear, and by 1015 the crewmen were climbing back aboard. But they now boarded a dead ship. The engineering plant had been shut down and secured when the order to abandon ship was given. Hours later some consideration was given to relighting the boilers, though the free oil floating in the interior of the ship made this a risky proposition.[30]

The *California* received several visitors during the afternoon of the seventh. Lt. Cdr. Lebbeus Curtis V, a Naval Reserve salvage expert passing through Hawaii on his way to the Red Sea, came aboard to lend his advice. He had arrived in Hawaii on Saturday for what was supposed to be a short layover. Curtis had been in temporary charge of the San Diego salvage base since 1940 and had been ordered to assist the British at the port of Mesewa in Italian Eritrea (now Ethiopia), where the retreating Italians had sunk a number of ships at the harbor mouth to deny the British use of the port as a repair base for their Mediterranean Fleet. The attack at Pearl Harbor derailed those plans, and Curtis immediately went to work in Hawaii. The fleet paymaster and fleet disbursing officer came aboard too, to remove records and funds from the ship's safe, lest they be lost if the ship should capsize. And there were others who left the *California* too, starkly illustrating the ordeal she had gone through. These were dead sailors, most killed by the bomb hit. Dozens of others were missing.[31]

With the concurrence of the Battle Fleet material officer, Cdr. Homer Wallin, the

California's commanding officer had ordered some starboard voids counterflooded to limit her list to 4 degrees. During the afternoon, boilers 5 and 7, both of them on her starboard side as well, were flooded when the list reached a precarious 16 degrees. Altogether, nearly 1,800 tons of water was admitted to the ship's starboard side, more than the weight of the *Shaw* burning a short distance across the harbor. The fire continued to be fought and was extinguished primarily with carbon dioxide, to limit the amount of additional water taken aboard. It was out by nightfall, and the effort to keep the *California* afloat continued throughout the night. More pumping capacity was needed. Using the ship's bilge pumps and drainage system to aid in pumping was a possibility fraught with unknowns and risk. The speed of the flooding prevented many of the drain valves from being opened, and no one wanted oil-laden water in the fireroom bilges if the boilers were lit off. At any rate, steam for the bilge pumps was available only when the ship had power, and that was not often on 7 December. Finally, there was no firm knowledge of the extent of the damage and the rate of flooding below decks. Allowing water to drain to the bilge so that it could be pumped out could have the result of simply increasing the rate of flooding to the ship's interior.[32]

There was a very real possibility that the ship could capsize; one had only to look at what was left of the *Oklahoma* a few hundred yards away to see that. A pair of oil barges had joined the other ships alongside trying to pump the water out of her, but drastic measures might be called for if her list grew again to 15 degrees. Her boats and a rangefinder had already been removed by a floating crane from the yard. The ship's crew, still manning her antiaircraft battery, organized working parties prepared to cast the port 5-inch/.51 guns over the side if there was no other means immediately available to land them by barge or lighter. Another party, equipped with acetylene torches, was ready to cut loose the port crane. If the ship were in extremis, the crew were even prepared to cut off the mainmast at the base and topple it overboard, to lower her center of gravity and keep her from rolling over.[33] Throughout Sunday night and into this Monday dawn, work had continued to keep the *California* upright. And afloat.

TWO

Birth of the Salvage Organization

At dusk on Monday the *Enterprise* entered the Pearl Harbor channel. The crew's first sight of the disaster, as it would be for many crews in the months ahead, was the beached *Nevada* at Waipio Point. The Big E's escorts had sailed silently into the harbor that afternoon, the men lining the rails in disbelief. Aboard the cruiser *Northampton*, Rear Adm. Raymond Spruance, commander of Cruiser Division 5, was stunned and badly shaken by what he saw. Later, in tears, he would tell his wife and daughter of the sight that had greeted him as the *Northampton* passed Ford Island.[1] Pearl was not the intact base he had left on 28 November but a smoky, oil-soaked disarray of crippled ships and dead, dying, angry, and frightened men.

The *Enterprise* tied up at berth F-9 starboard side to the quays on the northwest side of Ford Island at 1743, and a few minutes later the ship went dark as the exterior lights were extinguished. Ahead were more disheartening sights: the hull of the *Utah* and beyond her the *Raleigh*. The *Raleigh* now listed to starboard, a result of counterflooding. A deep-draft target sled was tied up outboard of the *Enterprise* to shield her from torpedoes. There might well be another attack, or perhaps a submarine lurked in the harbor, waiting for a chance to fire on a survivor of the attack. A carrier missed the day before would make a perfect target now.

Just before 2100 the first camels came alongside the carrier with provisions and supplies, and the crew turned to with a will, storing the crates below. The Big E would not stay in port long; she was headed back to sea to shield Hawaii from further strikes. Only one boiler was in operation, supplying steam for electricity, but the others were on two hours' notice. About midnight the *Neosho* came alongside and spent the next three hours pumping 463,000 gallons of fuel oil and 61,000 gallons of gasoline aboard. By 0400 the tanker had pulled clear, and more boilers were cut in on the carrier's main steam line. At 0420 she was under way, clearing the last channel buoy ninety minutes later. The cruisers followed, the *Salt Lake City* bringing up the rear. The *Enterprise* turned east, sailing past Waikiki Beach, then cleared Diamond Head, her escorts taking station around her.[2] The sun came up, and the *Enterprise* headed off to war.

The United States was now at war for the second time in less than a generation. "Congress Declares War," declared the front page of the *Stamford Advocate*, while the *Indianapolis News* headlined its Monday-evening edition, "Congress Votes War." President Franklin Roosevelt had delivered an address that day to an emergency joint session of Congress that began, "Yesterday, December 7, 1941, a date which will live in infamy, the United States of America was suddenly and deliberately attacked by naval and air forces of the Empire of Japan," and ended with a request for a declaration of war for the "unprovoked and dastardly attack." The president enumerated the unfolding disasters in the Pacific: "Yesterday the Japanese government also launched an attack against Malaya. Last night Japanese forces attacked Hong Kong. Last night Japanese forces attacked Guam. Last night Japanese forces attacked the Philippine Islands. Last night the Japanese attacked Wake Island. This morning the Japanese attacked Midway Island." Roosevelt's speech exemplified the mood, the shock, and the pure undiluted anger that Americans felt. The attack, he said, had been "planned many days or even weeks ago. During the intervening time the Japanese Government deliberately sought to deceive the United States by false statements and expressions of hope for continued peace." He admitted that there had been "severe damage to American naval and military forces. Very many American lives have been lost." Later there would be recriminations as Americans realized how badly they had been caught off guard, how thoroughly they had been beaten. They would ask who was responsible, how it could have happened. But that lay in the future. For now, as the sun and the smoke rose higher in the Hawaiian sky, the needs of the ships, and of the sailors, soldiers, and Marines, were more immediate.

Back at Pearl, even as the roar of Japanese aircraft died away to the north on Sunday morning, naval officers afloat and ashore were taking stock of the situation. Reports flooded Kimmel's headquarters, the Fourteenth Naval District, and the shipyard of damage real and imagined and of the ability of the fleet to strike back. Commander Wallin, who had celebrated his forty-eighth birthday the day before at an outdoor movie with his wife and children, made a quick survey of the cruisers in the Navy Yard on the afternoon of the attack to determine how many were ready for sea. The *San Francisco*, he reported, was still immobile owing to yard work and would remain so for another two weeks. The *New Orleans* was already having some superficial splinter damage repaired, and the yard was preparing her for sea within a day on three shafts. The *Honolulu* had three 5-inch and two 6-inch magazines flooded by a near miss that had passed through the pier and exploded underwater next to her hull. But aside from being slightly down by the bow, she was otherwise undamaged, and the flooding, said Wallin, was under control. The *Helena* was in the worst shape. Unaware as yet of the torpedo hit, Wallin noted that she had been ruptured by a "near miss" and that she had lost all power, her main battery being operated by a diesel generator. She could not get under way, as the freshwater supply for the boilers had been salted up and the evaporators were inoperative.[3] Hours after the attack the *Helena* was given first priority into Dry Dock 2, just as soon as the dock could be readied to take her.

Earlier in the day Wallin had submitted another report, listing the damage to the battleships. The tally was disastrous but merely confirmed much of what was visible from shore. The *Arizona* was a "total wreck," the *West Virginia* "sunk almost up to the main deck and . . . burning," the *Oklahoma* "sunk by capsizing to port." The *California*, he reported, "has a list of about 10 degrees to port and there has been a serious fire amidships." The *Nevada* "is on the South side of the South Channel with her stern apparently beached. She has had a fire, which seems to be entirely extinguished except well forward under the forecastle. The ship is considerably down by the bow with about a 3 degree list to starboard." There were only two optimistic reports. The *Pennsylvania* "was hit on the boat deck aft on the starboard side, which did considerable superficial damage. Otherwise the *Pennsylvania* is undamaged." The *Tennessee* was "possibly down by the bow somewhat . . . [but] appears undamaged." Wallin also noted four of the other more obvious casualties. The *Cassin* and *Downes* he reported to be "total wrecks." The *Shaw* was "gutted by fire forward, but the after part of the vessel seems to be intact." Finally, he reported simply, "the *Oglala* was sunk at the Navy Yard dock, having capsized."[4]

Despite the disaster there were a few good things to note. Damage to the base was slight. The dry docks, except for the one that had sunk with the bow of the *Shaw*, were nearly undamaged. The marine railway was operational. The Navy Yard itself was still functioning, and the oil storage tanks had not been touched. The shops had not been hit. The cranes and floating derricks were still in service. The repair basin piers were usable, unscathed except for some minor damage caused by near misses, including the one to the *Honolulu*. Experienced and knowledgeable men were in good supply under the able leadership of the commanding officer, Capt. Claude Gillette. The repair ship *Medusa* and the destroyer tenders *Dobbin* and *Whitney* were undamaged, and already their crews were hard at work on some of the damaged ships. The shipyard's welders, caulkers, carpenters, electricians, and draftsmen were ready to service the fleet. They could not, however, afford to get bogged down in the stupefying job of raising out of the mud and salvaging five battleships, a target ship, and an old minelayer.

Late that night Wallin realized that he had neglected to mention several other ships that had been damaged. So at 0200 on Monday morning he quickly wrote out another report, listing the capsized *Utah* on the west side of Ford Island and detailing damage to the *Raleigh*, noting that a Submarine Base diver would try to patch the bomb hole in her side at daybreak. From far across the harbor at Aeia, the repair ship *Vestal* had not yet sent in a report to Wallin, but from what he could see she was down by the stern 5 or 6 feet and on an even keel. What he could not tell, from his vantage point through binoculars, was that she was aground.[5]

The sight of the ravaged battleships had taken a psychological toll on some of

Battleship Row on 8 December 1941. The fire on the *West Virginia* was finally put out on Monday afternoon, but the wreck of the *Arizona* continued to burn until Tuesday.
Naval Historical Center 80 G 32596

the officers and men trying to get on with the repair work at hand. Many were pessimistic about the fleet's chances for recovery. As Wallin later noted, "It seemed very doubtful whether any of the vessels which were sunk could be returned to effective service, or whether some of them could even be refloated."[6] Over half of the battleship force was out of action. Japanese bombers and fighters had not yet landed back aboard their carriers on Sunday when the fleet maintenance officer, Cdr. D. H. Clark, reported the condition of the *Oklahoma* and *Arizona* as "beyond repair." The *Nevada* was not much better: "Doubtful if can be floated. 18 months to repair if floated." The *West Virginia* was similarly "doubtful," with a time estimate of a year to eighteen months for repair.[7] Wallin's update of 9 December lumped the *Arizona* and *West Virginia* together: "So far as the ship proper is concerned," he wrote, "these vessels may be considered as total wrecks." He recommended stripping them of anything useful.[8]

While his officers were compiling summaries of the damage, Kimmel was sending his own messages to the chief of naval operations, Adm. Harold Stark. Before dawn on the eighth he requested that Stark "send earliest time salvage personnel and equipment plus large number mechanics and material, particularly structural steel and electrical wiring. More details later." It was obvious that the repair and salvage efforts would quickly overwhelm the resources of the yard, and there was the possibility of additional battle casualties arriving any time. The *Enterprise* and *Lexington* forces were still at sea, and no one knew where the Japanese carriers were.

By midmorning on the eighth, Kimmel was able to amplify his initial attack reports. He was receiving word of the havoc wreaked at the Army and Marine airfields and at the patrol plane base at Kaneohe: "First attacks were against aircraft on ground at Pearl, Ewa, Kaneohe, Hickam and Wheeler and were so effective that none of these aircraft were immediately available with the exception of 10 patrol planes which were in the air." Kimmel had been informed of the various times of the attacks and knew a well-executed plan when he saw one: "Enemy bombing and torpedoing very effective and despite magnificent and courageous work by gun crews not more than a dozen enemy planes shot down." His recitation of the losses suffered was brief but shattering: "*Arizona* blew up, most of her officers and men including Admiral Kidd lost. Floating dry dock sunk. Total estimate of personnel casualties about twenty-eight hundred, with one-half dead. About two hundred civilians in Honolulu killed in bombing of docking facilities." A natural mistake to make, yet in fact almost all of the civilians had been killed by falling American antiaircraft shells. The liability of a single channel entrance to the base was underscored by the beached *Nevada*, and Kimmel wrote with simple relief, "Pearl Channel is usable."

The damage done at Pearl was only part of Kimmel's concern as he continued his reports to Washington: "Oahu not raided today. Blackout being carried out. Two enemy cruisers attacked Midway by gunfire evening of the seventh." He was now reacting to the attack with the forces left to him: "Own forces are at sea to cut off enemy. . . . My efforts devoted to location and destruction of enemy forces and dispositions made with this in view."[9]

Three days later, on Friday, Kimmel sent a personal, "Dear Betty"[10] letter to Stark. The weight of the attack was bearing heavily on him: "Needless to say we have been up to ours ears in getting re-oriented; so much so that we have scarcely had time to feel the terrific shock." He was beginning to feel it, however: "No amount of explanation can alter the results which are included in a letter which I am sending along to you today, giving in such detail as is now possible, the damage sustained." He knew, even as he rallied his fleet, that an explanation would be required, even demanded. He had, as always, praise for the conduct of his men: "During the action it was magnificent and their efforts since have been untiring and effective." Those efforts, in large part, had been devoted to the repair and salvage of his ships.

Kimmel amplified his initial damage report with a formal message to Stark that same day, briefly listing the known damage to each ship. The *Downes* and *Arizona* were total losses, but for each of the other sunken ships, including the *Oklahoma* and *Utah*, he noted simply, "Recommendations regarding salvage and repairs to be made later." But it would be Adm. William S. Pye, not Kimmel, who was to note those recommendations on the twenty-first. Husband Kimmel had by that time been relieved of command of the Pacific Fleet.

Repair priorities were quickly established by the yard Planning and Production Offices, though these were subject to frequent change as Gillette's men established a triage of sorts for the ships. The Navy Yard was naturally focused on the ships that could be made ready for action in the shortest possible time. There were task forces at sea, and they needed to be reinforced. Those ships that could not be immediately helped were bypassed for the moment. The "Summary of Damage Reported to the Planning Section [of the Navy Yard]" on December 7 did not even mention the *Oklahoma* or the *West Virginia*.

The *Honolulu* was reported to be stable, in little danger of sinking, but had major electrical problems. The near miss had ruptured a magazine sea-flood, which then flooded the connected magazines. The train, hoists, blower, and lighting circuits to turret 1 were grounded; the power and lighting cables to turret 2 were also subject to frequent failure due to grounding.[11] As for the damage to the *Honolulu's* hull, it was too extensive to be repaired by divers. As soon as the *Pennsylvania* was removed from Dry Dock 1 the shipyard planned to place her on the blocks.

The *Maryland* was given second priority into Dry Dock 2 so that the hole in her bow could be patched. Though the Battle Force had been crippled, the lightly damaged *Tennessee*, *Pennsylvania*, and *Maryland* were nearly ready for action. In fact the *Maryland* stood the best chance of getting back into the fight first. She was boxed in by the hull of the *Oklahoma* and could be maneuvered clear, though it would be a "tick-

The *Shaw* floats above *YFD*-2 on Monday afternoon. The *Nevada* first ran aground to her right. NA 80 G 32503

lish proceeding requiring careful planning and preparation by Yard pilot and tug talent."[12] But for now, Gillette's men planned to repair her as much as possible at F-5. The damage reported by Capt. Fred Earle, the planning officer, listed a bomb hole 23 feet below the waterline on the port side at frame 8, split seams in the hull, and splinter holes. Divers measured the hole on Monday. Fortunately the bomb had detonated in a canvas and life-jacket storage area, which absorbed many of the fragments, but the 1,000 tons of water that flooded the ship through the holes and fractures and from the flooding of some of the forward magazines could not be pumped out because of hatches that had been sprung by the blast. Eight submersible pumps had already been burned out in the effort. Windows on the flag bridge and in the pilothouse had been shattered by the *Maryland*'s own gunfire. But aside from additional damage that a second bomb hit had caused on the forecastle and main decks, wrecking the anchor chains and destroying some main-deck wiring, the ship was undamaged though down 5 feet at the head. A portable caisson was being altered so that it would fit over the hole, to allow the flooded compartments to be pumped dry.[13] The Navy Yard sent out a party to sound the depth of the water around and forward of the *Maryland*, to assess the chances of her grounding when she was towed out.

The rapid completion of Dry Dock 2 would do much to ensure the speedy repair of ships with hull damage. Upon request, the chief draftsman of the district Public Works Department provided Captain Earle with the dimensions of the new dock and the depth of water when it was flooded. The dock was 975 feet long with 45 feet of water over the sill and 43 over the 4-foot blocks. A damaged ship could draw no more than about 42 feet to be able to clear the blocks.[14] Fortunately work on the dock was months ahead of schedule.

The possibility of more attacks heightened the tension and strained already raw nerves. A Japanese midget submarine had grounded a few hundred yards off the beach near Bellows Field on the eighth, and one of the two crewmen had managed to swim ashore and had been captured. Still another submarine had been fired on and probably sunk by the destroyer *Ward* in the morning hours before the first bombs had dropped on Ford Island. Another had fired torpedoes at the *St. Louis* as she emerged from the channel during the attack. And the destroyer *Monaghan* had rammed a sub in the North Channel at the height of the attack. It was assumed that she had been sunk, but no one knew for sure; there hadn't been time to investigate. The destroyer *Case* got under way at 1655 on Sunday afternoon and headed for the North Channel, past the *Raleigh* and *Utah*. When she came to the last known position of the *Monaghan*'s sub, the *Case* dropped depth charges, then hove to off the coal docks in the Pearl channel. At 1900 she commenced circling Ford Island, listening with sound gear for the presence of more submarines. She continued her vigil until just after midnight but reported no further underwater contacts.[15]

Divers were requested from the Base Force to make an inspection of the antitorpedo net in the channel to determine if it had been penetrated before or during the attack. If it had, more midget subs could slip into the harbor undetected. But divers were also needed to make hull inspections and were unavailable for a few days. The net extended about 35 feet below the surface and was intended to prevent a submarine from firing a torpedo up the narrow channel at a ship entering or leaving. There was a section of the channel directly under the main gate varying between 45 and 82 feet in depth that had been dredged for damaged and flooding ships. The net could not be extended to cover this area because the sloping bottom on either side of the damaged ship channel would prevent a deeper net from opening all of the way.[16] The concern was that a particularly daring and intrepid miniature-submarine commander might enter the harbor underneath the nets.[17]

The waters around the island seemed to be swarming with Japanese submarines, too. The Fourteenth Naval District Control Post watch officer's log recorded an enemy submarine reported off Haleiwa Point on the eighth and another off Kaena Point on the morning of the ninth. Later that day a destroyer was reported to be depth-charging a sub off Ahua Point.[18] The destroyer-minelayers *Ramsey, Breese, Gamble,* and *Montgomery* had been under way on offshore patrol since the attack and repeatedly dropped depth charges on sound contacts. Task Force 8 seemed to be trailed by the entire submarine fleet of the Imperial Japanese Navy. Between the eighth and eleventh, as the force shielded Oahu against a repetition of the raid, the *Enterprise*'s log recorded over twenty different sound contacts, submarine and periscope sightings, and torpedo wakes. Her escorting destroyers dropped depth charges on some contacts, and several times the *Salt Lake City* opened fire on a suspected surfaced sub.[19] In exasperation, Halsey sent this message to his jittery sailors: "If all the torpedo wakes reported are factual, Japanese submarines will soon have to return to base for a reload, and we will have nothing to fear. In addition, we are wasting too many depth charges on neutral fish. Take action accordingly."[20]

Back inside Pearl, target rafts were placed in front of the dry-dock caissons. They had been ordered there by Kimmel on Sunday night, one alongside the caisson and one about 100 feet out.[21] But the rafts drew only about 20 or 24 feet, and Pye recommended that half-inch steel plates be suspended beneath the rafts on wire ropes to extend the draft to 35 feet.[22] Another kind of torpedo shield made from interlocking sheet piling was placed in front of Dry Dock 2 and the incomplete Dry Dock 3. Local companies were asked for wire of sufficient strength to manufacture nets. In the meantime wire fencing was torn down, welded to reinforcing rods, and suspended below more target rafts.[23]

The *Oklahoma*'s captain, Howard Bode, and his executive officer, Cdr. Jesse L. Kenworthy, had been in charge of a small group of battleship survivors since the seventh. Bode used them at West Loch to replenish the ammunition of the ships in the harbor still capable of action. On Wednesday he was ordered to organize the defenses of the Pearl Harbor channels and lochs. He obtained small yachts and sampans for a harbor patrol and asked the Inner-Island Drydock Company and the Hawaiian Tuna Packers, among others, to convert the boats for patrol duty. These were reinforced with motor torpedo boats and a destroyer. Boats from the *Oklahoma, California,* and *West Virginia* were transferred to the Fourteenth Naval District to augment the harbor patrol. Bode's small improvised staff also implemented mine watch stations and instituted a regular sweep of the harbor for mines.[24]

Aircraft, not submarines, had caused the damage at Pearl, and the antiaircraft defenses were strengthened, too. Given the damage to the Hawaiian Air Force's fighters at Wheeler Field, even the battleships on the bottom were needed to contribute to Pearl Harbor's air defense. The *California* and *Nevada* were each directed to organize an antiaircraft defense group of 450 men per ship. With power provided from the shore or from attending salvage ships, these men would man the 5-inch/.25 antiaircraft batteries and machine guns. The *California*'s men were quartered in the *Maryland*, while the *Nevada*'s group went to the *Pennsylvania* for their food and bunks.[25] A test was ordered to determine if the 5-inch/.51 secondary batteries could be used effectively against the low-flying torpedo planes. If the tests proved successful, each gun was to be supplied with fifty rounds with the standard mechanical time fuses.[26]

Phantom submarine contacts were accompanied by phantom air raids over the jittery fleet, leading to the shooting down of *Enterprise* planes trying to make a Sunday-night landing on Ford Island. Early the next morning the *Antares* signal log recorded a message about thirty enemy planes headed for Honolulu from Kauai, then another reporting that enemy planes were south of Wheeler Field. More planes were reported over Honolulu, and at 0547 the *Antares* recorded, "Anti-aircraft firing at Pearl Harbor. Appears as if P.H. is being bombed." The signal log also recorded the half-plea, half-order from Commander, Battleships, to "exercise more control over anti-aircraft fire."[27] Ewa Field had to be specifically commanded not to fire on any seaplanes. At 2314 on the eighth the Fourteenth Naval District log recorded "many planes coming fast SW of Kauai" and, at 0600 on the ninth, "seven sea planes and one land plane over Molokai."[28] But without exception the planes being tracked were either nonexistent or American. ComBatShips would later organize a school for the *Tennessee, Maryland,* and *Pennsylvania* crews on the identification of enemy aircraft. In time the jittery gunners around Pearl would ease up on the triggers as the men realized that for the time being, the Japanese were gone. But for now Pearl Harbor was a fortress under siege.

Siege or not, repair and salvage work notwithstanding, administrative duties continued aboard the ships. Rear Adm. Walter Anderson, Commander, Battleships, needed information from the *Nevada, California, West Virginia,* and *Oklahoma* survivors on the cause of the flooding—specifically, whether the machinery spaces had been flooded by the force of explosions and failure of bulkheads or by water entering through ventilation ducts, hatches, and piping. Action reports were due from each ship in the harbor in accordance with naval regulations and with a dispatch from Kimmel requesting information from the fleet on the action of 7 December. Some commanding officers sent theirs off almost immediately. The seaplane tender *Hulbert*'s report was written on Monday. So was the *Ontario*'s. The captain of the *Breese* wrote his on the ninth while on patrol off Oahu. More came to Kimmel's headquarters as the week wore on. The *Pyro* and *Vireo* reports arrived on the tenth, the *Pelias, West Virginia, Tennessee, Phoenix,* and *Vestal* reports on the eleventh. Many, like the *Avocet*'s, carried the simple heading

"Offensive Measures Taken during December 7, Report Of." The *Ramapo's* was a sober "Report of Japanese Raid of December 7, 1941," while Capt. R. B. Simons of the *Raleigh* jauntily headed his, "Report of U.S.S. *Raleigh's* Participation in the Battle of Pearl Harbor, December 7, 1941."

The reports varied in length and substance. The *Phoenix* report was a dry three sentences with an added chronology. The *Helena's* was lengthy and detailed, with sections on offensive measures, engineering, gunnery, damage control, repairs, casualties, and even lessons learned. "There is no reluctance of personnel to the use of steel helmets since they have once been under fire," reported her captain. The *Medusa* included a print of the harbor, with her position and that of "sunken submarines and destroyed planes" clearly marked. Capt. Joel Bunkley's report of the *California's* action attempted to trace the progress of her flooding, and there was a bit of confusion on the *Curtiss,* whose commander misidentified the nearby *Detroit* as the *Richmond.*

Commanding officers were universal in praising their crews. Capt. Daniel Callaghan of the *San Francisco* wrote, "No member of this command can be singled out for commendation; the performance of all hands was in keeping with the best traditions." The skipper of the *Phelps* was less formal: "The conduct of all hands was exemplary and deserving of the highest praise. Their initiative, willingness and coolness under fire were remarkable. No important item was left undone and every evolution required of them was accomplished smartly and enthusiastically." Many commanding officers singled out men for special praise, but Cassin Young of the *Vestal* gave perhaps the highest accolade: "The conduct of all officers and enlisted personnel was exemplary and of such high order that I would especially desire to have them with me in future engagements."[29]

One commander recommended the award of no fewer than eight Navy Crosses (seven posthumously) in his report dated 15 December. He no longer had a ship to command and had been given another job, one for which he had little preparation or training. He was Cdr. James M. Steele of the *Utah,* who had taken over the newly formed Base Force Salvage Organization the previous day. Steele was now in charge of getting the sunken ships off the bottom of Pearl Harbor.

James Mortimer Steele was a forty-six-year-old former submariner who had served in the Navy since his graduation from Annapolis in 1916. He had commanded the submarines R-6 and S-6, had served as the navigator of the *Nevada,* and had commanded the oiler *Brazos.* Before being ordered to take command of the *Utah* in July he had been on the staff of the Naval War College. He now found himself tasked with the creation of a new organization saddled with the enormous salvage job that lay ahead.

One of the many dilemmas facing the shipyard and the Fourteenth Naval District was the absence of a salvage infrastructure. The yard was not a salvage unit but a repair and maintenance facility. Vessels were delivered there for overhaul and renewal of damage. But the five battleships and the minelayer on the bottom were not within easy reach of its shops, cranes, and dry docks. The *Tennessee* was still trapped behind the *West Virginia* at berth F-6. The *Raleigh's* pumps were staying ahead of the leaks, and by

James Steele is awarded the Legion of Merit by Admiral Nimitz for his work organizing the Salvage Organization in the weeks following the attack. This photograph was taken on 8 January 1944. Within days Steele would take command of the battleship *Indiana*.
NA 80 G 207864

the fifteenth, reinforced concrete patches had been placed over the holes, but a long, precarious tow around Ford Island awaited her. A further complication was the salvage job facing the Navy Yard itself. The floating dry dock was vital to its success, yet it too was on the bottom, with part of a destroyer and a much-needed harbor tug resting on the dock floor. The rest of the *Shaw* was afloat, but she too needed a tow to a pier if the bulkheads held, or to a dry dock if they appeared on the verge of giving way.

What was needed was an organization built from scratch that could coordinate the myriad tasks necessary for salvage. Such an organization would spare the Navy Yard that daunting job so that it could get on with the task of keeping the fleet in the war from that vital forward base. The alternative was a long, time-consuming voyage back to the mainland yards at Puget Sound or San Francisco.

Adm. William Calhoun's Base Force was the logical choice for that duty. The Base Force tenders and repair ships carried out repairs and maintenance to the fleet when it operated away from port, and just as often those ships supplemented the yard. Navy Yard Pearl would be in operational, but not administrative, control of the Base Force Salvage Organization. It would issue the job orders outlining the work to be done. These orders would then go to the Base Force and thence to the Salvage Organization for completion. Steele would note, "It has been tentatively agreed to that the Base Force Salvage Organization will be considered, for the time being, an outside force of the Navy Yard, Pearl Harbor. Roughly, the organization will be something like that of the Production setup in the Yard."[30] In other words, the Base Force Salvage Organization would be another repair arm of the shipyard.

The Salvage Organization was a temporary means to an end. "A function of the Salvage Organization," Steele wrote on the fourteenth, "is to deliver ships and equipment to the Navy Yard for disposition. This is a guiding principle and must be thoroughly understood by all concerned."[31] There was, in other words, no other goal, no other mission for the force but to deliver the ships a few hundred yards across the oil-streaked water to the Navy Yard. The Salvage Organization was not to repair the ships in place, and work was to be confined to what was necessary to getting the ships off the mud and into dry dock.

Within days of the attack the tally of the missing, wounded, and dead was becoming clear, and it was massive. The heavy loss of life on the *Arizona* and *Oklahoma* was readily apparent, though accurate numbers were still not available. The casualty figures continued to climb, and ships were requested to provide the names of survivors they had aboard. Bodies were surfacing along Battleship Row, in the South Channel, and off Ten Ten Dock. Many were unrecognizable, missing limbs or heads. They had been blown overboard during the raid and had glided silently to the bottom, decomposition forcing them to the surface by midweek. Boats continued to tow the bodies ashore in what had become an all-too-familiar sight in the harbor. Most were so badly burned that they could not be identified. Bulldozers hastily prepared mass graves adjacent to the Navy Yard.

Within hours after the attack, the work of identifying bodies in the Naval Hospital morgue had begun. Clothing could sometimes be used for identification, but it was not a reliable means; the suddenness of the attack meant that many individuals had grabbed whatever clothes were handy. Fingerprints were taken where fingers remained. Each corpse was given a serial number for use on the casket, the grave marker, and the inevitable forms to be filled out. Plain wooden caskets by the hundreds were brought in. Officers who had been identified were buried in standard

Navy-issue caskets so that they could be later disinterred and reburied on the mainland if the family so requested.[32] Over three hundred dead had been brought to the Naval Hospital on Sunday, and burials began the next day at Oahu cemetery. That cemetery quickly filled, and another twenty-five acres were prepared at Halawa. Over the next twenty-two days, 532 service personnel were buried at those two cemeteries and another 18 over at Kaneohe Bay.[33]

The dead came from ships all over the harbor and from the Navy Yard and Ford Island, too. But the heaviest losses had occurred along Battleship Row. On 1 December the muster rolls of the Battle Line had totaled 766 officers and 11,334 enlisted men. By the nineteenth, nearly one-fifth of them had become casualties, with the list of missing eight times longer than the list of confirmed dead. Fourteen officers and 200 enlisted men had been listed as killed in action, 16 officers and 363 men were wounded, and 70 officers and 1,655 men were unaccounted for. The reports were continuously revised. On the thirteenth Captain Bunkley of the *California* reported an estimated 125 enlisted men killed and another 100 wounded, with 116 missing.[34] Nine days later the number had been lowered to 48 confirmed killed, with 58 wounded. Men had continued to check in to the receiving station and the temporary *California* assembly area on Ford Island, with the result that the number of missing had been reduced to 45.[35]

Of the total number of missing from the Battle Fleet, most were *Arizona* crew, 1,106 officers and men. Another 436 *Oklahoma* sailors and Marines were also officially unaccounted for, their presumed tomb just visible above the waves. Men who had escaped had reported about 125 men trapped on the third deck alone. Hobby had continued cutting into the hull where it was thought air pockets might contain survivors, but without success. At one point voices were heard near frame 70 and tapping at frame 76. More holes were cut into the hull, but no one was found. At 0900 on 11 December the *Oklahoma*'s first lieutenant reluctantly called off the search.[36]

For a few days tapping from within the *Arizona* was reported. One hundred thirty *West Virginia* men were missing too, and some believed they heard tapping coming from her hull. But it was hard to be certain. It ceased, at any rate, within a few days after the attack.[37]

Divers continued to sound the hulls of the submerged ships. It was a backbreaking job, particularly for the line handlers on deck. Each diver was lowered by rope 20 feet below the surface, where he pounded three times on the bow with a hammer. Moving 25 feet aft, he repeated the process, listening carefully, barely breathing, for a response. At the stern, the diver was lowered to the mud line, and the entire length of the hull was sounded again.[38] Then the procedure was repeated on the other side— except for the *West Virginia*. Several hundred feet of her starboard shell were wedged tight against the *Tennessee*, and no sounding was possible there when she was examined on the twelfth. Unknown to the divers—unknown to anyone—far below the surface, in a pair of unflooded compartments, *West Virginia* sailors still lived. Clad in blues, one group of three men in a storeroom had battle lanterns, rations, a small pocket calendar, and access to a freshwater tank nearby. A few others climbed on top of cold steam pipes in the after engine room, where there was a small air pocket. While men from the *Oklahoma* and *Utah* were being rescued, these *West Virginia* sailors waited. Surely they would turn up missing. Surely there would be a search for them. Surely it would be only a matter of hours, maybe days, until rescue came. They kept track of the time with a watch, marking the passing of days on the calendar: 8 December, 9 December, 10 December. And so they waited.

As the dead were buried and the wounded tended, the survivors of the sunken ships also had to be cared for. They came to the receiving station, they swam to Ford Island, they boarded other ships to carry on the fight. All had to be fed and quartered and their papers retrieved, if possible, while the Navy decided how best to utilize them. Pay was given to men whose records had been lost with their ships, but only from the seventh on. Back pay was not yet authorized, and the men had to sign sworn certificates stating which ship or activity had last carried their account, and any allottees carried. Not counting those men retained by a few battleships for antiaircraft defense or salvage work, there were thousands of sailors and scores of Marines to assist. There were places for them all. Many ships needed replacements for casualties or reinforcement to bring them to wartime strength.

Three-quarters of the *Oglala* crew were almost immediately pooled out to different ships. The *Pennsylvania* and *Helena* each received reinforcement for their antiaircraft crews and repair parties. The *Tennessee* received forty-five *Oglala* men to help fight her persistent fires. Another thirty went to sea on the destroyer *Mugford*. Seventy-five more went to the Naval Ammunition Depot to break out and distribute ammunition under Captain Bode. Many survivors of the *California*, having spent 8 December removing the bodies of dead shipmates, went to the cruiser *Astoria* when she returned to Pearl. Their place on the *California* was taken by *Oklahoma* men who loaded the last of the recovered bodies on boats for the journey ashore. The *California's* band was sent en masse to the fleet Communication Intelligence Unit for training.[39] Over five dozen *Utah* men went to the *Honolulu*, five dozen more to the *Detroit*. Thirty-six were assigned to the gunboat *Sacramento*. Others went to the *San Francisco*, to the *St. Louis*, to the *Maryland*.[40]

The Salvage Organization began work on Tuesday, 9 December, and officially came into existence on the Sunday following the attack, a Sunday that saw yet another false submarine alarm within the harbor. The new group was given an office near Building 129, close to the marine railway, in a small contractors' shack between Ten Ten Dock and the repair basin. A telephone was installed and an officer placed on watch twenty-four hours a day. This shack was the conduit through which all contact between the new organization and the Navy Yard was made. It had taken less than a week to assemble and organize a rudimentary group of officers to undertake the daunting job that lay ahead. The men were assembled from the Base Force (mainly the *Utah*), from the Navy Yard, and from the Fourteenth Naval District. A few others were brought in from the Eleventh Naval District in San Diego, but experienced salvage officers were few and far between. There was as yet no school of salvage engineers from which the Base Force could draw men familiar with the work ahead. There had been salvage training in the Navy for years, and many successful salvage efforts attested to the skill of the officers and civilians who had undertaken those jobs. But there was no formal course in salvage. A school was being formed, and in fact there were sixty prospective students in San Francisco at the time of the attack waiting to hear where their school was to open. These men were immediately sent to the new organization.[41]

In overall command was Commander Steele, who reported to Admiral Calhoun, the Base Force commander. Nine departments eventually reported to the former *Utah* commanding officer. The Ship Salvage Section was under Lieutenant Commander Curtis, the senior salvage engineer. His mission was straightforward: "Raise damaged ships in 14th N.D. and deliver to Navy Yard." Assisting him were a pair of officers from the Base Force staff, Lt. Cdr. Rufus Thayer and Lt. Cdr. James Rodgers; a pair of lieutenants on loan from the Eleventh Naval District; and two warrant officers, Carpenter W. A. Mahan, also from San Diego, and Chief Turret Captain Garland Suggs, a master diver.

The Services and BuShips Material Section was under Lt. Cdr. Solomon Isquith, also of the *Utah*. He had been her engineer and the senior officer aboard during the attack. It was he who had directed the men to abandon ship when she was about to capsize, and who later returned to the ship to direct rescue efforts. He led another ten *Utah* officers distributing equipment, material, barges, pumps, and cranes as well as maintaining the watch in the Salvage Office. The Ordnance Section was led by the *Utah*'s gunnery officer, Lt. Cdr. F. C. Stelter Jr., with five others from the ship. They would be in charge of removing guns and fire control equipment from the vessels and preserving them for future use. Salvage of ammunition was to be the charge of Lt. Cdr. Edward E. Berthold, gunnery officer of the *West Virginia*, with another officer, Gunner Roman S. Manthei, assisting him. Manthei was young but was held in high regard by Berthold for the knowledge and sound judgment he had displayed in the five months they had worked together aboard the battleship.[42] Personnel, including the office force of civilian stenographers and Navy yeomen, was under Lt. Hal C. Jones, the senior watch officer aboard the *Utah*. Jones was due for retirement on 30 June 1942, but in the meantime it was his office that would coordinate the massive job of assembling working parties. He would also have to find transportation and housing for the salvage force. There was a Diving Section, which would be crucial to the success of the jobs ahead, under the command of Lt. Cdr. J. L. DeTar, with Lt. Howard E. "Pappy" Haynes as diving officer. Haynes had been recalled from retirement to active duty in June 1940. A Salvage Stores Section was established under Lt. Emile C. Genereaux, who had just arrived from the Eleventh Naval District. He would procure and distribute the special salvage equipment that would be requested and keep an accurate accounting of it. Lt. Wilfred L. Painter, who had reported to the *Argonne* on the eighteenth, led the Public Works Section of the Base Force. He would coordinate construction activity with the Fourteenth Naval District's Public Works and with the civilian contractors on the base. Those contractors were represented on the organizational

Lt. Cdr. Lebbeus Curtis V
Lebbeus Curtis VII

tables by Dillingham Construction and by the Pacific Bridge Company, a heavy-engineering contractor now at work on Dry Docks 2, 3, and 4. Finally, there were two more repair outfits from San Diego under the command of Lt. Cdr. K. F. Horne. Known variously as the Mobile Repair Unit, Mobile Salvage and Repair Unit 1, and the Pearl Harbor Repair and Salvage Unit, these were formally called Advance Destroyer Base 1 and Destroyer Repair Unit 2, each made up of a dozen officers and five hundred enlisted men.[43] A few men from the units, mostly divers, had arrived right after the attack; the remainder shipped out on the liner *Lurline*, which arrived in Hawaii on 20 December. Horne's Mobile Repair Unit was actually under the Fourteenth Naval District rather than the Base Force but was available for any work that Steele's men needed.

On 10 December the yard succeeded in docking the *Helena*. She had been badly hurt by the single torpedo and was extensively flooded, but on 7 December there had been no place to put her: Dry Dock 1 was full, and Dry Dock 2 was incomplete. Yet within days Dry Dock 2 had been readied to take its first customer. Tugs eased the *Helena* away from Ten Ten Dock on Wednesday and placed her safely inside the drydock, lest another air raid reduce her from a repair job to a salvage effort off Ten Ten Dock. It took a frustratingly long time to pump the dock and land the ship on the blocks,

The hull of the *Oglala* can just be seen astern of the crippled *Helena* along Ten Ten Dock on 8 December 1941. The Navy Yard repair basin is just beyond.
NA 80 G 325002-6

since the standard pumps had not yet been installed and only small pumps could be used. A suction dredge was moved into position to take over the pumping so that in the future it could be emptied in only five hours.[44] While the ship was in the drydock the concrete floor would be poured, so that carriers could dock once the *Helena* was removed.

The oil coating the water was almost 2 inches thick and presented a problem each time a vessel was brought into one of the graving docks. When the caissons were opened, the oil flowed in on top of the water and coated the sides of the docks as the water level dropped. Eventually it covered the bottom of the dock and the blocks, too. Attempts to clean the sides with a steam and water mix were fairly successful, and Gillette installed a series of boilers around both docks, but the whole process had to be repeated every time a ship entered or left. The only permanent solution was to employ Wheeler oil-collecting systems to skim the oil off the surface and trap it in screens to be pumped into tanks ashore. Ridding the harbor of the foul-smelling and corrosive oil was to be a messy and time-consuming business.[45]

While at Ten Ten Dock the *Helena's* crew had shored buckled, leaking bulkheads and rigged jumper electrical and water leads above the damaged area to provide power and fire-main pressure to the forward part of the ship. Oil from the harbor was seeping into the third-deck spaces below the waterline between frames 61 and 82, and to slow the influx of more the draft was decreased by pumping out her undamaged fuel tanks and removing ammunition. Once the ship was in the dock, Wallin suggested that perhaps the *Helena's* wrecked number 1 engine could be replaced by one from the *Shaw*. The goal was to enable her to make the journey to the West Coast on just two shafts. Extensive repair work would now be done almost exclusively at Puget Sound or Mare Island. Pearl Harbor was now an emergency repair yard only. And it had a new commanding officer. Gillette would remain as the manager of the yard. But Adm. Claude Bloch, Commandant, Fourteenth Naval District, named Rear Adm. William R. Furlong, formerly Commander, Mine Force, with his flag in the *Oglala*, to the newly created position of Commandant, Navy Yard Pearl Harbor, on 12 December.

All overhauls in progress were ordered expedited, the installation of the *San Francisco's* radar on a not-to-delay basis. Dry dock priorities were established on the eleventh. Work on the *Pennsylvania* continued in Dry Dock 1. The *Helena* was to be made seaworthy in Dry Dock 2. The destroyer *Aylwin* was to be docked on the marine railway to repair near-miss damage suffered as she steamed out of the harbor. The *Maryland* and *Tennessee* were granted restricted availability while their damage was repaired.[46] So was the *Curtiss*, which had been crashed by one plane and bombed by another. But more damaged ships could arrive at any time from the sea, and there would soon be the added work of the damaged ships in the harbor. On the sixteenth, Kimmel issued a memorandum to the fleet outlining a plan to reduce the time in port for ships needing repair. Each type and force commander was to establish a liaison office ashore to coordinate the work to be done on a ship due for a yard period, so that everything necessary would be prepared for the ship before she arrived. Kimmel wanted the yard to be "utilized for the accomplishment of urgent repairs beyond the capacity of the forces afloat, and important military alterations which can be accomplished during short periods of restricted availability, and during short scheduled overhauls to be known as 'Interim Overhauls.' Work involving navy yard stays of one month or longer, excepting work which may be necessary to make ships seaworthy, will be undertaken at a mainland yard." Kimmel needed to be kept "continuously advised" of every detail regarding the yard time of his warships: how long they were to be in, limitations in speed or armament while the work was being done, and the time it would take to get under way while the ship was undergoing repair.[47] The commander in chief could plainly see out the window of his headquarters what ships he did *not* have. He needed to know what he had to fight with.

Kimmel's flagship, the battleship *Pennsylvania*, was one of the handful of damaged ships that did not come under the scope of the Salvage Organization, since she was already in the hands of the Navy Yard.[48]

The yard quickly reinstalled the three propeller shafts and screws, though the work was delayed by occasional precautionary flooding of the dock when an air raid warning sounded. Workers also began renewing and repairing the superstructure and upper decks. The gallery bulkheads were also replaced, as was part of the warrant officers' messroom bulkhead. By the following Sunday, stores and provisions were being carted aboard by the *Pennsylvania*'s crew as the ship made ready to get undocked and under way.

The seaplane tender *Curtiss* was also in yard hands. She had been moored in the North Channel and was crashed by a crippled Japanese plane a few minutes after 0900. The plane disintegrated on the boat deck, flaming gasoline setting the ship on fire. Less than ten minutes later the *Curtiss* was showered with bombs. Most were near misses, but one hit the starboard side of the boat deck and smashed through to the hangar before exploding. Casualties from this hit were heavy. Twenty were killed, two having been so badly burned that they could not be identified. Thirty-three badly wounded were sent to the Naval Hospital and to the *Solace*. Another twenty-five were less severely hurt and were treated in the ship's sick bay. One man could not be found. Despite the casualties, damage to the ship was relatively light. It was a lucky break for the Salvage Organization. The *Curtiss* could easily have been another of Steele's concerns.

The resources of the Navy Yard and Base Force had been further stretched by the damage to the repair ship *Vestal*, beached since Sunday morning off Aeia shoal. She had been tied up alongside the *Arizona* when the Japanese high-level bombers began to pummel the battleship, and just after 0800 she was hit by two bombs that were probably near misses on the bigger ship.

The first bomb hit on the starboard forecastle deck, plunged through three decks, and exploded in pipe and bar storage. The second bomb sliced through the carpenter shop, shipfitter shop, and oil tanks before boring a 3-by-5-foot hole in the side of the ship and exploding. More damage was caused on deck when the *Arizona* blew up

The *Vestal* beached off Aeia. Damage to this repair ship stretched the already limited resources of the Base Force and Navy Yard.
Naval Historical Center 80 G 19933

alongside, and at 0845 the mooring lines between the two ships were cut away. Tugs pushed the *Vestal*, listing to starboard and taking water aft, to a position off McGrew's Point while the crew continued to monitor the settling of the 520-foot ship. Launched in 1908, she was far from watertight, and the accumulating water flowing about her increased concern about her stability. Young decided to run her aground, and forty minutes after anchoring she was under way, her bow nosing into the soft mud of Aeia. Her bow settled 4 feet into the silt, and there she lay with a slight starboard list. Nine dead were sent ashore, including three "who may have been either the *Arizona* personnel blown over or *Vestal* personnel so badly burned as to be unable to identify."[49] Seven others were added to the rolls of the missing, and nineteen were hospitalized. For now, the *Vestal* was both out of the war and out of the salvage effort as the crew worked to float their own ship.

To keep the Navy Yard and Base Force informed of salvage activities in the harbor, Steele issued the first of his daily Base Force salvage memoranda on Sunday the fourteenth. The memo went to his own officers as well as to five of Gillette's men detailed to act as liaison with the salvage force, including Lt. Cdr. Francis Whitaker, just arrived from BuShips in Washington. It called attention to two looming logistical concerns: the tagging and identification of material recovered from the battleships, and the lack of storage space for recovered material and salvage equipment. The next day Steele's memo began with a third concern, the lack of manpower: "The Base Force Salvage Organization has a very limited number of men. . . . Thus, when projects are undertaken beyond the capacity of the salvage organization personnel it will become necessary to apply to outside sources."[50] To assist with that problem a temporary Fleet Pool of newly arrived men and survivors awaiting assignment was set up. Crews from ships in the harbor could also be used in an emergency. The manpower shortage meant that salvage activity, except for pumping, could be conducted only during the day. This did have the benefit of aiding the blackout and reducing the chance of accidents occurring while maneuvering heavy and delicate equipment in the dark, but it slowed the recovery. The shortage was alleviated for a brief time by the release of men from the *California*, *Nevada*, and *West Virginia* to the Fleet Pool. Those not required for the partial antiaircraft batteries aboard the *California* and *Nevada*, for manning the shore-based antiaircraft batteries being formed, or for salvage parties aboard each battleship were ordered to be made available for transfer. The security and salvage watch on the hull of the *Oklahoma* was also reassigned. By the nineteenth the ships had been ordered to further reduce as much as possible the number of officers retained, thus freeing more men for temporary assignment by Hal Jones.

The *Tennessee*, *California*, and *Nevada* were assigned the first project officers by Steele, as they had the most hope of a relatively rapid salvage. Thayer was given the *Tennessee*, Rodgers the *California*, and Genereaux the *Nevada*. In the week following the attack, the *California*, *Nevada*, and *West Virginia* were directed to assign a group of officers and enlisted men directly to the Salvage Organization as experts and advisers aboard their own ships. The *California*'s initial group included Lt. Cdr. M. N. Little, the ship's first lieutenant and damage control officer; Lt. Cdr. C. A. Peterson; Ens. W. A. J. Lewis; Lt. G. P. Garland; and Lt. Cdr. Oliver F. Naquin, the *California*'s engineering officer. Naquin had commanded the submarine *Squalus*, which sank in 240 feet of water off New Hampshire in May 1939. He, along with thirty-one of his crew and a civilian, had been rescued by diving bell, after which the submarine was raised by pontoons and towed to the Portsmouth Navy Yard. The *California* group also included four warrant officers and fifty enlisted men, including shipfitters, boatswains, machinists, electricians, water tenders, and gunner's mates. The *West Virginia*'s group was under Lt. William White, the ship's assistant damage control officer. He had with him the chief engineer, Lt. Levi Knight Jr.; four warrant officers; and fifty enlisted men, including eight chiefs. Steele ordered the groups whittled down within a week to just three officers and twenty-two men. Lieutenants White and Knight, Machinist M. S. Johnson, the eight chiefs, and ten first-class, two second-class, and two third-class petty officers comprised the *West Virginia*'s experienced group. The salvage groups aboard the other two ships were equally experienced, with fifteen chiefs assigned to the *Nevada*'s group.

The morning after the Salvage Organization began operations, Kimmel and the fleet were heartened by the arrival of the *Saratoga* from San Diego. She was a reminder that Pearl was still a hub, still the heart of America's Pacific defense, and that the salvage effort under way was but a small part of the war. But the crews aboard the *Saratoga* and her escorts were stunned by what they saw inside the harbor on the fifteenth. Newspapers had speculated on the extent of the damage, and the scuttlebutt hinted at the sights, but the real thing was something else again. The smoke was gone, the oil had mostly washed ashore or out to sea, and nearly all the bodies had been fished from the water or collected from the beach. And while Battleship Row was no longer burning, it looked even worse than it had during the battle. At least then the ships had looked like a fleet at war: the signal flags flew, antiaircraft batteries were firing, and ships went down fighting as the smoke poured forth and the crews fought back. Now, more than a week later, the Battle Line looked emasculated and helpless.

The *Saratoga* remained in Pearl only long enough to refuel before proceeding to Wake, carrying Marine fighter aircraft for the relief of the besieged garrison there. Wake had been bombed on the seventh, and an invasion attempt had been repulsed by the Marines on the eleventh. The *Lexington* group had departed on Sunday to support the relief with a diversion in the Marshalls. The *Tangier*, loaded with equipment and supplies, sailed the day the *Saratoga* arrived, and the Sara herself departed the afternoon of the sixteenth. The *Saratoga's* force included three cruisers, including the *San Francisco* after her expedited overhaul. Halsey's *Enterprise* force came into Pearl for fuel in the late afternoon of the sixteenth and left again for Wake on the nineteenth, clearing the harbor by 1020.

The Imperial Navy's Fourth Fleet tried again to invade on the twenty-third (Wake time) and this time came ashore to stay. The Pacific Fleet carriers were ordered back to Hawaii that same day. Wake, it appeared, was lost, and there was no sense risking the fleet with an unknown number of Japanese ships in the vicinity. Husbanding meager resources, not risky offense operations, was the prevailing mood at CinCPac. The fleet retreated east, to fight another day, while the waters of Pearl Harbor began to hum with activity. Salvage operations on a grand scale to resurrect the Battle Line had begun.

THREE

Getting Down to Work

Throughout Tuesday, 9 December, the *California* continued to settle lower into the water, down by the bow and listing to port. If she could stay afloat long enough she would be towed to Dry Dock 2 following the patching of the *Helena*. The *Maryland* could wait. But the *California*'s chances of staying afloat long enough were looking doubtful, and the yard began preparing to dry-dock the *Maryland* instead.[1] The small pumping capacity available from the attending ships seemed merely to prolong the fight to keep the *California* from settling to the bottom. More water was entering her than could be removed. There were about sixteen pumps aboard, the last of which had been placed that morning. Not all were in use at the same time. Twelve were 6-inch pumps, the other four were 3-inch, and they removed an average of more than 8,300 gallons per minute. Unfortunately, nearly 9,500 gallons of water were pouring into her in each of those minutes, a net loss of 1,200 gallons every sixty seconds, or 72,000 gallons an hour.[2] The ship was inexorably filling up, compartment by compartment. Still, Commander Curtis felt she could stay afloat until patches were placed over the holes in her port side. One patch had already been made, but the divers who had explored the forward torpedo hole had provided inaccurate dimensions, and the patch would not fit.[3] Adding to the trouble, the cables securing the ship to the quays had begun to part when she listed. Eight 8-inch Manila lines and the single $1^5/8$-inch wire hawser had been stretched so taut that a bollard on the mooring quay and part of a quarterdeck chock had been snapped off.[4] Lines parted all day Tuesday and Wednesday. To prevent the *California* from capsizing or drifting toward the channel, tugs were summoned to push her gently back against the quay so that additional mooring lines could be run. At 1500 on Wednesday a dredge came alongside to starboard and removed an anchor chain, dropping the anchor into the mud. An hour later the *California*'s crew began running the chain around turret 1 and securing it to the forward quay. It was no easy task, and it was another five and a half hours before the makeshift mooring was completed—at which point the last of the wires aft parted with a snap. Only the anchor chain held the bow in place while the stern continued to pivot outward a few inches at a time.[5]

By 1600 on Wednesday over 21,000 tons of water had flooded into the ruptures, and the *California*'s draft was at the point where she was assumed to be on the bottom of the harbor. But still she continued to settle, to slide away from the quays. Unlike the hard coral bottom farther up Battleship Row, the bottom in the lagoon at berth F-3 was silt that would not support her weight. The water that continued to pour into the vessel now carried mud along with fuel oil into the body of the ship at the third-deck level. Later in the day the quarterdeck was abandoned as the water came up over the gunwales to swirl around turret 3, encircle the barbette of turret 4, and begin to submerge the main-deck catapult and stern crane.

The pumping by this time had ceased; there was no point to it. The *California* had made the transition from a damaged ship to a sunken one, from a repair job to one of salvage, the moment her docking keels touched the mud. But now there was a new concern. Piles previously driven by Public Works into the harbor bottom in the vicinity of berth F-3 had gone through 125 feet of silt in some areas before hitting hard bottom.[6] Just how far would the *California* settle? How would this affect her eventual salvage? It would certainly complicate it. The ship might sink so far that the damage to her hull would be covered up, frustrating plans to patch the holes. Throughout the night she sank lower in the water. Turret 4 disappeared altogether, and only the three 14-inch muzzles, elevated and trained to starboard during the attack, were visible above the waves. The deck catapult disappeared. The water level rose up the ladders leading from the quarterdeck to the upper deck, and within hours that level was awash, too. Sometime late Wednesday night or early Thursday morning the ship came to an apparent halt, her hull encased in 16 or 17 feet of mud. Because of her list, the starboard edge of the quarterdeck was about 7½ feet under water while the port edge was over 17 feet below the surface. Almost all of the forecastle was submerged, the deck sloping up from port to starboard so that only the starboard gunwale was dry. Whereas the ship had been down by the bow initially, she had embedded herself more deeply into the mud aft. She was far down by the stern.

At Ten Ten Dock, hundreds of yards across the water from the lagoon, the *Oglala* had also been the focus of considerable attention and consternation immediately after the smoke from the attack had cleared. The shallow water at berth 3 had prevented her from completely turning turtle, and now she lay on the bottom on her port side obstructing the valuable pier. Her hull had been opened up—that much was certain, but little else was definitely known about her damage. She had been next to the *Helena*, outboard of her and port side to, when a torpedo had struck the cruiser minutes after the attack began. The torpedo had hit the *Helena* 18 feet below the waterline and exploded next to the forward engine room, sending flames throughout nearby compartments. As the *Oglala* drew only 16 feet of water, the concussion from the explosion caved in her hull near the turn of the bilge. The men of the *Helena* were positive that this torpedo had sunk the old minelayer, reporting that the *Oglala* "was sunk by

Heavy mooring lines secure the *Oglala* to Ten Ten Dock and prevent her from sliding into the channel. The fires on Battleship Row are nearly out in this view taken late on 9 December 1941. Naval Historical Center NH 60672

the mining effect of the explosion."[7] But the crew of the *Oglala* were not so certain. They reported that several minutes after the torpedo struck, a bomb landed between the two ships and exploded with equal violence, though the *Helena* never reported any such near miss.[8] Whether by torpedo or this near miss, or a combination of the two, the *Oglala* began to take on water in the fireroom. The bomb explosion possibly ruptured the hull further and flooded the engine room, and within a half-hour she listed 5 degrees to port. The power was out, which meant no pumps, and by 0900 she had been towed astern to clear the *Helena* so that she would not roll against her. The *Oglala*'s crew and sailors on the dock rigged additional mooring lines to try to stabilize her in an upright position, but it was no use. By 0930 she listed 20 degrees to port, and within thirty minutes she lay on the bottom, her masts lying on the dock. On 6 December she had been the flagship of the Pacific Fleet Mine Force. Now she was merely in the way.

Near the channel entrance the tug *Sotoyomo* and what was left of the *Shaw* lay inside the sunken floating dry dock YFD-2. The dry dock had been another, less spectacular,

The *Shaw* lies smashed and burned on 8 December 1941. To the right is the *Helena*, moored to Ten Ten Dock.
U.S. Naval Institute

victim of the raid. The *Sotoyomo* had entered the dock on 1 December and had almost been forgotten about in the aftermath, but the *Shaw*, having drifted part of the way out of the dock, had not. She had been hit by three bombs just before 0900, when the *Nevada* was being pummeled by five hits a short distance away. Two exploded within the *Shaw*, and a third appeared to have passed through her and detonated between the hull and the dock. At once the destroyer was afire, the flames fed by leaking fuel oil and the wooden blocks at the bottom of the dock. No water was available to fight the fires, and the forward magazines had blown up, with a spectacular explosion caught on film. The bow had been torn from the body of the ship just aft of the second 5-inch gun shield and was held in place by a few shreds of steel along the bottom. When the dock was flooded to prevent more damage to it, the unstable bow had fallen over to starboard and had slipped under the water. It was uncertain whether it was still attached to the rest of the ship.[9]

The after two-thirds of the destroyer was still buoyant, and how long it would remain so was a question to be answered as quickly as possible. The forward fireroom was completely flooded, bringing the ship well down by the bow. The bulkhead at frame $87\frac{1}{2}$, separating the flooded forward and leaking aft firerooms, had been deflected by the bomb blasts and by the water pressure against it. It needed to be shored. The yard Design Section under Lt. E. C. Holtzworth conducted a preliminary survey of the ship a few days after the attack, recommending removal of as much top-side weight as possible, including the pilothouse, chart house, forward stack, and centerline torpedo tubes. Holtzworth also suggested that the forward fireroom be pumped down a couple of feet in order to determine how much the bulkhead leaked, and from where. The forward fireroom was a large compartment. If a significant volume of water were allowed to slosh unrestrained from side to side, it could affect the destroyer's stability when she was towed out of the dock. Holtzworth asked divers to have a look at the bow section, to determine how it was connected to the ship. With both forward 5-inch guns attached, it was estimated to weigh about 300 tons. If it was cut in two and severed from the ship, a 150-ton-capacity crane could lift the sections off the bottom of the dock.[10]

Across the channel from where the *Shaw* was being surveyed, divers from the submarine salvage vessel *Widgeon* had gone to work on the *Nevada* within days after the attack. She continued to flood, and air bubbled to the surface even weeks afterward. Battleship anchors were sent out to the ship on Tuesday and were fastened to stern chains to prevent the *Nevada* from sliding forward into the deeper water of the channel. Divers reported that she was sitting on a large lava rock underneath her number 3 turret on the starboard side, and that her starboard screw was in about 4 feet of silt and mud.[11]

Steele wanted to know how much water would have to be pumped from the ship before she regained buoyancy, and he sent his inquiry to the Planning Section. Lieutenant Commander Whitaker gave it to the design superintendent, who replied to Steele a week later, giving four possible scenarios. Based on the present draft of 48 feet forward and 40½ feet aft, and assuming that all compartments were presently flooded but could be made watertight, Holtzworth advised that for the ship to regain a draft of just 30 feet, it would "be necessary to remove all the water in the ship or an amount equal to 46,300 tons or 12,100,000 gallons." Such a shallow draft was not necessary, however, and the deeper draft meant less water to be removed. The three other options presented assumed a target draft of 36, 38, and 40 feet. Dry dock 2 required no greater than 42. A 40-foot draft equaled 10,400 tons of water in the ship, with the level just a few inches below the second platform.[12] The memo gave Steele and his officers some idea of what to shoot for, and a rough estimate of the work involved. But first, they needed a look at the damage.

Men from the *Widgeon* made the first of what would eventually total over five hundred dives on the battleship and had a preliminary look at the torpedo damage. Measurements were obtained of the hole, and a party from the Navy Yard went out to the *Nevada*'s sister ship *Oklahoma* and lifted a template from the same spot on her hull, for use in fabricating a huge wooden patch. Carefully the divers began to cut away the jagged edges of steel that had splayed away from the hole so that the patch could be placed flush against the hull. It was hoped that it would be delivered to the ship by Tuesday the sixteenth, and that it would be in place by the twentieth or twenty-first.[13] That timetable turned out to be wildly optimistic.

Also overly optimistic was the hope that the diving equipment in storage at Pearl Harbor and on the repair and rescue vessels would be adequate for the task ahead. In terms of quantity, there was certainly enough; in terms of quality, the salvage team made an unfortunate discovery when the gear was inventoried: only a small portion of it was usable.

Just about all of the gear was overage in terms of the life span indicated by the manufacturer. Nearly half of it had been made in the 1920s. The telephone equipment was obsolete and virtually unusable. Also obsolete were the exhaust valves on many of the helmets. Some helmets had broken face-plate glass, damaged breast-plate straps, and deteriorated gaskets. Many of the rubber hoses and leather items were also badly deteriorated owing to age and to years of improper storage. There was a shortage of accessories and spare parts so that repairs were often impossible to effect. The hand-operated diving pumps had no testing or efficiency documentation, and most operated at less than half the rated flow. Fortunately there was an adequate supply of power-driven air compressors.[14]

A great deal of recently manufactured diving equipment, much of it belonging to Curtis's West Coast Salvage Unit, was immediately dispatched to Hawaii so that large-scale operations could begin on the *Nevada*. Nine divers from Destroyer Repair Unit 1 had been flown from San Diego with their gear to Kaneohe on the eighth to augment those from the *Widgeon*, the Submarine Base, and the Navy Yard, but for the time being there would be a shortage of usable equipment.

At noon on 10 December, as the *Maryland* was being eased forward beyond the hull of the *Oklahoma* and over to the Navy Yard, a meeting was held on the *California* to brainstorm ideas for refloating that ship. The chief engineer was there, as was the ship's first lieutenant, an assistant salvage officer, and a representative from the Industrial Department of the Navy Yard. Commander Wallin also attended. He had just returned from a quick visit to his family at their Waikiki apartment, where he had changed out of the soiled uniform he had worn since boarding the *California* on the morning of the attack.[15] Later Captain Bunkley joined the meeting. The officers discussed, and subsequently opposed, a plan to place "soft" wooden patches over the holes, pump out the ship, and tow her to dry dock. The problem, as they saw it, was the unstable nature of such a patch, and the inherent danger if the patch parted or came loose while the ship was under tow in the middle of the channel. The possibility was explored of using underwater welding to attach a much stronger steel patch over the holes, using scrap metal from the hull of the *Oklahoma* or the *Utah*. Doubt was cast on the feasibility of this scheme because of the lack of underwater welders and the danger of fire from the oil still surrounding the *California*.

By this time the ship was nearly on the bottom, but her decks were still above water. Another plan, separating the ship into vertical sections and pumping out each in turn, was discarded because of the stresses that would be placed on the ship's structure, given the head of water each section would have to withstand—stresses that the bulkheads and decks had not been designed to endure. She might break apart completely. Another "slow but sure" method was to pump out the vessel top to bottom, compartment by compartment, with divers tracing and sealing leaks as they were discovered. The unknown factor in this plan, and in any other, was the extent of the damage to the watertight integrity of the *California*. It was still believed that two or three torpedoes had hit her, one forward and possibly a pair aft. The damage to her torpedo bulkheads could not have been great, as the pumps had a relatively low capacity yet she flooded slowly over a period of about eighty hours. It was felt that the damage could not have been nearly as extensive as that to the *West Virginia* or the *Oklahoma*, which had gone to the bottom within minutes of being torpedoed.

A visiting officer suggested another possibility: driving sheet piling clear around the ship, then pumping out the water within the cofferdam. Rather than bringing the ship to dry dock, a dry dock would be brought to the ship so that repairs could be made to the hull. Ironically, this plan was met with skepticism just as plans were going forward within the new Salvage Organization and the Navy Yard for trying exactly that.[16]

The *Tennessee* had been moored just inside the *West Virginia*, tied to the pair of quays at berth F-6. Neither bomb that had hit the *Tennessee* had done any great damage—not structurally, anyway. A fragment from the bomb that had hit the center gun of turret 2 had mortally wounded the captain of the *West Virginia*, Mervyn Bennion, as he stood on the starboard wing of his bridge. The bomb struck the gun near the face plate of the turret, cracking the hoop, and fragments from it gouged both wing guns. Splinters also peppered the pilothouse and the air defense platform above it, as well as the conning tower platform, and punched a few holes in the deck to the left of turret 1. A sec-

The *West Virginia (outboard)* pins the *Tennessee* to the forward quay at F-6 on 10 December 1941.
U.S. Naval Institute

ond bomb hit the ship about the same time. It broke the starboard yard of the main-mast, smashing the catapult atop turret 3 before penetrating the roof of the turret and breaking apart without detonating. The left gun of the turret was knocked out of commission by the fragmenting bomb, and a small fire was started in the turret, but it was quickly extinguished. By far the worst damage suffered by the ship was from fire. Burning debris from the *Arizona* had started fires on the wooden deck aft of turret 4, and blazing oil on the water had cracked and warped the hull plating on both the port and starboard sides as far back as turret 3. The red-hot hull had ignited the paint on the second-deck bulkheads, gutting the officer quarters and prompting the crew to flood three magazines lest the nearby fire ignite them, too.[17] The *Tennessee* reported three dead and twenty injured, some seriously.

All of the ship's forward main battery guns were able to fire save one, and five of six after turret guns were similarly ready to shoot should Japanese surface ships appear on the horizon. Officers of the *Tennessee* were looking to the sinking *California* for replacement parts for the two inoperable guns. The high catapult atop turret 3 was also out, and consideration was being given to removing one of the *West Virginia*'s to replace it.[18] Nevertheless, once the fire was out the ship was ready for action—ready, that is, except that she could not move. When the *West Virginia* listed to port after being torn open by a barrage of torpedoes, her hull came up hard against the bottom edge of the *Tennessee*'s armor belt, possibly keeping the *West Virginia* from rolling further until counterflooding could correct her dramatic and dangerous 28-degree list. But when she settled back down to starboard she pinned the inboard battleship against the top of the forward concrete mooring quay. The *Tennessee* was trapped.

A party from the Navy Yard, led by Holtzworth and including electrical, shipfitting, and machinery estimators, plus a naval architect and a machinery draftsman, had visited the *Tennessee* on Tuesday the ninth. A yard pilot, whose job it would be to maneuver the battleship out of the confined area, was also there. The draftsman prepared sketches of the ship relative to the *West Virginia* and the mooring quays to decide how best to free her with the *Maryland* still moored a few yards ahead. It looked possible for the *Tennessee* to be towed astern and jockeyed out between the *West Virginia* and the *Arizona*, if she could be pulled free of the mooring quay that was wedged hard against her starboard side between her forward turrets. But either the *West Virginia* would have to be pulled outboard or the mooring quay itself would have to go. Moving the ship sideways, said Admiral Anderson, would be "work of major proportions."[19] That left removing the large masonry quay without doing any appreciable damage to the hull of the *Tennessee*.[20] It would take some time, and the yard issued orders for the quay's removal. In the meantime, repair work began while the ship was trapped.

The *Medusa* sent a party to begin the rehabilitation of the fire-damaged spaces. Much of officers' country had been burned out, including the wardroom, and the ship's general mess now served the officers. The warped plating on the stern was rewelded and caulked, and inside much of the wiring was replaced. The armor belt was inspected and found intact. Thousands of gallons of oil were removed to lighten the ship.

Merely chipping away at the huge concrete pier was not going to be enough. Officers of the Base Force and Lieutenant Commander Curtis decided to blast it apart with dynamite until enough had been removed to get some water between the quay and the hull. Not much was needed. It had been decided that the *Tennessee* would go out forward, once the *Maryland* was gone, rather than backwards between the stern of the *West Virginia* and the shattered bow of the *Arizona*.[21] But the blasting was slow going. The hull patching by the *Medusa* was temporary; the *Tennessee* would be far from watertight in a seaway, and many portholes were bent and would not close, but it was good enough. By the fourteenth, a week after the raid, about 60 percent of the quay had been removed, and there were four to six feet of water now between the side of the vessel and the quay—nearly enough to tow her clear.

Salvage of usable material from the *California* began even as she continued to settle. Tuesday evening, when it became apparent that she would soon be on the bottom, the crew and civilians from the Navy Yard began to strip the battleship of her port secondary battery before the water rose over the guns. There was no plan, only a hurried effort to get the guns off the ship so that they could be remounted and used elsewhere. Later a group of ordnance men, survivors from the *Utah* led by Lieutenant Commander Stelter, removed guns and fire control equipment from the *California* and other ships. Four of the five port 5-inch/.51 broadside guns were hastily removed. Wednesday morning the fleet gunnery officer ordered all accessible ordnance material, guns, ammunition, and fire control equipment to be removed as rapidly as possible from the *California*, and the Salvage Organization took over the job. The men, joined by a fire control party from the *Medusa*, continued to remove the 5-inch/.51s on the upper deck before moving to the port 5-inch/.25 antiaircraft guns. One 5-inch/.25 gun was removed on the thirteenth, three more on the fourteenth, and another pair on the sixteenth. Anything that could be removed was detached, unbolted, or disconnected and taken off the ship. Ready service lockers, 3-inch/.50 antiaircraft guns, catapults, saluting guns, 36-inch battle searchlights, 12-inch signal searchlights, rangefinder mounts, and gun directors were loaded onto lighters for shipment ashore.[22]

While men began to strip the *California*, others did the same aboard the fire-blackened *West Virginia*. She was too badly crippled for immediate salvage. She had been opened up more fully than either the *California* or the *Nevada*, had nearly capsized, and had gone down almost at once. Her recovery could take months, perhaps years. Yet the Japanese might be back in days, even hours. They had smashed the Army Air Force pursuit squadrons on the ground at Wheeler Field, shot up the bombers at Hickam, and thrown the entire island of Oahu into turmoil. An invasion force might be looming over the horizon. The fleet was out looking for the raiders but had seen nothing. Perhaps the enemy carriers were refueling, preparing to launch another attack at the Navy Yard, at the fuel tank farms, at the dry docks so vitally needed to repair the ships. The Japanese had struck once, when no one thought they would or could. Now they had proven that they had the will and the ability. Long before any help arrived, the Japanese Rising Sun might be flying from flagpoles on Oahu. Soldiers were digging in to repel an invasion, and all around the harbor gunner's mates and ordnance specialists were swarming over the crippled ships, stripping them of anything that might be useful.

Guns were removed from the *West Virginia* for island defense and to replace those damaged on other ships. A pair of machine guns went to the *Tennessee*, and on the ninth a 5-inch/.25 gun was removed from her undamaged starboard side by the men from the *Utah* and taken by barge to Dry Dock 1. There it was lifted aboard the *Pennsylvania* and installed, replacing one with a bulged barrel. The rest of the *West Virginia*'s antiaircraft battery of seven 5-inch/.25 guns was also removed. Four were set up as a shore battery at West Loch in Pearl Harbor. The heavy cruiser *Chicago* got one, and the *Salt Lake City* the other two. Gunner's mates from the *Maryland* took a boat to the *West Virginia* and removed the gas check pads and a range keeper from the main battery. On Friday the twelfth a 5-inch/.51 gun was also removed and taken to the *Pennsylvania* to replace one damaged by the bomb hit near the galley. Three of the five *West Virginia* port 5-inch/.51s were too badly damaged to be used elsewhere and were shipped to Mare Island (along with the damaged gun from the *Pennsylvania*). The remaining six were turned over to the Army for use in the defense of Oahu.[23]

Some semblance of normalcy returned to Pearl Harbor as the days wore on. The fresh-water supply to Ford Island had been severed when the *Arizona* sank on the 12-inch main and when bombing had destroyed the 6-inch temporary line to the south end of the island. Quickly a new 16-inch line was run from Hospital Point to Ford Island, and the supply of fresh water resumed. Within a week liberty was again granted, one-quarter of a ship's complement at a time, beginning at 0900 and expiring on board ship at 1700. Dress for officers was service dress whites, for enlisted men undress whites with neckerchiefs. Submariners and aviators could get by with khaki.[24] Liberty boats still had to make their way though the oil-choked water around the harbor, though, no more flipping cigarette butts overboard. Captains were directed to keep the oil away from the hulls of their ships and to take care to avoid igniting the fuel and trash that floated nearby.

A more orderly pace and a return to the voluminous paperwork that the fleet and Navy Yard generated replaced the hectic activity of the days immediately following the raid. Only now there was more. Pye issued a memorandum directing the Salvage Organization to maintain a careful and complete written and photographic record of all salvage work in the harbor. He was not concerned with the historical record so much as with providing "guidance in other similar work in and in connection with present and future practice as regards design and operation."[25] Aboard ship, action reports were now to be supplemented with war damage reports.

In October 1941 the Bureau of Ships sent a memorandum to all Naval Districts, Naval Stations, and Navy Yards, and all commanding officers of ships, advising that the bureau was "collecting all available information concerning war damage incurred by United States and foreign vessels." The information was to be used for design mod-ification and damage control procedures, and to determine the type of weapons, par-ticularly torpedoes and mines, that the enemy was using. The commanding officers were to include such information as the ship's location, course, and speed and the weather and sea conditions when the damage was incurred. For bomb or projectile hits the bureau wanted to know where the ship had been hit, what type of plating had been penetrated, and the damage caused. Underwater explosions were evaluated on the basis of the center of the strike, holes or indentations in the hull, damage inboard of the shell plating, the condition of watertight doors and hatches, and the progress of flooding. The Navy Yard or repair ship involved was asked to provide a supplement to the commanding officers' reports. In the aftermath of the 7 December raid, captains of the damaged vessels sat down to write these war damage reports. Months later they would be the nucleus of the Bureau of Ships war damage reports, which would include information gathered once the ships had reached dry dock and could be thoroughly surveyed.

Ashore, the work of creating a cohesive unit out of the new Salvage Organization continued. Each day at 1230 a conference was held aboard the *Argonne*, with the vari-ous ship representatives and section heads reporting to Steele, Calhoun, and Furlong on the progress of work in the past twenty-four hours and outlining plans for the next twenty-four. Curtis was on the phone early each morning updating Washington on progress in the harbor and requesting urgently needed men and material. These conferences aboard the Base Force flagship continued until Christmas Eve.

Many different ideas for refloating the ships were tossed about. One of the more novel was to seal the holes with an ice barrier. A lieutenant j.g. by the name of Ross, an assistant shop superintendent in the shipyard, suggested such a plan for the *California*. The technique had been used with success in the St. Lawrence River during winter, but the warm water of Pearl did not lend itself to such a plan. Moreover, the piping needed to freeze water over the 2,000 square feet of hull that had been ruptured was beyond what could be supplied. Still, Furlong did not discourage such unconventional thinking and congratulated the officer for his suggestion.[26]

Salvage equipment continued to arrive each day, and the influx quickly became a problem. There was nowhere to store it all. Lieutenant Genereaux, in addition to his duties as the *Nevada* project officer, was given the assignment of unloading the equipment as it arrived and of making an accurate inventory. The yard could spare only limited quantities of lumber, steel, pumps, hoses, lights, and craft to transport it all, so the Salvage Organization set about to purchase or rent what it needed. The loose gear was sent to the new Salvage Storehouse at Magazine Island. Later two buildings near berth 5 at the end of Ten Ten Dock would provide 4,000 square feet of storage where the equipment could be readily accessed. Equally pressing was the need to keep track of the material and equipment recovered from the ships. This had to be labeled, preserved if necessary, and stored out of the elements and out of the way. Lieutenant Commander Whitaker took this in hand, but by the end of the month the problem of storage had become acute. Barges filled with equipment removed from the ships were tied up at berth 5 and abandoned. There was no place to store the ready ammunition boxes, searchlights, catapults, backing-out slugs, muzzle clamps, breech blocks, elevating screws, and scores of other items removed from the decks of the four accessible battleships. What was unloaded from the barges was simply piled on the dock. The situation got so bad that on the twenty-ninth a halt was called to further shipments of recovered gear until the yard could figure out what to do with it all.

The officers and men of the Salvage Organization needed housing too, and the Fourteenth Naval District made a pair of houses near the Submarine Base available for Curtis and the other salvage engineers. Just after Christmas the Public Works Section was ordered to construct a new barracks with mess and toilet facilities on Ford Island across from the *West Virginia*. The barracks were to house the men who were to work day to day on the *Arizona*, *West Virginia*, *Oklahoma*, and *California*. The buildings were expected to be ready by the middle of January.

The list of items needing the attention of Steele's men was long and varied. A record-keeping system had to be set up, liaison arranged between the contractors, salvage crews fed, divers trained. Gasoline had to be obtained for the boats, vehicles, and equipment. Confidential and registered documents had to be recovered from the ships, boats and crews for transport procured, security with the Inshore Patrol and the Marines coordinated. Priorities had to be agreed upon between the Salvage Organization and the Navy Yard. The chain of command and lines of communication had to be established. The lack of floating cranes and the scarcity of resources and space were a constant worry. Stenographic help to keep track of these items and a hundred more was in short supply. It was a mammoth job, and the speed with which it was carried out spoke well of the training, maturity, and flexibility of the officers involved. Still, it was three weeks before Steele could report that all three entities involved in the salvage work, the Base Force, the Navy Yard, and the Fourteenth Naval District, had come to an agreement of mutual understanding and cooperation. During those same three weeks it was decided that the salvage job would ultimately be turned over to the Navy Yard. Just when that would happen, no one was yet sure.

The Base Force had quickly ordered the salvage of the *Oglala* be limited to her removal from alongside the pier. She occupied a valuable berth, one that was urgently needed, and for that reason alone her salvage was to have a high priority. By 17 December the *Oglala*'s removal from berth 3 had a higher priority than floating the *California* or the *West Virginia*, and the next day she had become the number one focus for Jim Steele. Fortunately the work on her was not complicated by the need to salvage her for later use. The initial plan was to secure a pair of pontoons to her with chains and pump enough air into the hull to float her a few feet off the bottom, then tow her to a beach or into drydock. More drastic methods were briefly considered, including using dynamite to break the ship apart so that her hull could be taken away in pieces. But divers would be needed to finish the dismembering under water, cranes would be needed to lift the pieces, and both commodities were in short supply and urgently needed elsewhere. Dynamiting the hull could also result in damage to Ten Ten Dock. So the Salvage Force focused their preparations on giving the hulk enough buoyancy to float and towing her ignobly away to be dealt with at a more convenient time. She would be beached or towed into Dry Dock 2 after the *Helena* had been removed. Parbuckling tackle would be rigged to pull her upright and set her on blocks so that the hull could be patched. But there were possible complications to this plan, and one officer noted that "careful studies are being made to guard against having the vessel get out of hand in the dry dock and thereby make it unavailable for other ships."[27] That simply could not be allowed to happen. The dry docks were absolutely critical to the war effort.

On Monday the fifteenth, Holtzworth outlined to Steele the weight that needed to be removed from the *Oglala* preparatory to the attempt to float her. Her propellers would come off, as would her mainmast, rigging, paravanes and booms, stack and guy wires, deck winches, anchors, chains, and ladders. The boat davits accessible on her starboard side would be cut away, the ensign and jack staff removed, the forward gun lifted clear. Equipment near the bridge such as the rangefinder and searchlights, as well as any wreckage that might drag along the bottom as she was towed, would also have to go.[28] On Thursday the eighteenth a detailed thirteen-part flotation plan was sent from Holtzworth to Steele. In addition to the ship being stripped of all possible weight, the leaking fuel tanks would be pumped out and the oil coating the hull would be washed off with hot salt water. Vent pipes would be closed or cut off and blanked, hatches dogged, and the upper mine track exit door secured so that the spar deck would be as airtight as possible. The deck would be shored, as it would be subject to great stress. Air would then be pumped into the spar deck through fittings as a test to see if the hull could hold sufficient pressure. That in itself was not expected to be enough to float the ship, and care was to be taken to prevent her from rotating. At the same time, salvage pontoons were to be attached to the hull via chains and stops. These pontoons would pry the *Oglala* loose from the suction of the mud and provide the bulk of the lifting force. The chains would be secured in such a way as to prevent the ship from rolling. The compressors would be placed on a barge so that continuous air pressure could be supplied while she was being towed away from the pier. Multiple hoses and careful monitoring would ensure that no one portion of the hull received undue pressure. There was, of course, some assumption of the *Oglala*'s stability built into the plan, and the salvors were ready to resink the pontoons should she become unstable. Holtzworth concluded his plan with the opinion that the option existed to dry-dock her on her side, rather than beach her, and that a plan would need to be developed to right her in the dock. All in all, he was optimistic that the plan would work as outlined.[29]

Fittings for air hoses were attached to the *Oglala*'s hull, and on Saturday the nineteenth, air was pumped into the spar deck as a test for the actual lift to take place on Monday. But the hull leaked badly. Caulkers from the yard tried to seal sprung rivets, but it was apparent that the hull did not have sufficient strength to hold the necessary air pressure.[30] Her removal was not going to be as straightforward as was hoped. Suddenly the *Oglala* was no longer the number one priority. She would not be removed any time soon, and in keeping with standard practice, attention was shifted to those ships that could be salvaged first. The Base Force salvage memorandum for 20 December read, "Because of the difficulties which have been discovered in preliminary work in refloating the *Oglala* the date set for her removal in Salvage Memorandum 4-41 (which was to have been Monday the twenty-second) is now advanced to 'indefinite.'" The *Oglala* would prove to justify that prediction.

Aboard the *Shaw*, the bulkhead between the firerooms had been shored, and a pair of 6-inch pumps had been brought aboard to reduce the water level in the forward boiler room. As the water level decreased, holes in the bulkheads were patched and the ship regained buoyancy. Plans were developed to attach two 80-ton submarine salvage pontoons to the side of the ship, between the stacks, to raise the forward part of the wreck even further.[31] Some good news was relayed by the Design Section to the planning superintendent on the sixteenth. Based on weight and buoyancy calculations and backed up by diver reports, it was learned that the bow had been torn completely loose from the ship. There was now no impediment to towing the *Shaw* clear of the dry dock.

Throughout the seventeenth the pumps tried to keep pace with the inflow of water into fireroom 1 while some of the *Shaw*'s ammunition was removed to a barge. The next morning she was towed clear of the sides of the dock and taken to berth 17 in the repair basin. Already plans were under way to attach a temporary bow so that she could get to the West Coast for complete repairs. For the moment, however, the yard busied itself with removing the three remaining 5-inch guns. The *Shaw* would have no need of them for quite some time. She had been thought a total loss after the attack, with good reason, but was now under repair, on her way back to a war that was barely a week and a half old.

Once the *Nevada*'s torpedo hole was more thoroughly explored, it was determined that a significant portion lay beneath the mud. A dredge began to clear it away ten days after the attack, and divers took new measurements of the damage, relaying their findings to the yard, which began to modify the patch, delaying its delivery. The divers, as they explored by touch along the 575 feet of her hull, found more damage. A 4-inch-wide gash, more than a foot long, was discovered just aft of the torpedo hit a week after the attack, and more damage was found the following Sunday. A large triangular hole was discovered along the starboard bow, and another, 6 feet in diameter, had been found on the port side almost at the turn of the bilge more than 100 feet forward of the torpedo hole. These had apparently been caused by the near misses that had showered the ship. In fact there was still some confusion over just what had caused the damage to the *Nevada*. It was even thought possible that she had struck mines dropped in the channel.[32] The explanation of which bomb or torpedo had caused which damage would come months later, when the ship was in dry dock and drained of water, permitting a thorough investigation. For now, it was enough to know that she had been hit several times below the waterline, was partially buried in the mud, and was full of water, mud, and oil. Wallin later reflected, "There was considerable doubt in most minds as to whether the ship could ever be floated, and there were very few who even dimly hoped she could be of any further military value."[33] There was some good news, though. Surveyors had determined that the *Nevada* was stationary. She was not sliding, nor was she settling further into the mud. But to the consternation of all, the *California* apparently was.

The Base Force salvage memorandum issued on Saturday the twentieth listed the salvage of the *Nevada* as the fourth priority out of twelve. The priority was "subject to change as circumstances demand, or as ordered by competent authority," but the memorandum listed the following jobs:

> Removal of main battery of *California*.
> Removal of *Oklahoma* from present berth.
> Salvage of A.A. guns.
> Refloating of *Nevada*.
> Refloating of YFD-2.
> Refloating of *California*.
> Docking of *Raleigh*.
> Removal of miscellaneous ordnance equipment and ammunition not mentioned
>   above.

Refloating of *West Virginia*.

Recovery of material under cognizance of BuShips and Bureau of Supplies and
  Accounts.

Recovery of Japanese submarine.

Recovery of sunken boats, torpedoes, tubes, and miscellaneous gear now in harbor.

There was a reason that the first priority was the removal of the *California*'s main battery, and it was not for the defense of the island or to overhaul it for reuse. The ship
needed to be lightened in a hurry.

While plans for raising her were centering on the idea of a cofferdam encircling
the ship, surveyors from the Public Works Section were trying to determine whether
the *California* was sinking further into the mud. She was thought to be stationary after
the eleventh, and work had continued removing rangefinders and gun directors as well
as guns and ammunition. Public Works had been of the opinion that she would not
sink any farther, that the bottom would support her.[34] But from the seventeenth to the
twentieth, it appeared the ship had settled by the stern again—not much, only
3 inches in those three days,[35] but enough to cause concern. The time estimates for
her salvage were not very optimistic. The sheet piling for the cofferdam was more than
a month away from Hawaii by rail and ship, and another month would be needed to
drive it into place.[36] Sixty days at a minimum. Five feet more into the mud if the current rate of settling continued. The mud was extremely soft, as evidenced by the depth
the ship had already become embedded, and might soon cover the torpedo damage
completely. The suction to be overcome would then dramatically increase. The
watery silt was at least 90 feet deep at F-3.

The main battery guns would have to come off. Only about 2,000 tons would be
saved, but it was something. The tops of the turrets would have to be dismantled, as
they were when the ship was regunned, though the Pearl Harbor Navy Yard had no
experience in that. Replacing these guns was a job handled by the Puget Sound Naval
Shipyard, and ordnance men and riggers from Bremerton had been requested. But for
now the Base Force, with assistance from the yard, would have to do it. Getting weight
off the *California*, in the hope of slowing her rate of settling as well as lightening her for
eventual raising, had become the first priority.

Guns and ammunition were also coming off the *Cassin* and *Downes* in Dry Dock 1. Both
ships were flooded, burned, mangled wrecks. Removal of the 5-inch/.38 guns was the
first step in floating these battered ships out of dry dock, the first step in stripping
them of anything useful. As warships, they appeared to be at the end of their short
careers. Like the *Shaw* and *Oglala*, they had been in the hands of the yard before the
attack. As with those two ships, responsibility for the work on the *Cassin* and *Downes*
had been transferred to the Base Force.

Both were in dry dock before the attack for work on stern tubes and strut bearings,
and some of their hull plating had been removed for replacement. The same wave of
Japanese bombers that had scored hits on the *Nevada* and *Shaw* had hit the *Cassin*, too.

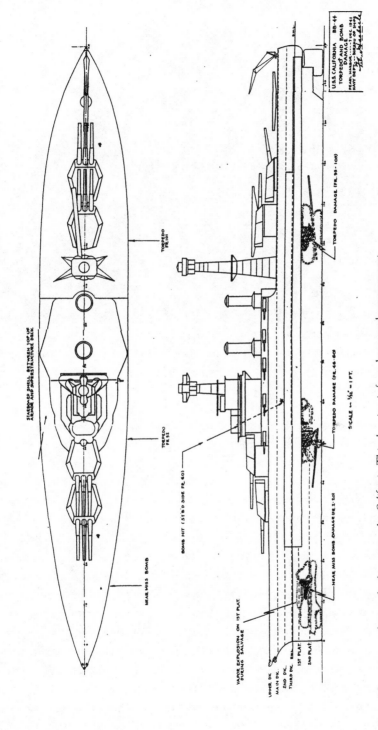

Near-miss and torpedo damage to the *California*. This drawing is from her war damage report.
National Archives

The *Cassin* (*right*) lies toppled next to the *Downes* in Dry Dock 1. Scaffolding was erected on the *Cassin* to enable ordnance crews to reach her guns. The battleship *Pennsylvania* is behind them. U.S. Naval Institute

A bomb passed completely through the destroyer and exploded against the dry dock floor, starting a fire, and more bombs struck the dock and cut off water and power. Another bomb passed through the hull and exploded in the dock, riddling both hulls. Fuel ran out onto the floor of the dock and caught fire, creating another column of thick black smoke in the sky above Pearl Harbor. It joined those billowing out from Battleship Row and from the floating dry dock. The *Downes* was hit by a bomb in her forward superstructure as the flames on the dock floor spread underneath both ships. The hulls glowed red beneath the fuel tanks and magazines, and both ships began to explode, further opening the hulls. The dock was flooded shortly after the fires began, but the blazing oil floated and rose up the sides of the ships. The heat ignited torpedoes on the *Downes*, and between 0915 and 0930 they exploded, tearing a huge hole in the deck. The water rising in the dock lifted the stern of the *Cassin*, but her forward section began to flood and stayed on the blocks. The dock was then pumped down to keep the burning oil on the water from reaching the depth charges that were perilously close to the bow of the *Pennsylvania*. Then the dock was flooded again. The *Cassin* by this time had lost her position on the blocks and was no longer stable atop them. Her hull was so full of holes that she was no longer buoyant. Her stern rose once again, water inside the ship sloshed to starboard, and the 1,500-ton destroyer toppled to the right and smashed against the *Downes*. The *Downes* had also filled with water as the dock flooded, her upper works devastated by fire and by exploding torpedoes. After the attack the pair lay half submerged, the deck steel hot to the touch, the water in the dock filthy with oil and debris.

As dreadful as the *Cassin* and *Downes* looked initially, the full extent of the damage became visible only when the water was pumped out of the dock. The ships were a shambles from stem to stern. Between them, lying on the dock floor, was the after stack of the *Downes*, bent, crumpled, and blackened by fire. Walking on the dock floor along her port side, crouching low under the hull of the toppled *Cassin*, her crew could see holes as large as 6 inches in diameter along the entire length of the ship. Below the after deckhouse the hull was riddled over a length of about 30 feet, shot full of holes in a particularly dense pattern. There was another such area behind the bridge. The hull plating of the *Downes* was badly warped, especially from the bow to between the forward 5-inch/.38 mounts, and beyond the missing shell plating there was a large hole in the hull, the result of a magazine explosion.

The *Cassin* was nearly as bad, the destruction accentuated by the fact that she lay almost on her side. The starboard damage to her was more difficult to see, as most of it was hidden by the dock floor. The bilge of the vessel lay on the floor from frame 72, beneath the mast, to frame 136, at the after deckhouse. By crawling along the drydock bottom, yard officers could see the terrific damage done to the ship's starboard side. It appeared as though a bomb had gone off in the dock beneath the *Cassin*, under the turn of her starboard bilge, and had torn holes in the hulls of both ships. Another bomb had apparently exploded between the two farther aft. The hulls of both were badly warped from the blasts, from the heat of the fires, and, in the case of the *Cassin*, from her tumble to starboard.

Topside the *Downes* looked to be beyond repair. She was badly burned, and her deck had been nearly demolished by the exploding torpedo tubes. The superstructure and deck plating of both the *Downes* and the *Cassin* were badly warped from the fire, and both already looked like the heaps of scrap metal they were almost sure to become.

American ships were not the only vessels undergoing salvage in the harbor. The recovery of the Japanese midget submarine that the destroyer *Monaghan* had sunk (and that the *Medusa* and others were claiming in action reports) during the attack in the North Channel was under way, though the Base Force Salvage Organization memorandum for 17 December noted, "This work is not considered particularly urgent." Divers fixed the location of the sub and marked it with a pair of cork buoys stenciled USS *Yorktown*, and within two weeks they began to tunnel into the mud underneath the conning tower in order to get a sling around it. A derrick was scheduled to lift the sub to the surface as soon as the slings could be rigged. But when the *California* was reported to be sinking further, the derrick was sent to F-3 to remove the weight being taken off the battleship. On the afternoon of the twenty-first the submarine was brought to the surface and taken to the Submarine Base for examination.[37] The com-

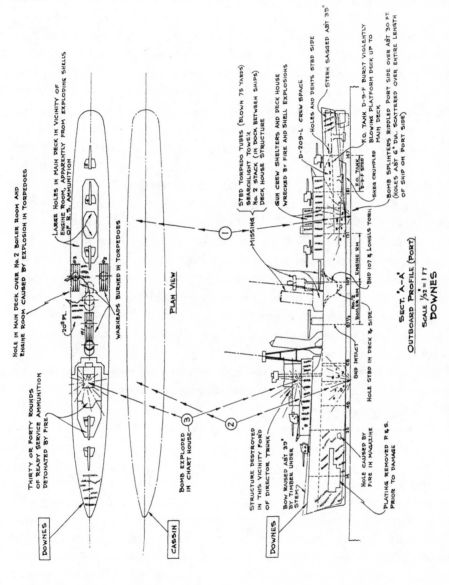

The extensive damage to the *Downes* is shown in this excerpt from the combined *Cassin-Downes* war damage report. National Archives

manding officer of the *Perry*, one of the many ships that had been shooting at it, wanted to know if there was a hole in the conning tower made by a 4-inch shell. No other ship, he believed, had been firing a 4-inch gun at it.[38] Interestingly, the dredging and rigging of slings led to rumors among the onlooking sailors that the submarine was not being salvaged but being captured. The two-man crew, the story went, had been hiding beneath a supply ship since the attack until it had been unceremoniously pulled to the surface. The story went so far as to call the Japanese sailors "embarrassed," as if a game of hide-and-go-seek had gone awry.[39]

Efforts continued to determine why the five battleships had been sunk. The *Arizona* was in a category by herself, of course, but information was needed on the other four as to their material condition and watertight status when the Japanese had pounced on the fleet. A Battle Force memorandum issued on 19 December stated, "It is evident that battleships were in as effective, if not better, material condition than called for by directive existing at the time." That directive called for Material Condition X-Ray, two levels below General Quarters and Condition Zed. Zed required the closure of all watertight doors, fittings, hatches, and valves, whereas X-Ray was the damage control condition in time of peace, when steaming in time of war in a location where attack was improbable or unlikely, or when in port where danger from torpedoes, bombs, and mines existed. This was the situation on the morning of 7 December. Zed was to be set immediately upon the sounding of the general alarm, but even though "there was no question about setting material condition Zed at the first alarm on December 7 . . . in view of the lack of time complete Zed closure was not attained on all battleships."[40] There had been no dereliction aboard ship. Surprise, the primary weapon of the Japanese that morning, had doomed the battle fleet.

While the men at Pearl Harbor struggled to recover from the attack and to understand its nature, the war continued to widen. On the tenth, as the *California* salvage meeting was under way aboard that battleship, two British warships, the *Prince of Wales* and the *Repulse*, were added to the toll of Allied capital ships lost when they were sunk by Japanese aircraft off Malaya. The reach of Japanese air power seemed to have no limits. That same day an air raid on the U.S. Naval Base at Cavite, in the Philippines, damaged a pair of submarines and a destroyer and sank a minesweeper. The following day, as bodies were still being fished from the water around Ford Island, Secretary of the Navy Frank Knox arrived in Hawaii for a firsthand look at the devastation. He was to be the eyes and ears of official Washington, of the president, and of a nation that could only imagine what had happened here. The magnitude of the damage was apparent everywhere Knox went, everywhere he looked. The visit to Kaneohe and to Pearl was a short one; he left the following day and flew back to Washington to brief the president on Sunday the fourteenth.

Knox's secret report to the president covered, among other topics, estimates of the time it would take to salvage the battleships now resting on the bottom. These estimates he obtained at a briefing from Lebbeus Curtis. The *Nevada*, Knox said, would be raised in a month, the *California* in ten weeks, the *West Virginia* by the middle of

March. Each would require an extensive overhaul, of course. The estimate for the *Oklahoma* was four months to raise her, with the advisability of an overhaul to be determined later. On the fifteenth, Knox released to the public the news of the loss of the *Arizona, Utah, Cassin, Downes, Shaw,* and *Oglala*. (Despite listing the *Shaw* as lost, the secret report described her condition thus: "The afterpart of the ship is still intact and can be salvaged and a new section can be built to replace that part of the ship now destroyed.") Knox recommended the expediting of men and material from the mainland to Hawaii, stressing the importance of the salvage operation and calling it "one of the most important pieces of defense work now underway."[41] His public report also informed the nation that the armed forces had not been on the alert on 7 December and that loss of life had been severe, and he posed two questions to be answered. Had there been any "error of judgment" on the part of those responsible for the defense of the islands, and had there been any "dereliction of duty"? Members of Congress were already calling for courts martial of those in command in Hawaii, and had been doing so since before the fires were out on the *West Virginia* and *Arizona*.

That was the future. For now, the Navy attempted to carry the offensive to the Japanese with what it had, including the submarines. The *Gudgeon* and *Plunger* left the Submarine Base for Japanese waters and revenge on the eleventh, though the *Plunger* returned shortly afterward because of a leaky hatch. The *Pollack* departed on the thirteenth and the *Pompano* on the eighteenth, leaving behind a Pacific Fleet bereft of its Battle Line, its plan for a battleship shootout in the Western Pacific drowned into the mud of Pearl, a fleet now reliant on the silent service and a small carrier fleet to carry the war to Japan.

"*Maryland* under way" was the message from the signal tower at 1548 on Saturday the twentieth, as the *West Virginia*'s sister ship slowly made her way out of Southeast Loch. She was followed twelve minutes later by the *Tennessee,* and less than a half-hour later the *Pennsylvania* made her way out of the yard and headed for sea, having completed repairs the day before. Four destroyers escorted the trio to San Francisco Bay and the welcome sight of the Golden Gate Bridge. The *Pennsylvania* arrived in the bay on the twenty-ninth and headed north to Mare Island, while the *Tennessee* and *Maryland* steamed up the coast to Puget Sound. All were to complete the temporary repair work begun at Pearl and then, joined by the *Colorado* and eventually the *Idaho, New Mexico,* and *Mississippi,* defend the West Coast from attack. As the remnants of the Battle Fleet left Pearl Harbor that Saturday afternoon, divers planned a survey of the damage to the *West Virginia*'s port side. An unknown number of torpedoes and bombs had opened up her hull, and a full two weeks were allotted for the examination.

FOUR

Trial and Error

No one yet knew how badly the *West Virginia* was damaged below the waterline. Her executive officer had reported three rapid heavy shocks along the port side minutes after the attack began. These presumably were torpedo hits and were followed by another explosion that threw him to the deck. By that time, he estimated, the ship had a list of 20 to 25 degrees to port. If the fourth hit was a torpedo, it had struck somewhere above the armor belt and above the ship's torpedo defense. Others reported more hits. The *West Virginia*'s navigator later recalled the ship being constantly shaken by bombs. It was generally believed afterward that she had been hit four times by torpedoes and once by a large bomb that struck her port side amidships. Quick-thinking officers and a handful of boatswains and shipfitters quickly counterflooded the ship. The *West Virginia* slowly righted herself and sank to the bottom with only a slight list to port, pinning the *Tennessee*'s starboard bow against the forward mooring quay. She was on fire and continued to burn until the following afternoon, the flames fed by oil from her tanks and those of the *Arizona*, until her decks glowed red and the steel warped.[1]

So wrecked was the Weevee thought to be, so beyond any timely return to duty, that she was not assigned a project representative by Steele. The Base Force salvage memorandum of 17 December listed her only as a source of equipment. "Remove serviceable Ordnance Material from *West Virginia* and deliver to Yard Ordnance Salvage Superintendent," the report read simply. She was to be stripped of anything useful to the fighting fleet, but that was all the action to be taken for now. Within days that had changed. By the twentieth she was being included in the priority list, and preparations for salvage work were under way. Nearly two weeks had passed since the attack, and the time had come for an appraisal of the work required to refloat her. Not only was a diving survey of the port side to be undertaken, but her decks were to be cleaned up. That job was given to the Mobile Repair Unit. Horne's outfit began cleaning the hulk of the *West Virginia* on Christmas Day.

The effect of the torpedo explosion and fire on the deck of the *Downes* is evident in this view taken on 8 December 1941. The after stack has been blown off, and there is a gaping hole in the deck on the starboard side where a torpedo mount exploded.
Naval Historical Center NH 54559

The *Downes* had been badly burned, and the main deck aft of the superstructure was a frightful sight. The exploding torpedoes had caused dreadful damage, and scores of holes peppered the hull. So extensive was the damage that Bloch recommended retaining the *Downes* only as a repository of spare parts for battle-damaged ships.[2] Kimmel had written Stark on the twelfth, expressing the same opinion; the *Downes* appeared to be a total loss except for her value as a spare-parts asset. The *Cassin*, he wrote, could possibly be returned to front-line duty as a destroyer after extensive repair. Officers from the yard and a few from the Bureau of Ships who had recently arrived from the mainland examined the ships on the Sunday following the attack and recommended a somewhat less ambitious plan. The *Cassin* should be patched enough that she could be righted when the *Raleigh,* which had been towed to the Navy Yard on 23 December, replaced the *Honolulu* in Dry Dock 1 in early January. Then she could be patched more thoroughly for a tow to Mare Island. Some sort of duty would await her—not as a destroyer, but perhaps as a patrol ship or convoy escort.[3]

But these were only initial reactions and recommendations, based in large part on visual inspection. As the weeks wore on, no firm consensus emerged about what to do with these two wrecks occupying a portion of one of Pearl Harbor's much-needed dry docks. The efforts on both the *Cassin* and *Downes* had so far been confined to casting loose the 5-inch/.38 mounts, the removal of ammunition and torpedoes, and the rigging of staging on the *Cassin* so that dock cranes could safely lift off her guns. That had been listed as the first priority for the Salvage Organization on the seventeenth, and already ammunition had been unloaded from the forward magazines of both ships. By Friday the nineteenth both forward magazines were empty. The after magazines were still full of water, and holes were to be drilled into the hull to drain them. At 0700 on Christmas Eve day the Mobile Salvage Unit began the laborious job of patching holes in the two hulls.

Emile Genereaux was the project representative on the *Nevada*, overseeing all aspects of her salvage and reporting the daily activity, progress, and requirements to Steele. He was assisted by the *Nevada*'s commanding officer, Cdr. H. L. Thompson, who had relieved Capt. Francis W. Scanland, and by her engineering officer, Lt. Cdr. George E. Fee. The forty-four-year-old Genereaux had been at sea since childhood and had been a master at the age of twenty-three. But it was his salvage experience, gained in years working with his father, a marine surveyor, that interested the Navy. In early 1941 he was offered a Naval Reserve commission and was called to active duty in August. When the Japanese struck he had been assigned to the salvage base at San Diego. Ordered to Hawaii, he arranged to have his equipment shipped to Oahu on the troopship *Harris* before hitching a ride to Pearl Harbor on Secretary Knox's aircraft. Genereaux's executive officer, a Reserve lieutenant (j.g.) from the Civil Engineer Corps named George M. Ankers, accompanied him. Genereaux's responsibilities quickly expanded to include the *Oglala* and then the *West Virginia*, and Ankers became the assistant salvage engineer for the *Nevada* job.

As divers explored the hull of the *Nevada* and recorded the location and size of the holes, and as the yard continued work on what was now known as the "big patch," Ankers arranged for members of the *Nevada*'s crew, who knew her compartments and passageways, to receive a brief course in diving. These men were to descend inside the dark ship to secure watertight doors, close valves, and isolate oil tanks. Others detailed to the salvage crew waded through the 4-foot-deep water on the main deck to retrieve loose equipment, burned furniture, wrecked lockers, and clothing.

Genereaux and Ankers were pleased with the progress of work on the vessel, and throughout the first weeks of the salvage effort they had little to report to Steele each day except that the patching work was proceeding according to plan and that they hoped to deliver the *Nevada* to the yard by 10 January. One hole in the bow made by an exiting bomb was beneath the waterline at the second-deck level and was sealed with a 4-foot-square patch on Friday the nineteenth. Two days later, divers found two more ruptures in the bow. One was a gash in the shell several feet long and several high portside at frame 7. Another was found on the starboard side at frame 13,

Emile C. Genereaux
David W. Genereaux

between the bow and turret 1, apparently caused by a near miss.[4] *Widgeon* divers also
measured a dished-in area along one seam 36 feet long and another vertical tear some
25 feet high. These two openings met in the shape of an upside-down L, and at the

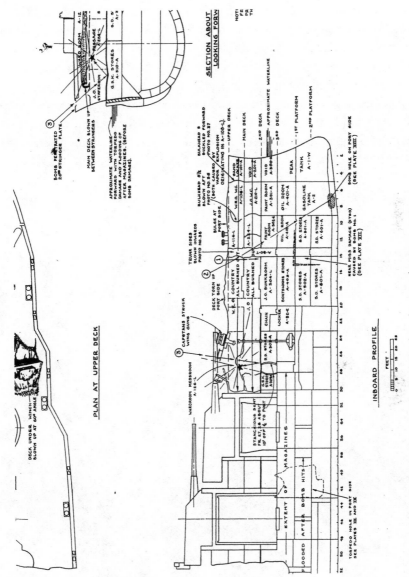

Bomb and torpedo damage to the *Nevada*'s bow, from her war damage report.
National Archives

point where the two tears met the corner had been pushed in 3 feet.[5] Measurements were taken by divers from the *Medusa* and a template was lifted from the hull. Fabrication of a window-frame patch began aboard the repair ship while *Widgeon* divers trimmed the ragged edges from this hole and the one at the port bow.

Ankers was having a bit of trouble obtaining equipment, but that was a common problem throughout the harbor as the salvage effort got under way in earnest and ship representatives badgered Isquith and his officers for pumps, compressors, hoses, diving equipment, and a host of other items in short supply. Divers cutting away the steel wreckage from the *Nevada*'s torpedo hole were slowed because only one cutting torch was available. Progress was further hampered by the restriction of work to daylight hours because of blackout requirements, insufficient manpower to organize another shift, and a lack of transport to and from the ships. But Ankers and his primary assistant, Carpenter W. A. Mahan, were fortunate that the removal of fire control equipment and guns had not been added to their salvage duties. There was no need to remove the *Nevada*'s ordnance for use elsewhere. She might need it herself soon.

On Christmas, Ankers reported that the fuel tanks inboard of the torpedo hole

The window-frame patch that divers secured to the hole in the *Nevada*'s port bilge. The ship had just been dry-docked when this photograph was taken, and water still drains from the patch and hull. Naval Historical Center NH 64494

had been filled with carbon dioxide as a precaution against fire. His only problem seemed to be the persistent delay in preparing the large patch. Finally on the twenty-eighth he was advised that it would be ready on New Year's Eve. Rigging for the patch was sent out to the *Nevada* the next day, and down-hauls and A-frames were installed on the forecastle. The A-frames would hold the patch while divers positioned it. The patch for the large rupture in the starboard side was delivered on the twenty-ninth, and by New Year's Eve both that hole and another had been covered. The fit was poor, however, and the holes far from watertight. More work on them would be needed. In the meantime pumps were being assembled for delivery to the ship. It looked as though she would be afloat by early January.

Lt. Cdr. James Rodgers was the salvage superintendent for the *California*, and it was he who was to oversee the plan developed for her salvage. It was an ambitious plan: the construction of a cellular (or, as it was sometimes called, "celluloid") cofferdam completely around the ship and her mooring quays. The idea was that of Capt. Edward Cochrane of the Bureau of Ships, who had come to Hawaii as the Navy Department's representative on the salvage. In fact, Cochrane proposed the same method for refloating each of the sunken battleships and had already ordered some of the needed material.[6] Twenty-six circular cells, each nearly 64 feet in diameter, would be constructed out of pilings driven 59 feet into the mud surrounding the *California* and joined by more pilings driven between them. Once the cells were in place, they would be pumped out and filled with coral or light rock to help anchor them in place. To counter the immense head of water that would press against the cells, the interior of the cofferdam would be packed with a heavier rock fill 20 feet thick, the water being displaced as the depth of the fill increased. The remaining 20 feet of water inside the cofferdam would then be pumped out. With the *California*'s list, the fill line would come up to the main-deck level on the port side and to the second-deck level starboard. Her torpedo holes had already been buried in the mud, and the fill above the mud line, taking the place of 40 feet of water, would keep her dry. She could then be pumped out until the waterline within the ship was below the manholes on the third deck. The manholes would be bolted down, those too badly damaged or warped replaced with patches.[7] The innermost torpedo bulkheads were assumed to be intact because the ship flooded so slowly, and therefore she would again be watertight. The fill would be removed from around the hull and water slowly released back inside the cofferdam until the ship came afloat. Enough of the cells would be removed to permit the ship to be towed outside her makeshift dry dock to the yard for repairs to enable her to sail or be towed to Puget Sound.

The complexity of this plan was matched by its difficulty. The time element initially caused the most concern. Rodgers advised Steele on the seventeenth that it would take until the end of December to get the sheet piling from the East Coast to California by rail. That estimate had been revised by the twenty-third, when he reported to Steele that although the first 120 tons of pilings were on a train headed for Alameda, it would take another three and a half weeks to roll all of them. Then there was the hazardous sea voyage to Pearl, and once on site, another month would be needed to drive all the pilings. It would be mid-February at the earliest before the cells were in place. Adding to the urgency, Rodgers was being given the disconcerting reports from Public Works that the ship was still settling into the mud.

Other plans were examined, variations on the first. Perhaps instead of a full cellular cofferdam completely around the ship the Salvage Organization could construct two smaller ones, in way of the torpedo holes. Fewer pilings would be needed; perhaps there would be enough in the first few shipments. Each of these mini-cofferdams would be made up of six cells, a little over 15 feet in diameter, extending in a semi-circle around each hole. They would be made of 20-, 60-, and 80-foot-long sheets of SP-4 steel, joined to make 100-foot lengths. Thirty-four of these would be used to make one cellular tube driven 60 feet into the mud and welded together with interlocks to keep them from sliding up and down. These would be shored by 6-inch timbers fastened to the hull by angle iron and bolts at the mud line. The bottoms of the cells would be weighted by 3 feet of concrete. The purpose of the cells was not to keep the water out but to keep the mud away from the hull. Once the two cofferdams were in place, divers would excavate the silt, construct a form over the torpedo damage, and seal the holes with concrete.[8] This involved placing a rich mixture of concrete underwater using 10-inch pipes, known as tremie pipes. Water would be forced out of the pipes, the end of the pipe blocked either by a valve or by air pressure, and concrete poured down the tube from a hopper. The end of the tube would be carefully controlled and kept constantly below the concrete line as the mixture was poured in horizontal gradients.[9]

A variation on this plan replaced the cellular cofferdams with two partial-walled cofferdams. Again the purpose was to keep the mud away from the hull so that the holes could be patched with tremie concrete. The forward section would extend from frame 44 to 58, the aft section from frame 98 to 112. These walls would be 90 feet in length, made from 60- and 30-foot lengths of SP-4 steel. Every third one would have a master pile for strength, a 2-foot-wide, 80-foot-long I-beam obtained from the coaling plant. Flat "shoes" of $3/8$-inch steel were to be welded onto the piles at the mud line if necessary to prevent settling. Each of the four end segments was to be constructed of sheet pilings driven into the mud at an angle to conform to the turn of the bilge. A fixed wale that supported and joined the vertical pile segments was to be secured to the armor belt, and movable wales, which could be lowered down the piles as the mud was excavated, were to be fastened as needed.[10]

While these plans were being drawn up by Fred Crocker of Pacific Bridge, and while the Salvage Organization pondered whether to wait for the steel to arrive or to try something else in the meantime, the work of removing the California's main battery went on. The thickly armored turret top plates were inspected to see what would be involved in removing them. One bit of good news was that the foreman of the riggers, who had experience in lifting Army guns, was of the opinion that Navy Yard Pearl had the equipment to do the job. What was lacking for the time being was the knowledge.

Aboard the *Medusa*, the workload had increased dramatically as fire control equipment came off the battleships to be inspected, repaired, and sent into storage. As early as 10 December some of her fire control men came aboard the *California* to begin casting loose rangefinders, range keepers, and directors. By 22 December the optical shop on the repair vessel had a two-month backlog of routine repair duties and salvage work. The shop also had to be ready to respond to the emergency requests that came in almost daily. So busy were the optical personnel that no more large parties could be spared to assist in the removal of rangefinders and other delicate equipment being taken from the *California, West Virginia,* and *Arizona*. About a dozen men were already working aboard the *Arizona,* and *Medusa* requested that Stelter send fifteen men from his ordnance group to assist the few *Medusa* men aboard the *West Virginia*. These men erected scaffolding around the turrets so that the long rangefinders could be gently eased out when work commenced on the twenty-third.

The work went on for weeks, and it wasn't until after Christmas that the *Medusa*'s men were able to remove the turret rangefinders from the *West Virginia*. All four of them, 33$\frac{1}{2}$ feet in length, went to the repair ship for overhaul before going into storage for future use. Other rangefinders, 20 and 12 feet long, were removed by personnel from the repair ships, overhauled, and put into store or turned over to the Marines. Sailors from the tenders *Whitney* and *Dobbin* lent a hand as well. Hurried as this effort was, careful records were kept as the material was removed to barges and lighters. Everything from "firing pin retaining screws" to "gasket rings" was noted on the daily log sheets that listed the items removed from each ship.

Not only was the *Medusa* running short of time and personnel; she was running short of storage space. The ship requested that the *West Virginia* and *Arizona* Mark 22 rangefinders be taken ashore to the Salvage Office, whence *Medusa* crewmen could retrieve them later. The fragile rangefinders each required about three weeks to be overhauled, and the ship did not have the space to work on a pair of the big Mark 22s at the same time. But space ashore was at a premium too, and the *Medusa* was forced to take aboard all four *West Virginia* rangefinders on 29 December until space could be made for them in the yard. Mark 19 directors were even more time-intensive, requiring about four months per instrument. A tally of man-hours spent on the equipment showed that about fifteen hundred hours had been spent on the *California* instruments and about twice as much time on those recovered from the *West Virginia* in the two weeks since the attack.[11]

Sometimes equipment was detached from the damaged ships faster than it could be taken ashore. Tug services were at a premium, and the valuable little vessels were everywhere, moving the *Tennessee,* moving the *Maryland,* and carrying out the myriad tasks that the captain of the Navy Yard required. Guns and mounts sometimes sat aboard a ship for days until a tug could be found to bring a barge alongside. Equipment continued to be removed from the battleships, and the workload continued to back up.

Only a few preliminary dives had been made on the *Arizona,* explorations to see how extensive the damage was and what might be recovered from the ship. The fires on

Still smoldering, the *Arizona* is visited by an inspection party on 9 December 1941. Along her port side the *Tern* continues to spray water onto the hot steel.
Naval Historical Center NH 97383

board had finally been put out on the ninth, though it was many hours before the steel was cool enough to walk on. The maintop still stood on tripod legs, but almost everything forward of it had been reduced to crumpled steel. The foremast had toppled over the bridge and conning tower, and the forward third of the ship had dropped nearly from view. Only the top of turret 2, the tips of the gun muzzles, and a mass of unrecognizable steel at the bow were visible forward of the demolished superstructure.

Definitive damage reporting was difficult because of the lack of survivors and the extent of the destruction. Lt. Alfred J. Homman, who had relieved Cdr. Ellis Geiselman as the *Arizona*'s acting captain, would later report eight bomb hits and would pass on the *Vestal*'s report that the battleship had been struck by a torpedo underneath turret 1. According to a damage report made more than a month and a half later, she had been pummeled by five bombs amidships, including one dropped down the stack.[12] Two others hit the quarterdeck, one ricocheting off turret 4. The eighth bomb struck near turret 2 and penetrated to the black powder storage below, which in turn set off the smokeless powder in the forward magazines. The extent of the damage caused by four of the reported bomb hits was not known, and the torpedo hit could not be verified because of the subsequent destruction to the forward half of the ship.[13] Whatever the actual number of hits, there was no doubt about the fatal one.

Amazingly, the magazine detonation had been captured on movie film by a doctor aboard the *Solace*.

Shortly after the *Arizona's* fires were extinguished, inspection parties went aboard onto the boat deck, the only deck above water. The ship settled for days, air bubbling eerily to the surface among the blackened corpses still bobbing to the surface. Other bodies lying on the superstructure deck were collected in pillowcases and sheets. Sometimes all that remained were ashes and bits of bone.[14] Recovering bodies below the waterline was more difficult, equally unpleasant, and much more dangerous because of the metal wreckage that was everywhere in the darkness. The recovery of bodies did not go on for long. Though the thought of the hundreds of bodies in and on the ship was becoming a serious morale problem, the ship was now being viewed as a grave site.[15]

Homman reported that the ship's personnel records, near the executive officer's office, had been burned. Pay records might be salvaged later if a large, well-equipped party were to cut through the side of the ship to the disbursing officer's cabin. The interior passageways were impassable in that area, but the effort might be worth it, as there was reportedly $135,000 in cash there besides cash receipts and the crew pay records. Another $4,000 was located in the ship's service safe, along with some bonds, and these could be reached by shallow-water divers. So could the ship's registered publications in the wardroom and some of the personal effects of the crew.[16]

Arizona survivors, with little or no diving experience, began to recover some of the paperwork and money on 8 December even while the ship still burned. A lieutenant, a carpenter, three chiefs, and a pair of gunner's mates made up the diving group. Their only equipment was a few items recovered from the ship. Nevertheless they pressed on, making thirty-three dives into the wreck of their ship in December alone. They would continue for months.[17]

A caisson similar to that planned for the *California* was proposed for the *Arizona*. Salvage parties could then work aboard her with ease, removing guns, ammunition, and equipment and collecting the hundreds of bodies inside for burial ashore.[18] Such a cofferdam had been built around the wreckage of the battleship *Maine* in Havana Harbor in 1911 so that she could be examined nearly a dozen years after she mysteriously exploded. But there was neither the time nor the resources for such a huge undertaking now.

On 22 December 1941 the work of stripping the hulk of usable equipment commenced. There wasn't much, and what there was came from aft of frame 70. Twelve-foot rangefinders and 36-inch searchlights were removed from the mainmast, and for the next five days yard burners cast loose a pair of secondary battery directors, 5-inch/.25 guns from her twisted boat deck, two saluting guns, 5-inch/.25 directors, the main battery directors, and some loading machines. All of it was taken to the yard by the Hawaiian Dredging Company crane barge *Gaylord*. Much could not be recovered. The secondary battery was beyond reach. Some of the guns were submerged, the rest charred. Sound-powered phones at the 5-inch/.51 splinter shields were burned beyond use, and there were about a hundred scorched metal helmets scattered around the boat deck.[19] By the twenty-ninth, after a one-day delay so that the *Gaylord* could pluck an Army plane off the bottom of the channel near Hickam, everything accessible had been removed, and the *Arizona* was abandoned once more.[20]

On 10 December the submarine rescue ship *Ortolan*, sister to the *Widgeon*, departed San Diego for Pearl Harbor carrying sorely needed divers, compressors, pumps, and salvage pontoons. Under the command of Lt. F. D. Latta, she arrived ten days later and after a brief stop at the Submarine Base tied up alongside the *Oglala*. The first test to pump air pressure into the *Oglala*'s hull had failed two days earlier, but work continued with the same plan developed by the Design Section, to raise her by air bubble and pontoons. She was still leaking oil, and the sludge removal barge *Intrepid* came alongside to pump out her tanks. But the balky pumps aboard the *Intrepid* refused to remove more than a negligible amount, at one point just thirty barrels in seven hours. When the *Ortolan* arrived the barge was moved out of her way. Divers were over the side almost immediately to seal the mine-deck hatch and to begin rigging the pontoons to the *Oglala*'s hull. There were six available, and as many as ten of them, each with a lifting capacity of 80 tons, would probably be needed. Steele ordered an officer out to the *Raleigh* to see if some of the pontoon gear could be released for use alongside Ten Ten Dock.

The patching, caulking, and welding of hull seams continued. By Christmas Eve, preparations were well under way to lower the two forward pontoons into place and to plug additional air fittings into the hull for the lift, but on Saturday the twenty-seventh Steele explained to Calhoun the impracticality of lifting the *Oglala* by air pressure and pontoons alone. The old ship simply did not have the hull integrity or the internal watertight subdivision necessary to isolate compartments. The pontoons available would not be enough without air in the hull, and the hull couldn't hold it. "Therefore," he reported, "work has been commenced on obtaining four one thousand ton lighters from Honolulu Contractors and fitting them for the lifting job." The hope of quickly dragging the *Oglala* clear of Ten Ten Dock had gone. "Lifting by this method," Steele continued, "is much slower and the *Oglala* berth cannot be expected much before the middle of February. A definite date will be given later."[21] Lieutenant Commander Curtis, personally in charge of the *Oglala* job, proceeded with the acquisition of the lighters with the assistance of the busy Genereaux and newly arrived Lt. Wilfred L. Painter. Bill Painter was a thirty-three-year-old former Marine Corp officer and civil engineering graduate of the University of Washington. He had resigned his Marine Corps Reserve commission in February 1941 to accept a commission as a Civil Engineer with the rank of lieutenant in the Naval Reserve and had been transferred from the Naval Operating Base at San Pedro to the Base Force staff following the attack.

Regardless of the method used to raise the *Oglala*, much of the superstructure, masts, and kingposts had to be removed to provide room for whatever would eventually lift the ship. Two parties of divers from the *Ortolan* worked alongside her daily, cutting away the top hamper and retrieving personal effects of the crew. The conges-

This view of the *Oglala*, taken six months before the attack, shows the amount of top hamper that needed to be removed by divers before pontoons or barges could be sunk alongside the deck and secured to the hull.
Naval Historical Center 19 N 25593

tion of debris and recovered material in the yard was still very much a problem, and pieces of the *Oglala*, some recognizable and some not, were piled atop a barge off Ten Ten Dock. Removing the superstructure in the murky waters of the harbor was a laborious, time-consuming process. With the decision made to lift and tow the *Oglala* clear of the pier with the barges, the team of engineers and divers had entered a new phase of her salvage.

Silent and abandoned, with dozens of her crew missing and presumed drowned inside her inverted hull, the *Utah* was virtually ignored by the salvage teams in the weeks after 7 December. The old ship was a valuable training vessel, yet she was not a combatant, and at the moment it was combatants the Navy needed.

Isquith, her engineer, had reported that the ship had apparently been hit in rapid succession just after 0800 by a pair of torpedoes at about frame 84. The flooding was immediate and extensive, and within ten minutes the ship had listed 80 degrees and rolled over. A bomb hit near the stack had also been reported, penetrating the upper deck to explode on the main deck in or around the bakeshop. Her watertight integrity was virtually nonexistent, and there had been almost no time to close the watertight doors. Even had there been time to counterflood, the obsolete *Utah* was not equipped to do so.[22] Steele had been ashore on leave the morning of 7 December, and by the time he reached Ford Island his ship had capsized. He had been visibly shaken by the sight.[23]

As yet divers had not examined the wreck to determine the damage to the *Utah*'s hull or even her position in the mud. None could be spared for what was obviously going to be a very costly and time-consuming righting and refloating job. There was no design or planning work under way by Steele or Gillette. Still, her 5-inch batteries and store of ammunition were of value. On 21 December, as the liner *Lurline* arrived from the West Coast with its load of workmen for the salvage force, Steele noted in his daily report, "Need for the 5-inch batteries of the *Utah* is considered urgent. Investigation will be made as soon as possible, giving low priority, to determine feasibility of removing the eight guns before righting the vessel. Ballistic houses are now installed which would drop off when cut."[24] Nothing was noted regarding the recovery of the bodies.

Nor was anything mentioned in Steele's daily reports to Calhoun about the four hundred or more sailors and Marines who had drowned in the *Oklahoma*. In fact, that ship was not referred to at all, even though Whitaker and Holtzworth had requested details about her damage from Steele so that the Design Section could decide how best to raise her. Captain Bode's action report of 18 December listed five or six torpedo hits, and he wrote, "Because of the condition of the *Oklahoma*, capsized and practically flooded, it has been impossible to ascertain the extent or details of damage sustained." Like the *Utah*, she had been torn open, her watertight boundaries either damaged, open, or in poor repair. She had rolled through 135 degrees of list within eight or ten minutes until her masts and superstructure had hit the mud. Unlike the *Utah*, she was a badly needed combatant. Yet the daunting job of righting her, in the midst of much more attainable short-term work, allowed only the most cursory brainstorming to be undertaken by the salvage officers. Day after day the remark next to the *Oklahoma*'s name on the salvage reports was the same: "No work."

On 30 December, from a float tied up abreast turret 2, divers from the Mobile Repair Unit began the underwater exploration of the *West Virginia*'s hull under Lt. (j.g.) F. G. Archbold, Horne's ship superintendent. The float had been moored there the previous day for the first of two diving parties organized to investigate the 220-foot span between the likely foremost and aftermost torpedo damage. This float and another one were to be moored at frame 102, just forward of turret 3, if enough wreckage could be cleared away by Horne's cleaning crew. Lieutenant White's crew had already made a number of dives to retrieve personal effects from crew spaces. Archbold's team was to make the first dives concerned with the monumental salvage effort to follow.

Five dives were made the first day directly below the float under the supervision of Garland Suggs. The divers explored a little forward of the hole at frame 46, and finding no additional damage in the immediate vicinity, they concentrated on the 50 feet of hull between frames 46 and 52. By touch alone, for it was too dark and murky to see anything at that depth, the divers found a split in the hull, just above the bilge, about

2 feet wide and extending 10 feet high, far below the lower edge of the armor belt. Aft of that, between frames 47 and 51, three small ruptures were found, the metal edges of the shell splayed outward as if from an internal explosion.

As the *West Virginia*'s anchors and chains were being removed, the survey continued on New Year's Eve. The work was dangerous. Jagged metal protruded outward from the hull, and divers had to proceed carefully and by touch alone to avoid being injured. There were four dives made that day. Archbold's divers worked their way aft of frame 52 to frame 60 without finding any damage. At frame 60, though, directly under the casemate for broadside gun 4, the shell became rough and wrinkled, and about 25 feet further aft they found a second major rupture, 8 feet high and up to 4 feet wide. A small hole was found at frame 70, and then they came upon a huge hole at frame 79, between the stacks. The bottom of this hole, as with the others, was about 37 feet below the main deck. This one extended aft 25 feet and was 17 feet high at its tallest point. The bottom was pushed inward, and this was assumed to be the impact point of the torpedo. Above this the shell had been exploded outward, evidently from the warhead detonation. The divers, becoming more familiar with their surroundings, began to work more quickly. After measuring this torpedo hit they felt their way aft again to frame 92 under the mainmast. Here an 8-by-4-foot hole was discovered. On New Year's Day 1942 the divers spent the morning examining the hull from the bow to frame 10 without finding any damage. Four additional dives were made that afternoon and the following day. From frame 10 to 46, the divers made their way by touch along the hull, from the surface all the way to the turn of the bilge. With the exception of some loose rivets near frame 46, the location of the first hit, no further damage was found. The stern of the ship, including the hit at frame 102, still remained to be examined, but for now plumb lines were rigged at each of the holes to obtain more accurate measurements.[25] Suggs himself made many of the measuring dives, spending hours under water running the lines so that patch dimensions could be calculated.

The exploratory dives would continue, but already there was some unexpected good news. Although Wallin would later report damage "so extensive as to beggar description,"[26] Archbold reported through Steele on 3 January that "investigation of underwater damage now discloses that the damage is not as great as expected." Little wonder that the *West Virginia*'s salvage had been initially regarded as doubtful. The destruction of her port side, though frightful, was less than had been assumed in the days after the attack. Now Curtis was of the opinion that the battleship could be "floated in a reasonable length of time by patching and unwatering."[27]

As the diving operations commenced on the *West Virginia*, work proceeded with the cleanup of the decks. They were a shambles. Officers from the Mobile Repair Unit had surveyed the upper and main decks on 23 December and found the once gleaming paint, brass, and woodwork covered in oil, blackened by fire and smoke. Charred clothing lay strewn about. Some of it had come from lockers torn open after the attack. Rumor had it that looters among the *West Virginia*'s own crew had been at work.[28] Thousands of pounds of burned potatoes rotted in the "spud locker" at the mainmast. Bread and pastries spoiled in the bakeshop. Tile and wood had burned off the steel deck. Ashes were everywhere. Far below, still listed among those missing and presumed drowned inside the ship, the three men trapped in a storeroom, their air supply growing foul with carbon dioxide, marked off another day on their calendar. It was to be their last.

The unit started cleaning the next day. The first order of business was to reduce the fire hazard, to clean up the oily trash and get it off the ship. Sand was spread on the decks to provide footing. Not only was the trash to be removed but parts of the damaged superstructure, too. The boat deck sagged where the supporting bulkheads and stanchions had either given way in the heat of the fire or been collapsed by bombs or torpedoes that hit above the armor belt. The Mobile Repair Unit and the few remaining crewmen under Lieutenant White turned to with a will.

By the final day of 1941, some 50 tons of debris and damaged equipment had been assembled in piles awaiting removal by lighter. The *West Virginia*'s boat deck had been cleaned up, as had the bridge, the compartments inboard of the casemates, and the upper deck all the way to turret 1. Stanchions and lifelines had been removed from her quarterdeck and forecastle; boat cradles, skids, and stanchions had been lifted from the boat deck. About half the doors and hatches in the superstructure were removed, and 150 fathoms of anchor chain were taken away. The charred wood decking was removed from the port side near turret 1. On Tuesday the thirtieth a 9-ton yard crane came alongside and began to transfer the debris and salvable material to a pair of barges.[29]

Some of the *West Virginia*'s remaining crew had been assigned guard duty on the ship since the day after the attack. It was depressing duty, and it could be nerve-wracking, too. Some men swore they could hear tapping from below. A few were told by officers that the noise was simply wreckage in the water bumping against the hull. But the men were not so sure, believing that some of their mates were trapped and signaling for help. It was a detail that some would never forget, would never forgive.[30]

Once the ship was rid of the clutter and debris and there was room to work, the unit began to lighten the *West Virginia* to aid in floating her. Orders had been issued on the twentieth from the Navy Yard to the Salvage Organization to remove the eight 16-inch guns, both masts, both stacks, the ship's cranes and catapults, and any other readily accessible and removable weight. Once the *California*'s main battery had been removed it would be the *West Virginia*'s turn.

While George Ankers reported little difficulty so far on the *Nevada* job, James Rodgers was getting frustrated aboard the *California*. Rodgers, assigned to work with the new organization but still attached to Calhoun's Base Force staff, let Steele know he was annoyed with the current state of affairs. "There has been," he wrote with irritation, "some lack of cooperation between the Design Section and the Salvage Engineers."[31] Though plans were still being drawn up involving some type of cofferdam, that option was losing its appeal. Not only were the cofferdam plans too time-consuming, Public Works was reporting that the mud surrounding the ship was too deep and too fluid to

Debris, trash, and charred lumber piled by the Mobile Salvage Unit on the forecastle of the *West Virginia* on 5 January 1942. Note the decking that had been removed along her port side.
National Archives

provide a good support for the piles. Perhaps if the hull could be made tight the ship could be pumped dry one deck at a time, from the top down, after a small cofferdam was built around the quarterdeck to permit access to the deck for the placement of pumps and compressors. That plan had been adopted on the eighteenth as a stopgap measure, and one that it was hoped would prove successful so that the cofferdam plans would not need to be attempted. No one could as yet provide a clear answer as to how Rodgers and his Base Force men and Little and his *California* crew were to proceed. The plans for her salvage were in a constant state of flux, the main difficulty being the still-evolving relationship between Gillette's officers and the Salvage Organization. On the eighteenth Rodgers notified Steele of the deck-by-deck unwatering plan, yet three days later he reported, "It is definitely decided to build celluloid cofferdam around the *California* to assist in unwatering the ship."[32]

Rodgers continued to be exasperated by the day-to-day activity aboard the ship. "Very little progress," he advised on 19 December, in sharp contrast to the normally upbeat reports received by Steele from his various ship superintendents: "Asked for derrick and barge yesterday for this morning. They had not arrived at noon." Rodgers wanted to land some of the recovered equipment and clear some room on the deck. This was only a temporary setback, though. The next day he was able to report that the requested derrick and barge had arrived at F-3 and were clearing the *California's* decks of debris and fire control equipment.[33]

Divers had begun plugging holes in the *California's* hull on the nineteenth, the same day Rodgers had vented to Steele. Scuppers, portholes, and fragment holes were located and either closed or patched. The ship was still flooding, as the constant stream of bubbles from her starboard quarter attested. Divers found the sources of the bubbles (missing rivets and split seams) and closed them with caulk and sheet lead. They also continued their exploration of the hull, searching for undiscovered damage.

Regardless of which plan was adopted to float the *California*, there was a consensus among the engineers that she had to be lightened by the removal of her main battery. Riggers from Bremerton had arrived to provide needed guidance. The armored plates atop turret 3 were laboriously detached and lifted off by the *Haviside*, one of the Hawaiian Dredging Company's crane barges, while work began on removing them from turrets 1 and 2. Next the face plates were removed from the turrets while the guns were cast loose. Turret 4, submerged and out of sight except for the tips of the muzzles trained out to starboard, was unreachable for the time being.

The work went on throughout the rest of December while two groups of divers continued to seal openings in the hull. On the twenty-seventh they discovered a new hole on the port side at frame 12. Rodgers wrote, "This is believed to have been caused by a third torpedo hit that many people spoke of but were not sure of."[34] One diving group was tasked to measure this hole for a patch, while the second continued the time-consuming job of sealing the hull. The method of raising the ship was still being debated, Cochrane's recommendation notwithstanding. Steele advised Calhoun on the twenty-eighth, "Further investigation points to the extreme difficulty of the cellular cofferdam around the *California*. The nature of the bottom at this berth is such that other and quicker methods are indicated. The matter is now under study. This does not mean that material ordered will not be used but does mean that it may be used in a different manner."[35] Yet Rodgers, on New Year's Eve, was not so definite. "The placing of the cellular cofferdam, previously reported, will probably be changed in character somewhat," he wrote Steele. "Consideration is being given to the possibility of concrete patches."[36] This was the modified cellular or partial-walled cofferdam. Clearly the plan for the salvage of the *California* would be created as the situation unfolded.

On 22 December, as the Japanese midget submarine was being examined at the Submarine Base and as *Ortolan* divers began cutting away the *Oglala*'s top hamper, a special commission appointed by the president met at the Royal Hawaiian Hotel on Waikiki Beach. This was the Roberts Commission, headed by Supreme Court Justice Owen J. Roberts. Knox's report to the president and to the nation on the magnitude of the defeat, and the resulting hue and cry in the press and in public debate, demanded that an investigation be undertaken to find out who was responsible for the debacle. Two generals and two admirals, along with Roberts, made up the commission. It had already taken testimony from those concerned in Washington, and now the five men prepared to interview Kimmel and Short.

Short was first, and it was not until Saturday the twenty-seventh that Kimmel was questioned. Thereafter, for the next thirteen days, the Roberts Commission interviewed officers and enlisted men from both services, as well as civilians, about the cooperation (or lack of it) between the Army and Navy; about the responsibilities of each service in the defense of Oahu and in particular Pearl Harbor; and about the attack itself. The commission left for California on 10 January, but it would be several more weeks before those in Pearl Harbor learned its findings and recommendations.

Steele and his officers had little time to reflect on the commission. There were still minesweepers providing power to the *Nevada* and *California*, and Public Works was looking into the possibility of running 125-volt land lines out to the ships, as was being done on the *West Virginia*. Transportation to and from the ships was still lacking, and Rufus Thayer was busy trying to secure more boats and boat crews, along with trucks and drivers. Berth 22, which had been used to move equipment to and from Battleship Row and the *Nevada*, was needed to moor ships under repair and was reclaimed by the shipyard. Steele's men now had to clear the surrounding piers of salvage and recovered equipment and move it to berth 5, near the end of Ten Ten Dock, which had become the new dispatching point. The Salvage Organization continued to lack adequate office space and clerical support, although several buildings were being prepared as a headquarters. Night movement within the harbor was extremely dangerous, and Steele put a halt to it pending the establishment of recognition signals with the Marines and the Inshore Patrol. Time was wasted every day ferrying men from ship to shore for their noon meal, and Lieutenant Commander Horne looked into providing box lunches for the men. It seemed like a little thing, but it wasn't. Some one thousand man-hours a day were being lost just in feeding the salvage crews.

The problems experienced by the Base Force were minor ones and to be expected. And they were being solved. Steele acknowledged this in his Salvage Organization memorandum of the twenty-eighth. "It is now felt for the first time since December 7 that there is a basis of mutual understanding and cooperation between the Salvage Organization, the Navy Yard, Pearl, and the Fourteenth Naval District," he wrote. "Because the Salvage Organization had to be started from scratch on December 7 it is felt that the regrettable delay in orderly prosecution of this work could not have been avoided except by planning before the enemy action took place."[37]

The Base Force was about to be removed from this triad. The previous week Steele had informed Calhoun, "Organizational details are going forward and it is expected that the Fourteenth Naval District will relieve Commander Base Force of the responsibility of all damaged vessels at Pearl in the very near future."[38] By "Fourteenth Naval District" he meant the Navy Yard. With its large, well-equipped shops and established infrastructure for major repair work, the shipyard was better equipped to permanently handle the salvage. The Base Force, after all, had an active and mobile fleet to service.

The shift of responsibility for the salvage work was mainly an administrative one. The table of organization would remain basically the same, though there would be some personnel changes. Steele was informed that he would soon be relieved and reassigned, probably to a staff position under Calhoun. Lieutenant Commander Curtis was also advised that his position as the senior salvage engineer was temporary, and a number of *Utah* officers were also told to expect transfer. Salvage engineers for hull work and machinery had been requested from Washington, as were more officers for Isquith's busy Services Section.

While the Fourteenth Naval District prepared to absorb the Salvage Organization into the yard command structure in early January, the yard itself continued its busy schedule of preparing the fleet for war. Dry Dock 3 was under construction at an accelerated pace, and Drydocks 1 and 2 were full. Number 1 had the two destroyers and the *Honolulu*, which had replaced the *Pennsylvania* on the thirteenth. Number 2 had the *Helena*. She was to be followed in the dock by the *William Ward Burrows* so that the transport could have her rudder straightened. The submarine *Narwhal* and the *Shaw* were to follow the *Burrows*, the *Narwhal* for repair of an oil leak that had plagued her on her last patrol, the *Shaw* to have a false bow installed for the trip to Mare Island.

Over on the marine railway the *Tracy* was hauled out of the water on Christmas Day for an overhaul. She was part of a constant stream of ships that were being docked by the huge chains of the railway. The *Aylwin, Dolphin, Mugford, Southard,* and *Shaw* had all preceded her. Among the ships docked at the repair basin were the destroyers *Selfridge* and *Farragut*, both having torpedo tube mounts renewed. The *Craven* was having her number 1 gun shield repaired, and guns removed from the *Helena* were being installed on the *Phoenix*. The *Curtiss* had been maneuvered over to the piers for a period of restricted availability beginning on Saturday the twentieth for repairs to her damaged hangar and main and second decks. The minesweeper *Rail* had been replaced alongside the *Nevada* by the *Bobolink* so that she could have a main engine cylinder replaced. Preparations were also under way to repair the *Lexington's* main motor stator as soon as the carrier arrived back at Pearl from the aborted Wake Island relief mission.[39] Now, in addition to this work, Navy Yard Pearl was to take over the salvage operation.

The Pacific Fleet now had a new commanding officer. Kimmel had been relieved on the seventeenth, temporarily replaced by the commander of Task Force 1 and of the Battle Force, Vice Adm. William S. Pye. Selected to take command was a polite, soft-spoken Texan named Chester W. Nimitz, currently a rear admiral and the head of the Bureau of Navigation. He arrived in Hawaii on Christmas Day. Like many who had arrived on Oahu since the attack, Nimitz was depressed by what he saw in the harbor, his gloom amplified by the rain that pelted him as he stared at the wrecks along Battleship Row. Bloch briefed him on the security measures put in place since the seventh. The nets were now closed at all times except when ships were entering or leaving. The harbor patrol had been reinforced, and PT boats armed with depth charges were kept on standby in case a submarine managed to enter. Everyone was jumpy, convinced that Japanese fifth-column agents had been at least partly to blame for the success of the raid. The day Nimitz's plane landed in the oily waters of Pearl Harbor, Combat Intelligence and the captain of the yard were notified that carrier pigeons, perhaps carrying enemy messages, had been observed landing in a tree near berth C-5, off Aeia.[40]

Preparations to ward off another attack continued. Air raid shelters were under construction for Navy Yard employees and residents of the nearby housing areas. Fuel and water tanks had been camouflaged and the windows in the Navy Yard painted black.[41] Carriers and battleships moored at Ford Island's few available quays were now protected by the modified target rafts at all times. So were cruisers out in East Loch. The possibility existed that Japanese aircraft or submarines could damage a ship transiting the narrow harbor entrance, so tugs were alerted whenever a large vessel entered or left Pearl Harbor. They would attempt to beach any ship in danger of sinking and blocking the channel.[42] Nimitz was also given a tour of the harbor by Wallin and a briefing on the status of the salvage operations and the ongoing work to expedite completion of Drydocks 2 and 3. Wallin's natural optimism had reasserted itself after the initial shock of the attack had worn off, and he assured Nimitz, while the two toured the *Nevada*, that the sunken ships could be and would be refloated. Nimitz was not convinced, but Wallin was undeterred. As he wrote more than two decades later, "It is well for Salvage Officers to remember that ships are designed to float, and they will float if given half a chance. The main objective should always be to isolate damage in order to recover buoyancy, and to unload everything possible as necessary. The earlier work at Pearl did not comprehend many of the facts of Naval design because the work was being guided by salvage experts who were experienced in rigging work such as required for pulling ships off the beach, etc."[43]

In a quiet ceremony aboard the submarine *Grayling* on 31 December, while the *Helena* was being removed from Dry Dock 2 and made ready to sail to the coast, Nimitz assumed the rank of full admiral and took command of the fleet that Kimmel had trained for war and that the Japanese had bloodied three and a half weeks earlier.

FIVE

The Navy Yard Takes Over

On 9 January 1942, Homer Wallin replaced the newly promoted Capt. Jim Steele as the salvage officer of what was now the Salvage Division of the Navy Yard. Steele was assigned to Calhoun's Base Force staff. He had done a splendid job, despite being badly traumatized by the attack, the tremendous loss of life, and the sinking of his ship. Though he had always enjoyed telling stories, he would never again speak of the events of that time.[1] Wallin was from Washburn, North Dakota, was a graduate of Annapolis, class of 1917, and had earned a master's in naval architecture from the Massachusetts Institute of Technology in 1921. He was well informed about the progress of the salvage work to date but had not been the first choice to head the new Salvage Division. Furlong had requested that the Navy Department send him either a commander or a captain with sufficient salvage experience to take over from Steele. No one, he had been advised, was available. Wallin, also just promoted to captain, requested that he be allowed to take the job, but because there was not a suitable replacement for him as material officer, this request was denied. On 5 January, Wallin requested the assignment as extra duty on a voluntary basis. As this arrangement seemed to be the best solution, he received his orders the following day and replaced Captain Steele.

The transition was a smooth one, though Wallin was not altogether happy with the freedom that Lebbeus Curtis had enjoyed as senior salvage engineer. He acknowledged that Curtis had expedited delivery of salvage equipment on his own authority, and he praised the progress that had been made in an organization built from scratch only a month before, but he complained to the yard management that this freedom had also resulted in unnecessary expenditure of money as well as equipment that could not be accounted for. Curtis, in telephone consultation with Cdr. W. A. Sullivan, supervisor of the newly established Navy Salvage Service since 13 December, had ordered the sheet piling for the *California* cofferdam, about $1.5 million worth, but when the caisson plan was abandoned only about two-thirds of the order could be canceled. When the plan to lift the *Oglala* with an air bubble was replaced by a scheme to lift her with barges available in Hawaii, Curtis, wrote Wallin, "decided on his own responsibility that the barges previously considered satisfactory should not be used, and he arranged with Commander Sullivan for the procurement of four 1,250-ton steel lift barges with suitable compartmentation for this work." Wallin also complained that some thirty pumps, "unsuitable and not needed for the work now in view," had been ordered either by Curtis or in his name from the Peerless Pump Company, in the amount of $150,000. Wallin was also frustrated by the lack of accountability for the equipment that had been ordered while Steele was in command. "I am quite sure," he continued, "as a result of discussions with some of the personnel and with Captain Steele that a sizable quantity of the material is adrift in the yard and on ships without proper identification—it may be difficult to locate and account for all of the property which has been delivered." Though he accepted Curtis's "expert knowledge and recognized ability," he made it clear that any further procurements by Curtis or his officers would need to be "confirmed by memorandum so that yard personnel may have due knowledge thereof."[2] On 13 January he wrote to Curtis, requesting a complete accounting from him and from Commander Sullivan of all the equipment and material the Bureau of Ships had ordered for delivery. Clearly Wallin did not intend to be bypassed by anyone. He was responsible now, and he intended to be involved in the decisions concerning his new command.

Since Christmas, Steele had discontinued wide dissemination of his daily reports, and only Calhoun and Admiral Furlong received them. Wallin continued these noon summaries, now sending them to Furlong and to Captain Gillette. There was no pause in the work. Progress was being made, albeit in small increments. But more equipment and more men were arriving all the time to assist. The early pessimism was nearly gone. In fact, the Salvage Organization had received some welcome news less than a week earlier.

On 3 January, at a 1430 meeting attended by engineers and ship superintendents, Curtis had advised the group that it would not be necessary to lighten the *West Virginia* to raise her. This conclusion was based on the initial diver survey, which had found that the damage to the ship's port side, while severe, was not beyond patching. The work to seal the hull would be extensive, but once it had been completed, the *West Virginia* would regain her buoyancy. The mathematics (and the salvage work was all mathematics and construction work) were clear on the fact. With Lt. Louis Lefelar in charge, the work of disassembling turret 2 had already begun on 29 December. The guns of all turrets were first preserved by sponging them out and hand-applying a coat of mineral grease inside the barrel. Tompions were obtained from yard storage and the guns sealed. The turret top plates were removed over the next few days, but at the 3 January conference Curtis recommended that the guns stay in place. This was significant in terms of the labor and time saved in the salvage, and in the rebuild that would follow once the ship was raised and sent to Puget Sound. The salvage engineers were keenly aware that any equipment removed would delay the ship's return to duty.

Her gunnery officer, Berthold, now with the salvage group, gave the officers at the meeting the good news that the ship had been due for regunning at her next West Coast overhaul, and that the work would be expedited at Puget Sound by reinstalling only the outside bolts on the top plates. Forty-five minutes after the meeting began, the dismantling of the turrets was halted and the yard crews began putting them back together.

On the fifth, while the top-plate bolts and studs were being reinstalled with a coat of litharge and glycerine to ensure a watertight fit, and while a patch was being placed over the bomb hole in turret 3, divers making a further survey of the *West Virginia's* hull located the tail assembly of a Japanese torpedo at frame 80. A line was attached to the remnants of the torpedo, and it was pulled to the surface and taken across the harbor to the Submarine Base for an examination. Luckily, a look at what was left of the weapon confirmed that the warhead had exploded and was not still lying on the coral alongside the ship.

The work of the salvage officers was ever changing, responsibilities being added or removed as more men arrived and others were reassigned. The same day the torpedo was pulled from the murky water alongside the *West Virginia*, Berthold was reassigned to the yard as ordnance salvage superintendent, and his place was taken for the time being by Stelter, who was now in charge of both ordnance and ammunition salvage. Four days later, as Steele was replaced by Wallin and as Captain Gillette received orders detaching him from the Navy Yard as soon as his relief arrived, the job of reassembling and preserving the *West Virginia's* main battery was completed, and the remnants of her crew and the engineers began the long job of making her ruptured hull watertight.

On his first day as the new head of salvage, Wallin was treated to the welcome sight of the floating dry dock being raised to the surface. For over a month YFD-2 had sat on the bottom offshore, with just the tips of its sides visible at a 15-degree list. It had sunk from underneath the *Shaw* partly as a result of precautionary flooding to limit damage as the destroyer was pounded by bombs, and partly as a result of the dozens of fragmentation holes in her watertight compartments. The dry dock officer had managed to open valves and flood compartments on the port side, but the intense fire had prevented him from opening the starboard valves, and the dock had sunk on an uneven keel just as the attack was ending. It wasn't until about 1430 that day that the starboard side, riddled with holes from the explosion of the *Shaw* and from the bomb hits, finally sank, taking the *Sotoyomo* with it to the bottom.[3] An oil fire that scorched the dock floor and spread to the water did considerable damage to the dock walls as well as to the little tug.

Salvage of the dock and the tug was assigned to the Salvage Organization, which in turn gave the job of raising them to the Pacific Bridge Company. After a brief survey, and after the rest of the *Shaw* had been towed away, pump hoses were run into some of the dock's watertight compartments on 18 December. As unwatering began and leaks were discovered, Pacific Bridge divers patched them. By the twenty-third,

significant progress had been made and the water level within the flooded compartments had been lowered. The minesweeper *Turkey* was moored alongside on Saturday
the twenty-seventh to supply steam to the dock pumps and to permit use of a steam-
water solution for washing off the oil as the water receded. The level was lowered significantly on Sunday, but Steele wrote in frustration on Monday afternoon,
"Discontinued pumping because marines refused to permit lights last night. All work
during the day was lost. In accordance with the general permission, the marines were
instructed that the Salvage Unit has permission to show sheltered lights at jobs. These
will be extinguished in case of an air raid. It is hoped that there will be no further interruptions of this kind." He also reported to Calhoun, "As the USS *Turkey* is operating
non-condensing it is necessary to supply boiler water to her. Public Works is investi-
gating supplying steam to YFD-2 so the USS *Turkey* can be released."[4] Even three
weeks after the attack, the Base Force was still forced to rely on jury-rigged setups to
accomplish its tasks: a small minesweeper running a temporary steam line to the dock
and being supplied with fresh feedwater from shore because it was unable to condense
the oil-polluted salt water.

Though the repair of the dock was considered a Navy Yard job, it was being carried out under the control of the Base Force and under the direct supervision of the
Pacific Bridge Company, which had diverted some of its divers and equipment from
the job of completing Dry Docks 2 and 3. Both Pacific Bridge and Hawaiian Dredging
had, the day after the attack, purchased over $1 million worth of equipment and mate-
rial and recruited men from the mainland for the salvage operations. Pacific Bridge,
under its general manager A. E. "Jack" Graham, was placed in charge of any contractor
work to be done in conjunction with the yard and the Base Force. By the thirtieth
there was some concern with the progress of the company's work while it operated
under the direction of the Base Force, and Gillette's officers took over direct supervision. Four Pacific Bridge deep-well high-head pumps were then brought over to the
dock to expedite the unwatering. It came afloat on 9 January, but because many of the
patches were of a temporary nature, it was still unusable. Graham's divers installed a
40-square-foot patch under the bottom shell, creating a working space 4 feet deep in
which to effect more permanent repairs to the dock frames and bottom shell plates.[5]
The result of this ingenious setup was that the YFD-2 would not require dry-docking
in Dry Dock 2 to complete repair.

There was still some grim work to be done on the floor of the dock, which was littered with the wreckage of the *Shaw*'s bow and the burned *Sotoyomo*. The *Sotoyomo* was
floated clear on the seventeenth, but not what was left of the *Shaw*. The *Shaw*'s bow
was fairly intact forward of frame 32, between the 5-inch/.38 guns, but had been
shredded aft of that point. It lay on its starboard side, the shield over gun 2 crushed
and the deckhouse it sat on twisted to port. There were dents in the starboard side
from the impact with the keel blocks, and the hull plating was badly wrinkled from the
intense fire on the dock floor and the water. Men from the Mobile Salvage Unit had
begun cutting the wreckage into sections even before the dock was raised. On 10
January several bodies were removed from the wreckage, men who had gone down

S.S. SHAW   11 JANUARY 1942
...W OF FOREDECK OF SHAW AS IT LIES ...
...DE IN THE FLOATING DRY DOCK ...

Men probe the wreckage of the *Shaw*'s bow on the floor of the floating dry dock after it had been raised. The *Sotoyomo* lies just out of view to the right.
Naval Historical Center NH 84000

with the bow when it was torn away. Ordnance was taken to the Naval Ammunition Depot: a torpedo warhead, 5-inch/.38 and .50-caliber rounds, and a Thompson submachine gun.[6] An anchor was recovered, a pair of chains, and a few bitts and chocks, too. Holes were cut through the sections for riggers to run hoisting chains, and on the seventeenth they were lifted into a barge. The bow was taken to Waipio Point, where the burners from Horne's outfit cut it up for scrap. One of the guns had been removed while the ship was still in the dock and had been deposited over at Ten Ten Dock. The other was still attached to the bow. The nuts had been removed from the bolts holding it in place, but the bolts themselves had been bound. The ordnance crew from the Mobile Repair Unit were having a difficult time removing it.[7]

"This afternoon an inspection was made of the exposed hull of the *Utah* with a view to preliminary investigation and ultimate recovery of such ammunition that is accessible from the bottom."[8] So began a 6 January 1942 memorandum from Lieutenant Commander Stelter to Captain Steele, outlining the Ordnance Section's plan to cut their way into the hull of the target ship and remove ammunition from the "A" group of forward magazines. Stelter had approached Curtis with the plan, and it had been approved by the salvage engineer. On 7 January, divers from the *Ortolan*, under the direction of her skipper Lieutenant Latta, made an inspection of the submerged upper-works of the *Utah*, to determine how firmly the mast, conning tower, cranes, turret tops, and gun shields were in contact with the bottom. If these were holding the *Utah* at her present angle, then a sudden collapse of one or more might cause the ship to shift position violently, endangering anyone working inside. The divers reported good news: the masts and towers had broken off, and the upper deck of the ship was resting firmly on the mud. Unlike the silt beneath the *California* or under the *Oklahoma's* bow, this was firmly packed soil, solid enough for a diver to stand on. There was no danger of the *Utah* moving.

Shipfitters and carpenters from the Mobile Repair Unit were summoned to the far side of Ford Island, and a 50-ton covered lighter was obtained to serve as a base and for storage of recovered equipment and ammunition. On the tenth the lighter was moored on the inshore side of the ship, and staging was built as a working platform. Two days later two holes were cut in the hull, starboard of the centerline, at frames $32\frac{1}{2}$ and $40\frac{1}{2}$, next to the hole that had been cut on 7 December to pull Jack Vaessen from the hull.[9] The holes were cut, not burned, because no one could be sure if there were flammable gases trapped in the hull. Stelter was unsure exactly where on his ship the working parties were in terms of frame numbers. The booklet of plans he was using listed the location of a docking keel incorrectly and threw off his measurements. New openings in the shell, 3 feet square, were cut on the thirteenth and entrance was obtained to the hold deck. These locations were chosen for their access to trunks adjacent to the forward group of magazines. Air hissed out of the openings as they were cut, indicating that the hull was holding pressure and was probably not flooded to the outside waterline. The work party entering the hold found several inches of water topped with a half-inch of oil. Another party made its way into the hull from a hole cut near frame $32\frac{1}{2}$. Progress was very slow in this upside-down world. Divers descended into the trunks to close hatches, vents, and doors in the vicinity of the magazines as far down as the third deck, and a 10-inch pump was lowered into the spaces. Plugs were driven into vent lines and ducts to stop the inflow of water as the pumps took suction. It wasn't until nine days after they began that the first equipment was removed. The door leading from the trunk at frame $32\frac{1}{2}$ into compartment A-34, the forward magazine, was jammed closed by debris on the inside. Another hole had to be cut in the deck above so that a diver could go in and clear the door. It was opened on 22 January, and tanks of 5-inch/.38 powder were removed. Additional openings were made for 10-inch pumps clearing the original passageway for the removal of ammunition. The sailors were wearing gas masks, since hydrogen sulfide had been detected coming from frame $32\frac{1}{2}$, probably from the decomposition of bodies and the sulfur in the fuel. Throughout the remainder of January the group removed what they could from the ship, including machine-gun and 5-inch/.25 ammunition from the magazines at frame 40. To the relief of the divers, nothing was seen of the fifty-eight men missing and presumed drowned inside. The work was miserable enough, as Stelter noted: "Work below decks is laborious and very uncomfortable for personnel as they are required to work in hot, gas contaminated spaces while wearing respirator masks."[10]

Seven months later Furlong would request extra compensation for men "working in unwatered compartments of damaged vessels when, due to the presence of toxic gases, it was necessary to wear face masks with compressed air supply." The Bureau of Naval Personnel would deny that request.[11]

The patch for the *Nevada's* torpedo damage had been under construction for weeks, the time waiting for it well spent. The A-frames and chain falls were in place and the equipment overhauled and made ready. Small patches had been placed on the fragment holes in the hull, and on New Year's Day *Medusa* divers placed a 10-by-12-foot patch over the big rupture in the starboard side. Despite the bustle of activity, Nimitz was still pessimistic about the chances for salvaging the battleship. Admittedly she was still full of water and oil, with numerous small holes and a gaping torpedo hole in her hull, dead in the water and beached. But the men of the Salvage Organization and her crew were learning more about their new trade all the time and making slow, steady progress each day. If Nimitz was not optimistic, Ankers and his crew were.

The first pump, a big 10-inch Jaeger, was hoisted aboard the *Nevada,* set up on the forecastle, and tested on New Year's Day. On 3 January, while the Pacific Bridge divers were idle, the salvage crew rigged 17-foot slings and shackles on the A-frames

After weeks of delay, the "big patch" for the *Nevada* is brought to Waipio Point. Note the supports inside the patch and the two hatches for diver access.
Naval Historical Center NH 45464

to receive the big patch, now rumored to be only a few days away from delivery. Sections of 10-inch steel casing for discharge lines and five 10-inch centrifugal pumps were loaded onto the ship while oil was skimmed from the water around the barbettes and wardroom beneath the forecastle. A sketch of what had become known as the "big patch" was taken to Shop 11 so that an outline of the torpedo hole could be painted on. It was 6 January before the patch started on its long journey out to Waipio Point. Over the next couple of days it was lifted by the floating derrick *Gaylord* and slowly brought out past the Navy Yard piers, passing between the submerged YFD-2 and the *California*. A group of photographers from the Fleet Camera Party were there to record the event. So was a motion picture camera team. Work aboard the ship didn't stop for the patch; three 10-inch pumps were set up on the quarterdeck to begin draining the ship aft. It was nearly time to start pumping her out.

All three of the accessible turrets on the *California* were being worked on simultaneously, with top plates, 14-inch shells, and backout slugs being lifted to barges. Inside the turrets ordnance men methodically removed "flame shields and weather stripping of all guns. Removed cap squares, fulcrum arm segments to trunnions, locked up fulcrum arms."[12] The equipment was carefully labeled and preserved for the day when it would be reinstalled in a repaired *California* returning to the fleet. Bolts holding the turret plates had to be cut, splinter protection removed, and bore gauges, centering pins, shell-hoisting equipment, counterrecoil cylinders, and other equipment disconnected, labeled, and removed. Gun-loading platforms, eccentric adjusting bars, elevating screws, and dozens of other items had to be disassembled while overhead girders were taken out and the water in the lower reaches of the turrets pumped overboard. The process was delayed by the need to dry-dock and repair the *Haviside* after she was pierced by a projection from the *California*, and by the busy schedule of the yard's 150-ton floating crane. The work continued on into the second week of January.

By the first part of the month Pacific Bridge had developed a plan for building a wooden cofferdam around the entire quarterdeck and along the port side of the forecastle. This huge fence would be made watertight, and water over the main and upper decks would be pumped overboard. Then the interior decks could be dewatered level by level without the dangerous weight of water overhead. At the same time, a patch would be fitted to the hole in the bow now believed to have been caused by a near miss. A partial single-wall cofferdam would be driven into the bottom around the torpedo hits so that they could be cleared of mud. Forms for concrete patches would be attached to the hull and concrete poured through tremie pipes to seal the holes.

The face plate of turret 3 was finally removed on 8 January by the repaired *Haviside*, and a 6-inch pump was used to lower the water level in turret 1 so that ordnance men could begin to disassemble the guns. The *Gaylord* removed the face plate of turret 2 the same day, and all three guns were readied for lifting. But the 150-ton crane requested from the Navy Yard did not arrive. To make room for the unwieldy crane barge the *Gaylord* had maneuvered away on the ninth and the *Haviside* on the tenth, but the yard did not send it over. It did not arrive on the eleventh, either. Meanwhile, word reached Pearl that the *Saratoga* had been torpedoed five hundred miles to the southwest and would arrive back in Hawaii in a few days. Dry Dock 1 was still occupied by the *Cassin, Downes,* and *Raleigh,* but Dry Dock 2 was empty now that the *Helena* had been removed and the concrete floor had been completed. The delay in the construction of the *Nevada*'s patch assured that the Sara could be landed there if necessary.

Finally, on Monday the twelfth the huge crane was brought alongside the *California.* Turret 3's right gun was lifted in the morning and the center gun in the afternoon. The derrick was needed elsewhere in the harbor, and it was more than a week later, on 20 January, that it was returned to remove the third gun from turret 3. It was then moved forward, and the right and center guns of turret 2 were taken away. Two days later the left gun was landed, and two days after that all three guns were removed from turret 1, the water level having been reduced sufficiently for the *Utah*'s ordnance men to disengage the barrels.

An ensign still flew from the *California,* but she was no longer in full commission. The first salvage memorandum of 1942 had begun,

> Shortly after December 7, 1941, the Commander in Chief, United States Pacific
> Fleet ordered the Commander Base Force to conduct salvage operations on dam-

A 14-inch gun barrel is lifted from turret 3 of the *California*. Only the upper half of the stern crane and the top of turret 4 are visible, illustrating how deeply the quarterdeck had been submerged.
U.S. Naval Institute

aged ships at Pearl Harbor. As no organization for this work was in existence, a start was made to organize a group of officers and men to undertake this work on December 9, 1941. On December 29, 1941 the Commander Base Force took cognizance of the following vessels in commission in ordinary: (a) USS *California* (b) USS *Oklahoma* (c) USS *West Virginia* (d) USS *Nevada* (e) USS *Arizona* (f) USS *Oglala* (g) USS *Utah* (h) USS *Downes* (i) USS *Cassin* (j) USS *Shaw*.[13]

The *California* and the others were still in commission but in reserve—"in ordinary," as it was called. How long they would remain so was uncertain.

A month after the attack the salvage effort was in full stride, and the waters off Ford Island, Ten Ten Dock, and Waipio Point bustled with activity and resonated with the noise of hammers, diesel engines, and air compressors. Barges loaded with hoses, generators, boilers, tools, lumber, steel, and other salvage equipment went out to the ships and returned filled with recovered equipment, ammunition, and heaps of trash and wreckage. Work crews were shuttled out by small boat, as were box lunches and hot coffee for the midday meal. A daily summary was still prepared from reports submitted to the Salvage Office by the ship representatives. The summary of 4 January provided a snapshot of the projects under way on one day of salvage work in the harbor:

> Status of Work as of Noon Today:
> *California:* Main battery removal progressing. The *Haviside* will not be available until January 9, 1942. To avoid further delay, will investigate the removal of face plates, turrets II and III with 150 ton crane. Began removal of starboard 5-inch/.25 battery and will have those four guns, eight 5-inch/.25 ready boxes, six .50 caliber machine guns and mounts with hand pumps, eight .50 caliber ready boxes, five 3-inch/.50 ready boxes at Berth-5 at 1400 today. Continued diving operations along starboard side.
> *West Virginia:* Main battery removal was stopped and the battery will be placed in suitable condition of security until the ship is placed in Navy Yard hands. The *Gaylord* was returned this morning and work will proceed on the removal of 5-inch/.51 guns. Continued diving investigation. Now measuring a hole at Frame 46.
> *Oglala:* Completed removal of house on superstructure deck and removal of bulkheads in superstructure.
> *Nevada:* Waiting for patches.
> *Arizona, Oklahoma* and *Utah:* No work.
> *Cassin, Downes* and *Shaw:* In Navy Yard hands.
> 1. While recovering a catapult for the *Raleigh* at Berth F-12, wire straps in use parted. Another attempt is being made today. One group of divers is working on the USS *Grayling.*
> 2. The ammunition group section is removing the remaining serviceable .50 caliber ammunition (about eighty-three hundred rounds) and about one thousand belt lengths from *California* incident to the removal of 5-inch/.25 and .50 caliber battery.

Also continued inspection of damaged ammunition at West Loch and NAD [Naval Ammunition Depot].[14]

Although no firm decision had yet been made on the fate of the *Downes* and *Cassin*, their removal from Dry Dock 1 by refloating or scrapping was an immediate necessity. With the floating dry dock raised but not yet repaired, with the limited capacity of the marine railway, and with work remaining on Dry Dock 3, Gillette and Furlong badly needed the two big graving docks available without the space limitations imposed by the destroyers. Floating them might not prove the fastest alternative, but it offered a repair option if that was feasible or cost-effective. From 2 January to 9 January the Salvage Organization daily report had merely noted that the destroyers were in Navy Yard hands. Actually they were being worked on by Horne's Mobile Repair Unit, which had taken over the job of preparing the ships for flotation at the next opportunity. That opportunity now looked like the undocking of the *Raleigh* in early February. The *Raleigh* had replaced the *Helena* in the dock after the *Helena* had replaced the *Pennsylvania*.

The salvage work on the destroyers in Dry Dock 1 was an example of the close cooperation needed between the naval commands on Oahu. Initially it was the ordnance group from the *Utah* that had boarded the ships after the fires were out to remove the guns, ammunition, torpedoes, and fire control equipment. The *Downes's* 5-inch/.38 gun 5 was removed on 17 December, and guns 1 and 4 on the nineteenth. Mark 33 directors were taken off both ships on the twenty-first, and on the following Monday guns 3 and 5 came off the *Cassin*. Yard cranes hoisted them clear after taking a strain on the cables so that the last of the heavy nuts securing them could be loosened on the steeply listing deck. Gun 4 was taken off on Christmas Eve, gun 2 on Christmas Day. The yard had supplied the heavy equipment, the Base Force the men, and now the Fourteenth Naval District pitched in, ordering Horne to assign a detachment of the Mobile Repair Unit to finish the ordnance salvage and begin the long process of patching. A Reserve ensign named Hulings from the Salvage Ordnance Section took over this phase of the job under the supervision of Stelter, who was overseeing the ordnance removal on the damaged ships.

While the Mobile Repair Unit crew went to work with welding torches and sheet metal to patch the holes, Hulings's men carefully removed a couple of torpedoes from damaged mounts on the *Cassin*. It wasn't easy working on her. The deck slanted too sharply to walk on and was still slick with oil, so scaffolding and staging were erected. By the thirtieth, all of the guns and torpedo mounts had been removed as well as all the ammunition from the flooded magazines on both ships. Twelve damaged torpedoes were removed from the *Cassin* and taken to the Submarine Base. Eight damaged "fish" had been removed from the *Downes*, one in pieces. The other four had been destroyed by an explosion. One 5-inch/.38 mount from the *Downes* went to Ewa as part of a four-gun battery, with the other three guns coming from the *Shaw*. A gun director, rangefinder, and loading machine from the *Cassin* also went to the Ewa battery. Of the other nine guns taken off the two destroyers and delivered to Lieutenant Commander

Henderson in the yard, three of the *Cassin's* five were only lightly damaged and able to be refurbished. Only one or two of the *Downes's* guns had any hope of being repaired.[15]

Yard officers took over for Stelter and Hulings and directed Horne's men as they inspected, cleaned, and removed machinery and equipment. Just cleaning the topside of the *Downes* was a formidable job. From the superstructure aft she had been completely gutted by fire. The last few days of December and the first few days of January were spent removing 50 tons of debris and 200 tons of jagged, scorched scrap metal. About half as much debris, and only a little scrap, was hauled away from the *Cassin*. She had been far less severely damaged on deck.

The machinery and boiler-room spaces of the *Downes* were inspected, too. Boiler 4 had suffered the most damage, its turbines, economizers, and superheaters "demolished" by the detonation of the torpedo tube directly overhead. The other three boilers were in fairly good shape except for some slight damage to the casings. Steam lines and valves were also serviceable, but the starboard throttle had been crushed and broken beyond repair. The high- and low-pressure cruising turbines showed no obvious damage, though the casing and foundation for the starboard turbine had been distorted and broken. The majority of the auxiliary equipment was also in decent condition. A similar examination of the *Cassin* showed her machinery to be almost untouched, the only damage having been caused by immersion in salt water and oil.

Three vats were set up to clean valves, parts, and fittings. Ferrous items were dipped into a solvent of lye and kerosene, nonferrous items were cleaned with boiler compound, and boiling water was used to wash electrical machinery and parts. On the dock floor, working parties tried to dissolve dried oil from the hulls with live steam but had little luck. Other parties cut away jagged and torn hull plates so that the holes could be measured for patches. The floor of Dry Dock 1 was laboriously cleaned and sanded after each flooding brought in a new, but progressively lighter, coating of oil.

The Mobile Repair Unit began to strip the *Downes* of equipment, starting with boiler 4. The steam lines of the forced draft blowers were broken loose and removed and the blowers themselves disassembled. Torches cut holes in the overhead so that the boilers and eventually nearly all the machinery could be lifted clear by crane.[16]

While the cleaning of the *Downes* was limited to that which facilitated equipment removal and preservation, the crew working on the *Cassin* were trying in earnest to clean the interior and exterior of the vessel while leaving the machinery intact. A hot, caustic compound called Turko was used on the shell plates, particularly where welding was to be done, to reduce the fire hazard. Turko, a mixture of sodium hydroxide, soda ash, and trisodium phosphate, was also used to wash down the compartments, which were steamed afterward to rid them of hazardous gases. The manhole plates over the oil tanks were overhauled to ensure that they would be watertight at the next flooding. In addition to Turko, more old-fashioned methods of cleaning the ship were tried. Sailors with hand scrapers and hot water scrubbed away at the oil and coating of scum. It was very difficult work, slowed by the angle of the destroyer, by the makeshift nature of the cleaning facilities at the bottom of the dock, and by the lack of proper equipment.

Work on both ships had been temporarily suspended on 2 January when the dock

Part of the deck of the *Downes* was cut away to facilitate removal of her boilers and other machinery. This photograph was taken on 2 February 1942. The sloping deck of the *Cassin* is visible just beyond. Naval Historical Center NH 54558

was flooded and the *Honolulu* towed out. The next day, after the blocks had been reset, the *Raleigh* was brought in, safely completing the journey around Ford Island and across the South Channel that had begun twenty-seven days before. As the water drained once again out of Dry Dock 1 and out of the holes in the *Downes* and *Cassin,* the last of the *Raleigh's* ammunition, which had been retained on board for stability, was inventoried and removed while onlookers got the first look at the torpedo holes that had nearly capsized her.

On Tuesday, 6 January, the first twenty patches were welded to the hull of the *Cassin* beneath the after deckhouse at frame 136, which had been badly mutilated. Twenty more holes were patched the next day, and a flexible U-shaped patch, about 8 feet long and 4 feet wide, was fitted to the hull at frame 99 under the after stack. For the next few days blocking beneath the ship was reset for better support and to permit greater access to the hull, as more debris was removed and more patches were welded to the hull.[17]

Some of the sheet-metal patches welded to the *Cassin* and *Downes* closed holes made by the ships' crew and by Berthold's ammunition group when they drilled into the magazines to drain them of water. Those holes, and those made by fragments, had been useful when the dock was flooded, keeping the ships on their blocks and pre-

The *Cassin* after her hull was reblocked and shored on the floor of Dry Dock 1.
Naval Historical Center NH 55061

venting more damage if they moved. But there was no need to keep the shell open any longer. When the *Raleigh* was removed in a month or so and the *Vestal* placed inside, the *Cassin* would have to be watertight so that she could be righted and set down properly on a new set of blocks. The *Downes* would also be floated, and it was Gillette's hope to remove both destroyers from the dock and restore it to full use at that time.

In the repair basin the *Shaw* had been measured and fitted for a temporary bow while she was on the marine railway. She had been dragged ashore on 19 December so that her weakened fireroom bulkheads could be strengthened and shored and her damaged superstructure addressed. The bridge had nearly melted away, and the entire structure had toppled forward slightly. Everything forward of the stack was cut off down to the main deck. The wreckage was burned off at frame 60 to provide a clean fit for the new bow. Her three remaining 5-inch/.38 guns had been removed the day before her docking by the *Utah*'s busy ordnance salvage group.

The *Shaw* stayed on the railway until Christmas Eve, when she was towed to a berth in the repair basin. She was in the hands of the Navy Yard now, the only mention of her on the daily salvage memo being a brief notation reflecting that fact. Draftsmen were now completing plans for the temporary bridge and navigation stations to be built for the trip to the mainland.

The temporary bow was lowered by crane and welded to the *Shaw* while she was waterborne in the repair basin. A tripod mast was installed in place of the bridge, with an observation platform and a yard for signal flag halyards. The pole mast was relocated just aft of the number 2 stack. An emergency bridge was placed atop the after deckhouse, and a single 5-inch/.38 gun, taken from the *Cassin* and minus a shield, was reinstalled at the number 3 position. Firing would be under local control only. She had eight torpedoes aboard during the attack (four being overhauled ashore), and these had been removed. Her scorched boiler-room machinery was overhauled. All that remained was for the false bow to be made secure to the hull and watertight, and for this a dry dock was needed. As soon as the YFD-2 was ready, the *Shaw* would be, too.

As the last of the *California*'s accessible 14-inch guns were removed, the patch for the near-miss hole in the port bow was delivered and secured in place by divers. It was hung on an A-frame on 25 January, lowered into place on chains, and secured by divers using hook bolts. Painter, who had taken over as assistant salvage engineer from James Rodgers, watched in irritation as the floating crane that delivered the patch, the YD-27, left the ship after the patch had been delivered. He had wanted to use the crane to lower the patch alongside the hull since he thought it was easier to use the crane than the cumbersome chain falls. But as Curtis reminded him, the YD-27 was assigned to the Navy Yard, was a delivery unit only, and could not be arbitrarily appropriated by the salvage division. Curtis too was frustrated by the lack of equipment and the constant juggling act that was required to work on multiple salvage projects without dedicated equipment assigned to the organization.[18] It took two days for the divers to get a tight fit on the hull. As they worked in the darkness alongside the *California*, a foundation was built on the upper deck for a boiler. Water tanks, oil burners, and other equipment were being prepared ashore so that the ship would soon be able to produce steam for equipment, for lights, and for cleaning.

By 25 January, Pacific Bridge engineers under Fred W. Crocker had completed the plans for the quarterdeck and forecastle cofferdams, and much of the lumber had been assembled in the yard. The quarterdeck cofferdam was to consist of nine port sections, nine starboard, and one at the stern. Most of the sections varied between 30 and 24 feet in length, with the largest being 30½ feet, the smallest 19½ feet. The aft section was to be placed across the stern and link the final sections on the port and starboard sides. The sections themselves were to be built of vertical planks 8 inches thick by 12 inches wide and anywhere from 16 to 20 feet in length, tied together with 12-by-12-inch horizontal wales and bolted to the deck edge. They would be shored by massive beams, 8 by 8 inches on the starboard side and 10 by 10 inches on the port side, where the head of water was greater. These would be wedged at an approximately 45-degree angle to the deck and be secured to more beams bolted to the deck or to the turrets. The barbettes would have a band of steel welded to them 10 inches wide, ½ inch thick on the port side, ⅜ inch thick on the starboard side. To these would be welded L-shaped stiffeners with the shoring beams bolted to them. To counteract the natural

The patch for the port bow of the *California* goes into the water on 25 January 1942. In the background is the rebuilt *Shaw*. She would enter the floating dry dock the next day. The mast of the *Raleigh* in Dry Dock 1 is visible, as is the carrier *Saratoga* undergoing repair for torpedo damage in Dry Dock 2.
National Archives

buoyancy of the wood, the sections would be weighted with sandbags in boxes built into the inside of the fence.

The forecastle cofferdam was to be less work. It needed only to encompass the port side, as the starboard side of the deck was above water. There were to be eight sections, including one that would join the other seven to the superstructure deck, ranging in length from 26 to 31 feet. These would be made from 4-by-12-inch planks shored in the same manner as the quarterdeck fence, with 6-by-8-inch beams running at deck level and along the upper wale. These were to be anchored to 6-by-10-inch beams bolted to the deck. Unlike the quarterdeck structure, only a few shoring beams would be run to turret 2, and none to turret 1. The depth of water over the deck, and the head of water that the fence sections would have to withstand, was far less than it was aft. Shorter shoring beams, anchored to the deck, would suffice.

Unfortunately, work on building the sections was running behind schedule. The Salvage Division had not been able to round up nearly enough carpenters from the shipyard and had only a few of its own. The lumber, timber lugs, drift bolts, tie-down rods, sand, and other materials had been in place in the Navy Yard since the twenty-fourth, and about fifty carpenters were needed for two or three weeks to complete both cofferdams and the patch sections proposed for the *West Virginia*. By 6 February Wallin had been able to obtain fewer than ten men. He relayed his difficulty to Nimitz's assistant chief of staff, who told Wallin that Nimitz placed a high priority on clearing the berths along Battleship Row and could be counted on to issue any necessary directives so that Wallin could get what he needed. Armed with this assurance, Wallin told Furlong at the morning conference on the sixth that Nimitz could be counted on to help clear any obstacles to obtaining the needed carpenters.[19]

The work of plugging the scuppers and airports was nearly complete while the salvage officers struggled with the lack of carpenters. The gun casemate openings on the port side were closed off by the end of January with steel cover plates secured on the inside with strongbacks. But aside from diving for the fleet paymaster's safe, plugging leaks in the casemates, and removing the after catapult and motors from the interior of turret 3, work on the ship had slowed to a standstill. Painter's men were waiting for the first cofferdam sections to be delivered to the ship. A few electric pumps had been hoisted aboard, but they would be of no use until the cofferdam could be built.

The big patch for the *Nevada* arrived alongside that vessel at 0900 on 8 January, and almost immediately the supporting framework inside the patch was cut away while *Widgeon* divers made final checks on their equipment. The day before, a diving team had completed planking and wedging the window-frame patch on the hole at the port bow to seal it completely. Preparations for unwatering the ship were well under way, and five more 6-inch pumps and another 10-inch pump were sent from Salvage Stores. Curtis and Commander Thompson had requested an open-deck barge for debris, a freshwater barge for steam and hot cleaning water, another barge for lockers and their contents as the crew spaces were pumped down and the decks cleared, and a crane to place the pumps on deck and transport to the yard any equipment or machinery that needed immediate preservation. Two minesweepers were also requested. Curtis also noted to Steele on 30 December that the yard would need ground transportation when the barges unloaded at the dock. Gasoline storage, assumed to be about 800 gallons, would be removed before the ship was dry-docked, but Gillette would have to decide if the remaining powder and ammunition should be removed as well. The *Nevada*'s crew would need to be supplemented by another hundred men each day to help clean each deck as the water level dropped. Lines would be strung on Waipio Point for drying the clothing that was recovered, and additional showers would be provided for the men diving into the bilge to check for and plug leaks.[20]

All but the two center tension members were cut out of the inside of the big patch before it was lowered into the water, then *Widgeon* divers cut those away, too. It was brought back to the surface where slings were run to the A-frame. The *Gaylord* released its hold on it and shoved off, the patch now being supported by the *Nevada*'s A-frame. The Navy divers were assisted by those from Pacific Bridge, diverted again from their work on Dry Docks 2 and 3. The following day the first problems with the patch arose. It was too big, projected too low under the hull, and was evidently running into mud and coral. The *Widgeon* was shifted forward alongside the *Nevada* to siphon and jet away the mud. The next day an attempt was made to fit the patch, but again the bottom was hanging up on something. Divers went down beneath the bilge and found more mud, which was probably obstructing the bottom edge of the huge patch. This mud would have to be cleared, but it wouldn't be easy. It covered a layer of hard coral, which would also have to be removed, and the dredge now in position was having a tough go of it.

In the meantime the pumping had begun on the seventh using one 6-inch, one 3-inch, and three 10-inch pumps on the forward hatch. That first night the water level had gone down 9 inches, and a start was made in cleaning out the first few compartments on the main deck. By the twelfth the *Nevada* had been unwatered to just below the second deck. A steel patch was welded to the inside of the bomb hole made through the hull at frame 14 in the junior officers' quarters because the exterior window patch was failing to keep out the water. The ship was an unbelievable mess inside. The otherwise staid war damage report noted, "The filth left throughout the compartments as the ship was unwatered can perhaps be better imagined than described."[21] Oil coated everything and had ruined many things. Heaps of rotting clothing and bedding had to be hauled up on deck by hand and out to the debris barge moored alongside. Paper had disintegrated and shredded so that books, diaries, reports, and newspapers had become a heavy, sodden mass. Meat and other provisions had rotted, and the smell was overwhelming. Temporary lighting was rigged in each compartment as the water level receded, but it was still dark and dank on the main and second decks where crews now worked. Lockers were emptied and the sometimes unrecognizable contents piled together and taken away. What could be identified was preserved, but much could not be, or was beyond salvage. Tables and chairs, light fixtures, desks, cabinets, and chests were filthy and coated with fuel oil. All had to be removed by the parties that worked day after day in these sewerlike conditions.

The crews worked methodically through each compartment and each deck. Salt water, heated by a boiler on deck, was used to wash the spaces and passageways clean of oil and mud. An oil skimmer, called a Wheeler unit, then skimmed up the sludge where it collected at a low point on the ship's sloping deck. Hot fresh water followed; then men wiped down the area with rags. Wiring was scrubbed with fresh water and brushes; then it too was wiped down with more rags, which were taken ashore each day to be laundered. Machinery was sprayed with a thin-film polar compound known as Tectyl, which absorbed water and coated it with a thin protective film. Small gauges and fittings were dunked in containers of it. Warm fresh air was circulated through the compartments to dry them out. Wherever possible the men worked from the centerline of the ship outboard, to avoid tracking mud and oil through areas already cleaned.[22]

Sometimes the work crews were too zealous in their efforts. Many of the chairs, lockers, and bunks and much of the galley equipment were undamaged except for a coating of oil. Yet loads of this gear were being turned over to the yard every day rather than being cleaned aboard ship. The weight reduction gained by removing these items was slight, and they were in no condition to be turned in to general storage. The Nevada's crew were instructed to cease sending any and all such recovered material ashore and to make it serviceable themselves using the hot water and rags provided on deck.[23] In the meantime they continued washing bulkheads and decks and descended each morning into the dimly lit corridors to pick through the slime and garbage that littered the ship after six weeks' submergence.

"Work will continue in lifting the ship from present berth, using barges for buoyancy." So read the Oglala's entry on the 3 January 1942 Base Force salvage memorandum. It was still the hope of the salvage team to lift the Oglala off the bottom while capsized and tow her either to a shallow beach to be dismembered or to Dry Dock 2 to be scrapped or righted using a parbuckling arrangement. The barges needed to be secured to the ship as close to the hull and deck as possible, and the slow work of dismantling and removing the superstructure continued. Divers also recovered what they could from the ship: an X-ray machine on the sixth, officers' personal effects on the fifteenth and sixteenth. Meanwhile the Design Section studied the new plan to raise the ship with barges. The engineers worked over their calculations again and again: the mass of the ship, the stress points on the hull, the strength of the bulkheads, the lifting capacity of the barges and their placement around the hull for maximum effectiveness. A number of plans had already been developed detailing various aspects of the pontoon and air bubble combination; plans for pontoon arrangement and deck reinforcement; a method of emptying the fuel tanks; the location of the plug cocks and the air line; the sequence for blowing the pontoons. But those plans had been shelved in favor of the lifting-barge method. Lt. Cdr. James A. McNally, the salvage planning officer within the Planning Section, called a conference for the sixteenth to discuss the new plan, to review what had already been accomplished and what needed to be done to get the Oglala clear of Ten Ten Dock using the barges. Curtis was there, as were James Rodgers, Lieutenant Holtzworth, and the two assistant salvage engineers on the project, Lieutenants Genereaux and Painter.

Painter had delivered a copy of one of the original pontoon plans to the Design Section, with the proposed placement of the barges marked on it. He had been assisted on the lifting scheme by Pacific Bridge engineers. Painter seemed to be everywhere at once, always cheerful, always optimistic. But his enthusiasm was met with pessimism among Holtzworth's men. It would be "impossible to raise the *Oglala* using four 1,000-ton barges with the arrangement shown [in Painter's plan], without supplementing the lifting effects of the barges by means of an air bubble within the hull, or additional lifting effort from some other means." In fact, the Design Section was of the opinion that not only would the barge plan as presently constituted fail to lift the ship sufficiently to clear the bottom and permit a tow, it would not even pry the *Oglala*'s port side out of the mud.[24] Holtzworth was unsure of exactly how much air pressure had been applied to the hull in the original test and whether the test had been completed. The Design Section had not been involved in that process, and his men needed to know conclusively whether or not there was a way to pump enough air into the hull to permit the barge scheme to work.

Work on the *Oglala* ground to a halt on 20 January while a study was made of the original air pressure test and more calculations were made based on the idea that the barges could, with additional lift, raise the ship off the bottom. Except for a dive to recover an emergency radio generator on the twenty-sixth, there was no salvage work done on the ship between 20 January and 9 February. By the end of the second week in February, work was to begin in Shop 11 altering the barges to permit greater control over their attitude during the lift. They also had to be able to take the strain at the lifting points. A longitudinal bulkhead was to be welded about three-quarters of the length of each barge. Two transverse bulkheads would further divide them into several watertight compartments that could be flooded or drained as needed. Piping was to be installed for controlling trim and list, and strengthening supports were to be added to the corners where lifting wires would be fastened. More welding needed to be done to the tops of the barges so that the lifting wires could be fastened. It added up to significant work for yard shipfitters, specialists who could not easily be spared from other jobs.

Some problems had become clear as the plan was refined. The center of gravity of the capsized *Oglala* was such that it would be nearer to one set of barges than the other, vastly complicating the lift. The procedure had to be precise, lest the ship be torn apart, and it did not look as if the barges, even with the alterations, would be able to provide that sort of delicate touch. There was still a question of whether the *Oglala*'s hull could hold enough air pressure to supplement the barges' lifting capacity. Finally, all of this work, all this diversion of men and time, would still result in a ship that had simply been moved, without the possibility of being reclaimed for future use. The more the plan was examined, the less enthusiasm there was for trying it. Perhaps there was another way. Perhaps the salvage job going on across the water in the lagoon at berth F-3 would provide an answer.

The shortage of carpenters that was slowing work on the *California* was also to have an effect on the plans for the *West Virginia*. Curtis's decision not to remove the main battery, stacks, and conning tower meant that the prospects for raising the ship in the late spring or early summer were favorable. A system of patches would have to be devised, patches unlike any built before, to cover the damaged area beneath turret 2 and the huge expanse of destroyed hull and deck between the masts. But first the splayed metal on the boundaries of the torpedo holes had to be trimmed away so that precise measurements could be made and to ensure a snug fit when the patches, yet to be designed, were lowered into position. Two groups of divers went to work cutting away the damaged shell on 7 January. They would be at it for two weeks.

On the upper deck, a team of shipfitters burned away some of the collapsed superstructure and upper deck to provide a working area free of obstruction. Horne's Mobile Repair Unit detachment had not stopped clearing away the trash and wreckage that littered the decks, and had piled the rubbish in heaps for removal. Ashore, a process for dealing with these barges loaded with scrap and recovered material from the damaged ships had finally been put into place. Yard salvage superintendents had been placed in charge of each of the four categories of equipment being brought in: hull equipment, ordnance and ammunition, machinery, and sound and radio gear. Each superintendent, Whitaker for hull, Berthold for ordnance, Lieutenant Commander McNally for machinery, and Lt. H. A. Booth for radio, would direct the disposition of the material as it was unloaded. Trash, and there was a lot of it, would go directly to the dump. Scrap metal that could be melted down and reused went to a temporary storage area at the Richardson Recreation Center. Guns, catapults, cranes, masts, armor plating, and other such heavy but still useful material were taken to Waipio Point to be stored by the Industrial Department, while smaller items such as ladders and davits were taken to the supply officer at Pearl City. Items in good condition went into storage. Those that needed minor overhaul, especially items that were urgently needed by the fleet like telescopes, rangefinders, and searchlights, went to the appropriate shop within the yard for renewal before also going into storage. The salvage officers aboard the ships were ordered to ensure that usable items were painted with the ship's name or given a waterproof identification tag and were cleaned and preserved as much as possible before shipment ashore. They were to notify the yard in advance about the contents of each lighter so that officers could meet them at the pier and expedite the removal of the contents. There would be no repetition of the scene at the repair basin in late December, when heavily loaded barges were simply left tied up alongside the piers with no place to dump their loads.[25]

On 10 January, as the Mobile Repair Unit finished cleaning and prepared to leave the ship to the engineers, the *West Virginia's* commanding officer, William White, who had taken command of the ship for her period in ordinary, sat down in his office and penciled a few words on the first of the new daily salvage record forms. White had graduated from Annapolis in the class of 1926 and had been aboard the *West Virginia* since May 1939. He, along with Levi Knight, was now a lieutenant commander and had been part of the original salvage party from the ship's crew. The form on White's desk had four categories. The first was "Location and extent of underwater damage discovered." Here White wrote, "Shown on sketch in office of Lt. Cdr. Curtis, Salvage Engineer." The second was "Interior damage discovered that affected the flooding of ship, and steps taken to remedy same." As the survey of the damage had thus far been limited to what was visible on the main, upper, and boat decks and what the divers had found along the port side, White wrote simply, "None found as yet." The third category addressed the question of the watertight integrity of the ship at the time of the attack and how well the ship had been prepared to withstand the torpedo attack: "As each compartment is unwatered, a report to show, in detail, whether or not the 'X,' and 'Z' closures are opened or closed, and the probable source of flooding of each compartment." This information would be useful in preparing a war damage report and in recommending design changes and modifications. There wasn't anything for White to report in this regard; his ship had yet to have an ounce of water pumped from her. He jotted down, "No unwatering operations in progress" and moved on to the last section, "General progress of salvage operations." Detailed reports could come later and could be written by Painter, Genereaux, and Knight. For now, White summarized, "Diving survey and cutting away of underwater wreckage in progress." He scribbled his name at the bottom and went back to work.[26]

Much more than the opening and closing of watertight doors was on White's mind each day he walked the decks of the Weevee. Mustering the crew and identifying the dead in the hectic days after the attack had shown seventy West Virginia men to be unaccounted for. They were still missing a month later, in all likelihood entombed below decks of the hulk that was now White's first battleship command. When the time came to unwater the ship and record the "X" and "Z" closures in the various flooded spaces, White knew they would be collecting dead shipmates from those same compartments.

There was no plan for salvaging the Arizona, at least to return her to the fleet. There had never really been any consideration given to major work on the battleship other than removing weapons and ammunition. Salvage meant stripping the ship. From 30 December to 6 January, nothing was done aboard her. But the threat to Oahu was still very real, the defenses still very weak. The war continued to go badly for the United States. Japanese troops had landed on the Philippine island of Mindanao on 20 December and at Lingayen Gulf two days later. Wake had surrendered the following day while Japanese troops invaded Borneo. Christmas Eve saw more enemy landings at Lamon Bay on the island of Luzon. Manila had fallen on 2 January, and Japanese submarines had shelled U.S. installations on Pago Pago and Palmyra. They had even fired on Kauai, Maui, and the big island on New Year's Eve.

Nimitz had written to King on 7 January:

The attack of 7 December will be followed by others. The enemy has exploited the element of surprise. He can however, use it again, although to a lesser extent because of local alertness measures, if adequate search is not maintained. In any case, his strength in carriers and heavy ships is such that he need not depend on surprise. His objectives in the first assault were aircraft and ships. There remain untouched the very important and tempting objectives of fuel supply, navy yard industrial establishment and dry-docks, commercial docks and the city of Honolulu. There remains, further, as an ultimate objective the taking of the island of Oahu itself, retention of which is by no means assured with the forces now available to us.[27]

The *Arizona*'s 14-inch guns could still defend against the Japanese, but they would have to do it as shore batteries.

On 7 January a small party of shipfitters and riggers went out to the *Arizona* by launch to survey turret 3. Now that the *West Virginia* was to retain her main battery, the resources were available to remove the *Arizona*'s. By the eleventh the necessary personnel and equipment had been brought out to the ship, and within a few days the key plate, directly over the breeches, had been loosened and the partially burned catapult lifted off by the *Haviside*. Scaffolding was built on either side of the turret, and a party from the Mobile Repair Unit removed the rangefinder on the eighteenth. They delivered the delicate instrument to the yard, since the *Medusa* was still overloaded with work and had no room for *Arizona* equipment. On the twenty-fourth a second team of yard workers began to disassemble the top plates of turret 4. Removing these guns would be more difficult, as the ship had settled so that the quarterdeck was nearly 2 feet under water, bringing the water level just over the barbette. The rangefinder from that turret came off on the twenty-seventh while other items (turret train indicators, angle and deflection indicators) were taken by boat to the *Medusa* for overhaul. Small dams were constructed across the inside of the rear of turret 4, to prevent the turret from flooding when the rear plate was removed.

It wasn't until the first week of February that cribbing was hammered together underneath the guns of turret 3 to support them when they were cast loose, while a few feet away the cofferdamming of turret 4 continued. The lower pit doors would have to be closed off, the vent fittings blanked off, and pumps used to keep the water level below the disassembly locations. The work was slowed a bit by the similar but higher-priority job on the *California*. The *Arizona* had been at the center of the maelstrom on 7 December. Now she was merely a repository of guns and ammunition.

On 20 January the assistant engineers assigned to the nine ships under the Salvage Division were instructed to prepare periodic reports for Admiral Furlong, outlining the progress of the work, with a description of the methods that had been considered and tried as well as those that were under contemplation for future use. Mention was also to be made of any particular difficulties that had arisen. Hal Jones was responsible for drafting the reports for Furlong, based on the information supplied to him from the assistant salvage engineers, supplemented by any additions Curtis wanted to make. Genereaux was to submit a report on the *Oglala* on the twenty-second and, with Stelter, another on the *West Virginia* on the thirtieth. George Ankers had one to prepare for the *Nevada* on the twenty-fourth. Horne was to submit one each for the *Cassin* and *Downes* on the twenty-fourth and one for the *Shaw* on the twenty-sixth. Bill Painter's report on the *California* salvage effort was due on the twenty-sixth. Stelter was to be the busiest writer. In addition to helping Emile Genereaux with the *West Virginia* report, he was to co-write the *California* report with Painter and to write one on the *Arizona* due on the twenty-fifth and one on the *Utah* for submission on 2 February.[28] Painter was also assigned the *Oklahoma* project, but he had no report to prepare. No work on her was even contemplated for now.

Fortunately, these officers now had help. Early in January a group of six officers and sixty-two enlisted men had arrived at Pearl. They had been members of the Navy's first formal salvage school but when the war started had been waiting in San Francisco to learn if Pearl Harbor, or some other base, was to be the location of the school. The Japanese made that decision for the Navy. On-the-job training, rather than formal schooling, would be the education for these men. Though lacking in salvage experience, these Reserve officers were extremely well educated.

The enlisted men reported to Horne's Mobile Repair Unit as a separate organization within that unit while Wallin and Painter detailed the assignments for the officers. Lt. W. Walker, a civil engineer, was to be in general administrative charge of this sub-unit, a technical adviser to Curtis, and was also assigned to the *California* by Painter. Lt. (j.g.) James Darroch, an electrical engineer, was given to McNally as a planning assistant for recovered material. Another civil engineer, Lt. (j.g.) Wilbert Bjork, was to be Painter's assistant on the *California*, as was Ens. James W. Greely, a diesel engineer. To the *West Virginia* project went Ens. Earl Liedstrand, who had a background in naval architecture and mechanical engineering. The sixth officer, Ens. Edgar Beauchamp-Nobbs, who had studied marine engineering and naval architecture, was originally supposed to be Genereaux's assistant on the *West Virginia* and *Oglala* but was instead ordered to help George Ankers on the *Nevada*. The workload on both the *West Virginia* and the *Oglala* was soon to be too great for one officer, and Genereaux was replaced at Ten Ten Dock by Lt. Marshall L. McClung.

These men would work with both the commanding officers of the ships and the ship superintendents, who were liaison between the Salvage Division and the ship's company. Lt. F. W. Angrick was the *Oglala's* superintendent before being relieved by Lt. (j.g.) James Heal; Lieutenant Commander Garland was the *California's* superintendent under a new commanding officer, Captain Bunkley having been relieved by C. A. Peterson, the ship's engineer. The *Nevada's* damage control officer, Cdr. George Miller, was her first superintendent before being relieved by her engineer, Lt. Cdr. George Fee. The *West Virginia's* superintendent was her chief engineer, Levi Knight.[29] This was the nucleus of the salvage team of officers who would work closely together on these monumental jobs for the next five to six months.

SIX

The Sound of Hammers and Saws

Seating the big patch on the *Nevada* proved more troublesome and time-consuming than had been anticipated, but by 14 January, Ankers was able to report that the forward end was nearly in place, the aft end 7 feet out from the hull. That gap was narrowed to just 1 foot the next day. Suction lines were being snaked throughout the second deck forward, and more discharge lines threw brown water and sludge over the starboard side of the battleship, away from the divers working below.

The patch, so close to being secured, could not be nudged any closer. Mud had been jetted and siphoned from beneath the turn of the bilge, down to the coral layer beneath, and divers chipped that away with pneumatic mucking hammers and wedges. The coral was "very tough, apparently green, and will not split off," reported Ankers on the seventeenth.[1] Nevertheless they pressed on in shifts, hacking away at it for sixty to ninety minutes at a stretch before being relieved.

Now there was another wrinkle. The leading edge of the bottom of the patch, having been maneuvered past the coral, was hitting the forward end of the wooden docking keel. The port and starboard keels took the weight of the hull when on blocks in dry dock, and this section of the port one had to come off. The keel, like the coral, was extraordinarily tough, and cutting it away was slow and difficult work. On the twenty-eighth a new method was proposed: small charges of dynamite. A stick was packed into a 6-inch length of hose and the charge was set off next to the keel, blowing a hole 10 inches deep and 6 inches wide. A hole was burned into the keel the following day for a larger charge, which blew about 4 feet of keel several inches away from the hull. It was a promising start.[2]

The unwatering of the ship was going well, minor leaks from drain and sanitary lines being plugged as they were discovered. A steel plate with a rubber mat gasket had been placed over the hole in the first platform deck made by the bomb that had exited near the keel, and this helped limit the inflow of water to a trickle. The steel patch welded over the hole at the second deck had helped seal that one, but two other holes continued to leak, their location making it impossible to isolate them from the inside. Ankers still hoped to remove enough water, stores, fuel, ammunition, and equipment to raise the draft to 32 feet and get the *Nevada* into Dry Dock 1 following the removal of the *Raleigh*. In order to do that the patches, particularly the large one, would have to be secured as tight as possible to restrict the inevitable influx of water to an acceptable rate and permit the pumps to stay ahead of the flooding.

As the water receded, pumps were set up to take suction on the next level down. The pumps not only had to draw the water from below but had to lift it through discharge lines to pump it overboard. There was a constant balance between placing the pumps low in the ship to minimize the suction lift and keeping them as close to the deck as possible to reduce the head of the discharge line. By the twenty-third, as divers labored to chip away the coral beneath the bilge, two 10-inch pumps had been placed on the second deck forward. With the exception of a few inches of water aft, the second deck was dry. Five days later the pumping of the third deck commenced, and the *Nevada*'s own fire and bilge pumps were rigged in the starboard engine room to drain the after group of blisters. Lights and freshwater pipes were installed on the second deck, as they had been on the main and upper decks, so that working parties could remove trash and equipment and wash down the compartments.

Unwatering the ship, even at this slow rate while the patch was being fitted, was a balancing act between deceasing the draft of the battleship and maintaining equilibrium between the water pressure outside and inside of the hull where it had been opened by the torpedo. The more water that was removed, the more buoyant the ship would become and the better the chances of docking the ship in Dry Dock 1. But that would mean pumping water from the spaces between frames 20 and 48, inboard of the damaged torpedo bulkheads and the patch. The pressure difference between the water level outside the hull and that inside the hull might collapse the patch as the ship was being towed across the channel to the yard. It was assumed that the patch had the strength to withstand a head of water of 10 feet—that is, a difference of 10 feet in the water levels on each side of it. Much less than that and insufficient water would have been removed from the interior to obtain a satisfactory draft. Much more than that and, while the draft would decrease satisfactorily, the head of water would also increase, with a corresponding increase in water pressure exerted on the exterior of the patch.

Holtzworth had worked out a careful sixteen-step process of unwatering compartments, usually fore to aft, deck by deck, excepting the area flooded between frames 20 and 48. His plan would ensure a safe head of water on the patch but, unless the strength of it had been dramatically underestimated, would not allow a docking in Dry Dock 1. His unwatering plan also took into account the adhesion of the mud to the hull. Rather than try to overcome the suction of the mud along her entire length, the ship would be rocked gently up and down and peeled away from the bottom.[3] With the docking keel being blasted off and the coral painstakingly chipped away, it was hoped that it would not be long before Holtzworth's plan could be tried and the *Nevada* would be afloat.

The findings of fact and the conclusions of the Roberts Commission were presented to President Roosevelt on Saturday afternoon, 24 January. The report was released to the nation's newspapers in time for their big Sunday editions. The blame for the disaster, for the loss of life, for the shattered and sunken ships that Wallin's men now worked on, was placed almost squarely on the shoulders of General Short and Admiral Kimmel. The report stated bluntly that the pair had not coordinated their defensive efforts:

> It was a dereliction of duty on the part of each of them not to consult and confer with each other respecting the meaning and intent of the warnings and the appropriate means of defense required by the imminence of hostilities. The attitude of each, that he was not required to inform himself of, and his lack of interest in, the measure undertaken by the other to carry out the responsibilities assigned to each other under the provisions of the plans then in effect, demonstrated on the part of each a lack of appreciation of the responsibilities vested in them and inherent in their positions as commander in chief, Pacific Fleet, and commanding General, Hawaiian Department.

The report went on to state what had been obvious: that the attack had been a complete surprise. "Each failed properly to evaluate the seriousness of the situation. These errors of judgment were the effective causes for the success of the attack."[4]

Dereliction of duty. Errors of judgment. It was a blistering condemnation of Short and Kimmel. Had the American people been able to see photos of the salvage work in the harbor, their shock and anger might have turned into overwhelming fury at Kimmel. As it was, calls for Kimmel's scalp echoed in the halls of Congress, in the editorial pages, and in living rooms across the nation. It wasn't fair, of course. The Roberts Commission, while it had imputed some contributory negligence to Washington for its obscure warnings that emphasized probable Japanese moves in the Far East, had singled out Short and Kimmel for blame to the exclusion of almost everyone else. It was not to be the last investigation of the disaster by any means, and there were many, especially in the Navy and War Departments, who sympathized with the pair and believed that they had been made scapegoats. But what was done was done. Short and Kimmel, disgraced in the eyes of many of their countrymen, applied for retirement within days.

Back at Kimmel's former command, while diving parties continued to smooth out the *West Virginia*'s hull and close portholes forward of the damage, the catapult atop turret 3 was lifted clear, as were the main battery directors. On 25 January, as the citizens of the United States read the stinging conclusions of the Roberts Commission report over Sunday breakfast, a diving party surveying the hull farther aft than any before made a shocking discovery: the ship had been hit in the stern by another torpedo. The damage began at frame 140, just above the port inboard screw, and extended back to the sternpost. The rudder was gone, but the divers quickly found it lying in two pieces in the mud nearby. Also in the mud was part of the torpedo that had inflicted the damage. Like the other, it was hoisted to the surface and taken to the Submarine Base for examination. For now, the main focus would remain on the wrecked area amidships. But this new damage would need a further examination both inside and outside the hull to determine how badly the watertight bulkheads had been ruptured.

That same day the first material for constructing A-frames was sent to the ship by barge. As on the *Nevada*, these A-frames would support and lower the patches into place so that Pacific Bridge divers could bolt them to the hull. The frames, two beams fastened together in the shape of a capital A, extended out over the edge of the deck. The legs were bolted to angle iron that was either welded or bolted to the deck, and the tops were adjusted and restrained by 3/4-inch wire rope preventers secured to padeyes welded to the deck and bulkheads. An I-beam, running parallel to the deck, was fastened to the frames with clips at the level where the patches would be lowered into place. These would serve as a track for the chain falls, which could maneuver the patch horizontally and vertically.

The first supports for the small patch between frames 43 and 51 were completed by 30 January, and more lighters of construction material were delivered for the larger set between frames 63 and 99. Work on the patch sections continued, although the *California* job had priority and carpenters were being diverted there to complete the

The stern of the *West Virginia*, wrecked by the torpedo hit that went undiscovered during the initial diving inspection. Exploratory pumping revealed substantial damage and complete destruction of the ship's watertight integrity aft. This photograph shows the extent of the patching that was subsequently required.
National Archives

cofferdam sections. Four of the A-frames for the large patch were put in place rather quickly before work was halted so that proper shoring could be constructed for the legs of subsequent frames on the damaged deck.

The sound of hammers and saws, the flash of welding equipment among the twisted, buckled steel, the men in hard hats and overalls looking over plans or moving lumber and tools between lighters and the deformed decks—it all made the battleship seem more like a construction site than a ship of war. Shipfitters welded supports and braces so that frame legs could be bolted where the deck had been badly distorted or was missing altogether. By 9 February nine of the A-frames for the long patch had been built and were being lined up. A platform was nailed together over the port deck edge from foremast to after stack for a working area to handle the chain falls and patches. Forty feet aft, another group began the delicate process of cutting down the *West Virginia*'s mainmast. The turrets and conning tower would remain, but some weight savings, stability, and room would be obtained by removing the tall cage and top. Day after day, well into the second week of February, while the patches were being built on shore, the preparatory work on the charred deck of the *West Virginia* went on.

Throughout January, work on the *Cassin* and *Downes* proceeded. The effort to completely patch the *Cassin* for righting was coming along nicely. The *Downes* was being gutted, all serviceable machinery being removed and preserved. The fate of both ships was still being debated.

The A-frames for the *West Virginia*'s forward patch on 16 March 1942. Extending over the deck edge, the frames were restrained by preventer wires. Chain falls for holding the patch sections run along an I-beam attached to the frames.
National Archives

New quarters for *West Virginia* personnel on Ford Island, 4 May 1942.
National Archives

Not only had the ships been badly burned and holed, but the hulls had been badly distorted. The war damage report written several months later for both destroyers stated, "The partial flooding and draining of the dock bent this ship [*Cassin*] as a whole, and the keel, main deck and intermediate structure failed by buckling almost completely around the hull at frame 97, near the midship section." Taut-wire measurements had shown that the bow of the *Cassin* had been forced up about 2 feet. The *Downes* had similarly been twisted:

> Structural damage on this ship included the destruction or distortion of the main strength members of the hull to such an extent that the longitudinal strength was decreased about 65 percent. The hull was twisted and hogged. The forward third was about ³/₄ inch to starboard; the middle third was nearly 4 inches to port; and the after third about an inch to port. The bow was pushed up 39 inches, the keel was up 4⁵/₈ inches amidships, and the stern sagged 39 inches.[5]

The repair work to make these ships seaworthy again was obviously going to be enormous.

Gillette's main concern was restoring Dry Dock 1 to full use at the earliest possible date, with the disposition of those vessels, whether by salvage or stripping for parts, a secondary concern. He had suggested in early January that when the *Raleigh* was ready to undock the *Cassin* be either righted in place or towed to Dry Dock 2 and placed there with the *Nevada*. If that was feasible, he recommended that the *Shaw* be docked there as well. Unfortunately that would solve only half his problem. The work on the *Downes* would have to be expedited, because once the *Nevada* had landed on the blocks in Dry Dock 2, Dry Dock 1 would become the sole reliance for docking large vessels until the floating dry dock was fully repaired. Gillette recommended that the *Cassin* be repaired sufficiently to proceed to the West Coast on her own or under tow,

Patching of the *Cassin* and *Downes* continues on 23 January 1942. Nearly all of the *Downes*'s superstructure had been removed by this time. The hole in her starboard deck, caused by the torpedo explosion, is clearly visible.
Naval Historical Center NH 54562

and that the *Downes* be declared a total loss, with all salvageable fittings, machinery, and equipment removed from her as quickly as possible.[6]

It is easy to sympathize with Gillette's position in the debate. As manager of the yard he had much more to consider than the fate of a pair of badly damaged destroyers. The yard had a busy schedule of repair and upkeep work ahead. The *Medusa* had to have her boilers altered. The *Vestal* needed a period in dry dock to repair small leaks from her bomb damage. The *Rigel* was still completing conversion from a destroyer tender to a repair ship and was awaiting installation of boilers, evaporators, generators, and a distilling plant for fresh feedwater. Completion of the *Rigel* and *Vestal* was a top priority since they could then lend their repair facilities to the effort. The hardworking minesweepers *Bobolink*, *Vireo*, and *Turkey* were also in need of yard time. The *Bobolink* was overdue for a general engineering overhaul, and all three needed additional splinter protection, removal of their foremast, and installation of .50-caliber machine guns. And these were just Base Force ships.[7] Gillette had every right to be concerned about the destroyers taxing his already overburdened repair facilities far beyond their value to the war effort. Nimitz's destroyers, cruisers, and carriers needed upkeep, and the Japanese could add to the workload at any time.

Yet not everyone agreed with Gillette. Pye, who had reverted to commander of the Battle Force after Nimitz relieved him as CinCPac, did not want the *Downes* scrapped except as a last resort. The need for fleet escort vessels was acute, and the *Downes* could either fill that role after considerable repair or be reconstructed as a smaller escort vessel for convoy duty, which would free destroyers for the fleet. Gillette deferred to Pye's opinion, and in early January he agreed to convene an informal board to discuss the immediate fate of the *Downes*. It met on 7 January. Capt. Fred Earle, Gillette's good friend and the head of the yard's Planning Division, was there, as was Wallin, who was about to assume command of the Salvage Division. Capt. R. S. McDowell attended from Calhoun's Base Force staff, as did Whitaker from the Salvage Planning Office, Commander Lyttle, the planning superintendent, and Horne from the Mobile Repair Unit.

Wallin presented Pye's position, noting the extreme scarcity of ships, and said that even if the *Downes* proved inadequate as a convoy escort she should be used in some capacity. He also took issue with Gillette's concern with the need to free the dry dock, since the only advantage would be that the *Enterprise* and *Yorktown* (and soon the *Hornet*) could be docked in Dry Dock 1 if the destroyers were removed. If the carriers required dry-docking after damage resulted in an increase in draft, they would have to go to Dry Dock 2 in any case. Further, if the destroyers were to be placed with the *Nevada*, whether in Dry Dock 1 or 2, they might as well stay there as long as necessary because it looked as if the *Nevada* would require a long time in dock.

McDowell thought that a new hull could be built around the *Downes* machinery, but he was thinking in terms of Navy Yard Pearl building the hull, not Mare Island or Puget Sound. Construction plans existed but had long been filed away in dusty cabinets and would need to be dug out and examined. There was doubt about the possibility of obtaining material from the mainland to construct a hull from the keel up, and there was considerable hesitation about the yard engaging in what was essentially new construction in the middle of a war. McDowell refused to commit himself to an opinion one way or the other but finally stated that he would recommend stripping the ship of machinery and installing it either in a new hull at Pearl or in a repaired *Downes*. The others spoke mainly about the extent of the damage. Whitaker had toured the ship and was optimistic about the condition of the crew living spaces and the boiler rooms. He thought she could be returned to duty. Lyttle said that the wiring was a total loss and would have to be completely redone, and he was not optimistic about returning her to duty within a reasonable length of time. He agreed with Gillette that the decision about the fate of the *Downes* should be based on how quickly she could be removed from the dock. Horne focused on the machinery, saying that some of it, particularly boilers 1, 2, and 3, were in good shape. He advised preserving the boilers in place aboard the ship. In the end, the board agreed with Horne that the boilers should be left aboard. They also recommended to Gillette that the ship be treated as a "recoverable vessel," machinery preserved aboard her or in the yard until enough wreckage had been cleared away to permit a detailed structural examination of the interior. Only at that point would it be decided whether to return the ship to service or to complete the scrapping.[8]

By 17 January boiler 4 had been removed by Horne's men, along with the main condenser, the main feed pumps, and the number 1 main circulator. More machinery was lifted through the hole in the main deck in the following days: lubricating oil service pumps, main reduction gears, lubricating oil strainers, fire and bilge pumps. Horne reported that enough of the *Cassin's* hull had been patched to float her when Dry Dock 1 was next flooded. Patching the *Downes* continued, too. Some 243 holes had been counted in the port side alone.[9] Seams were split, sometimes to a length of 4 feet, and hull plates were missing. The ship was less damaged starboard, but it added up to an immense amount of welding and patching to be done by the busy Repair Unit.

On 3 February the heavy cruiser *Chester* passed the *Nevada* as she steamed up the channel to the Navy Yard. She had been escorting Halsey's *Enterprise* task force in a hit-and-run raid on the Japanese-held Marshall Islands, the first significant counterstroke of the war by the United States Navy. The *Chester* had been hit by a bomb that killed eight men and wounded dozens of others and had returned to Pearl for repair ahead of the rest of the force. At Waipio Point the salvage crew barely paid the cruiser any notice. The *Nevada* had been unwatered down to the third deck, and the last of the docking keel had been dynamited off. Only minor trimming of wood scraps remained to be done. Two anchors had been set on the offshore side of the ship, in deeper water, to hold her off the beach when she became waterborne. The diving teams now began their last efforts to place the patch, free, it was assumed, from any further obstructions. Pumping continued, and calculations indicated that the *Nevada* would float when the water level was 6 inches below the second platform deck.

As had been the case for weeks, there was close cooperation between the civilian diving crew, that of the *Widgeon*, and the team from the *Ortolan*, which had been sent over from Ten Ten Dock while the *Oglala* job was reevaluated. Ankers's 4 February report read, "1200. Continued work on pulling patch into place. Civilian divers down. Continued slow dewatering of third deck and clearing of dry spaces. 1530. Patch almost in place; began preparations to run hogging lines. 1600. *Widgeon* divers down to burn holes for hooks and rig hogging lines. 1700. *Ortolan* diving party relieves *Widgeon* on rigging of lines. 0000. *Widgeon* takes over burning and rigging. Opened hatches in patch."[10]

So far the salvage effort had been hot, dirty, unpleasant duty for those cleaning out the compartments aboard the *Nevada*, but it had been relatively safe, except for the divers. That changed on 7 February, when a lieutenant by the name of Clarkson, while in a trunk at the first platform level, was testing for the presence of water in an adjacent compartment. He unscrewed the air test cap at the doorway, and as water squirted out, he collapsed. A machinist's mate first class, Peter Cornelius DeVries, rushed to his aid and also collapsed. DeVries fell into the water and either died from whatever had stricken him or drowned before he could be pulled free. More men rushed over, and another four collapsed almost immediately. All were rushed to the Naval Hospital, where Clarkson later died. The other four recovered, though all were seriously ill. It was thought that perhaps the men had succumbed to carbon monoxide, but blood samples failed to bear this explanation out. Dr. C. M. Parker, from the Navy Yard's Department of Industrial Hygiene, borrowed a hydrogen sulfide indicator, a carbon monoxide indicator, and some other equipment from the Honolulu Bureau of Sanitation and went below on the *Nevada* to analyze whatever toxic gas had killed and injured those men. The odor of sewer gas, hydrogen sulfide, had been present throughout the unwatering, and many of the crew had been taken slightly ill, but it was not thought to have been hazardous. The rotten-egg smell was caused by the disintegration of organic material: paper, cardboard, shoes, clothing, food, and human remains. Under considerable water pressure, the gas was odorless and lethal. In a concentration of 1,000 parts per million, it could kill within minutes, and it was at this level where the men had succumbed. In some compartments the concentration in the water itself could be as high as 300,000 parts per million. The gas dissipated quickly as it rose and was found in concentrations of 40 to 100 parts per million on the second and third decks. Blowers and ventilation pipes were immediately run deep into the *Nevada* to bring fresh air in and force contaminated air out.[11]

As shocking as this discovery was, and as tragic as the deaths were, the salvage operation barely missed a beat. Measurements indicated that the stern had risen about $2^1/_2$ feet. The ship would soon be waterborne, and the question remained: Where would the *Nevada* be dry-docked? Oil was still being pumped out of the blisters into lighters in an effort to lighten the ship as much as possible. Lighters of canned goods, coffee, furniture, bunks, wiring, and clothing were still being removed. The stern rose another 6 inches between 9 and 10 February, necessitating additional pumping from the forward compartments on the first and second platform decks to reduce the pivoting pressure on the keel. Divers continued to fit the patch to the hull, but it just would not seat. By the twelfth the vessel was rising about a foot a day. The watertight bulk-

Divers from the *Ortolan* (left) and *Widgeon* work with the *Haviside* to attach the big patch to the *Nevada*. The *Ortolan* had been moved to Waipio Point while a new plan was devised to raise the *Oglala*.
National Archives

heads beyond the patch were still holding as Ankers and his men carefully regulated the water being removed. At 1300 on the thirteenth, Ankers officially reported his charge waterborne. The *Nevada* was once again afloat, sixty-eight days after her valiant run for the sea ended on the shore of Hospital Point.

By now the ship was scheduled for docking in Dry Dock 2 on the eighteenth. The *Saratoga* had left the dock for Bremerton after temporary repairs to her torpedo hit. Wallin had reported to Earle, the planning officer, that "the gas hazard which has developed on that vessel has very greatly limited the amount of work which can be performed in lightening ship, and it has therefore, been concluded that efforts to reduce the draft sufficiently to get into Drydock #1 should be discontinued—especially in view of the fact that Drydock #2 is available."[12] Wallin anticipated that the patch would be in place, as a safety factor more than anything else. Divers reported that the patch extended 2 feet below the keel, and they were still examining the underside of the ship for projections. Still, every bit of decrease in draft helped. As the *Nevada*'s magazines were unwatered, 14-inch powder cans were unloaded to ammunition lighters for the trip to the Naval Ammunition Depot. On the seventeenth, tugs ran lines to the *Nevada*'s stern and towed her out to deeper water in the channel.

Finally Ankers decided, with Wallin's concurrence, to remove the big patch altogether. He was taking a risk. Even though for some reason the patch could not be brought up tight against the hull, it would still serve as a bulwark against water surging into the torpedo hole while the ship was towed across the channel entrance.[13] The pressure could burst the inner bulkheads. But the deciding factor was that once the ship was waterborne and a thorough examination of the bottom was possible, divers had found the bottom of the patch extending not 2 feet but nearly 4 feet below the keel. This would prohibit the docking of the ship no matter which dock she headed for. Accordingly, a Hawaiian Dredging Company derrick came alongside the *Nevada* on the seventeenth and plucked the patch from the chain falls, delivering it to Waipio Point.

Throughout the night of 17–18 February, pumps continued to drain the ship while a careful watch was kept on the bulkheads behind the torpedo damage. Fortunately they continued to withstand the pressure head that Ankers and Mahan had so carefully maintained. Should the bulkheads suddenly fail, there would be very little time for tugs to beach her again before she sank or capsized. Two months of work could go to waste in a matter of minutes.

Work had begun in Shop 11 on modifying the barges to lift the *Oglala*, but there was not much enthusiasm for the plan. The Design Section continued to study it and even recommended augmenting the barges and air bubble with pontoons to gain the necessary lift. Divers from the *Ortolan* went into the ship daily, rigging safes for lifting, bringing chairs, decoding machines, typewriters, and the silver set to the surface. Captain Hull's cabin was searched for valuables, as were the other officers' cabins for their personal effects. It was the best use of the time being spent waiting for the Design Section to arrive at a decision.

Holtzworth's team finally decided to abandon the lifting scheme altogether in favor of a new plan to right the ship using submarine salvage pontoons to roll her over. Her salvage engineer, Lieutenant McClung, outlined the new scheme:

1. Clear debris from the area between the USS *Oglala* and the Ten Ten Dock.
2. Run pilot cables under the ship to pull chains through.
3. Rig fittings for securing chains and chocks for guiding chains around starboard gunwale.
4. Pull chains under hull.
5. Secure chains to pontoons.
6. Place pontoons, and secure chains to ship.
7. Test pontoons and chains.
8. Dredge outboard of ship.
9. Roll ship.
10. Close all openings in ship.
11. Place pumps and arrange vents.
12. Pump out ship.

Over three weeks were allotted to run the chains under the *Oglala* and secure them to pontoons, and the righting of the ship by blowing the pontoons was scheduled for 29 March, just over a month away.[14] If the fence cofferdam proved successful on the *California*, perhaps it could be used on the *Oglala*, too.

In Dry Dock 1, at the head of Ten Ten Dock, work patching the destroyers was nearing an end as the date for the next flooding of the dock grew near. By 24 January the preliminary patching of the *Cassin* was complete, with only the unseen damage on her starboard side, the portion that rested on the dock floor, yet to be repaired. The hull of the *Downes* was surveyed the next day by Horne and some of Gillette's officers to determine how much more patching was necessary to make the ship floatable. They decided that by expediting the patching and replacement of shell plating, the *Downes* could be completed in time. The shell plating in the bow that had been removed when the ship was first docked was replaced, as was plating that had been torn away by the detonation of the starboard torpedo tubes. The last equipment to be removed before flotation, the main reduction gear housings, came off the ship on 1 February, the shell plating had been completely renewed by the fourth, and the final patches were applied that same afternoon.

On the *Cassin*, welders finished repairing the last seam ruptures and small holes that were still being discovered up to the morning of Thursday the fifth. Water was let into the dock at 1310 that afternoon as a huge crowd assembled to watch the *Cassin* pulled upright. Lines had been run from the ship to the shore capstan, and when 3 feet of water had been let into the dock, a strain was taken on the lines. The *Cassin* lifted slightly off her blocks, rolled heavily to port, righted herself, and settled down on the dock floor with a 2-degree list to port. She was upright, but more damage had been inflicted on her starboard side by the shoring, particularly beneath her after stack.

All three ships remained in the dock on the fifth, and it was again pumped dry. Lieutenants Wildman and Camm of the Mobile Repair Unit examined the *Cassin*. Since she sat directly on the dock floor rather than on blocks, the condition of the bottom of the ship could not be ascertained. But the extent of the damage to her starboard side was alarming, and it was obvious that her stay in the dry dock would be extended. The *Downes*, though, was ready to undock. The following day, as Halsey's *Enterprise* task force steamed into Pearl, eleven new holes were burned into the *Cassin's* hull so that she would settle evenly when the dock was reflooded. The *Cassin* was shored from the dock bottom on her starboard side and from alters to port, and Dry Dock 1 was flooded just before noon. The water was 2 feet over the forecastle deck, but she stayed on an almost even keel. The *Downes* followed the *Raleigh* out of the dock at 1530 and was towed to Ten Ten Dock. Work on the *Cassin* was suspended on Saturday the seventh, when the *Vestal* was towed into Dry Dock 1 for final repairs to her hull damage. The Mobile Repair Unit resumed work the next day as welders again applied patches to the *Cassin's* ravaged hull.[15]

A strange-looking vessel took to the waters of Pearl Harbor on 8 February, one with a stubby, barren bow, a spare foremast with an old-fashioned crow's nest, and a single uncovered 5-inch/.38 gun amidships. But the number on her stern was a familiar one, 373. Aesthetically she was ungainly. From a practical standpoint, the *Shaw* represented a tremendous success.

Repairs to YFD-2 were not yet complete; the floating dock still did not have full buoyancy restored, but it could dock a destroyer, and the one that settled inside on 26 January was the same that had been there on 7 December, the USS *Shaw*. She was in the dock for ten days, having her new bow firmly secured for the journey to Mare Island. Undocking on the afternoon of 4 February, she was maneuvered to Ten Ten Dock with the assistance of a pair of tugs for the last of the repair work to be completed. The explosion that had ripped her apart had been spectacular, second only in magnitude to the shuddering detonation that had destroyed the *Arizona*. She had burned fiercely but by a combination of luck and design had stayed afloat. Now she was at sea again, under her own power, preparing to steam for Mare Island, where she would complete her rebuild. After more trials off the harbor entrance the *Shaw* was pronounced fit for the journey. The ninth found her at berth 6, near the Salvage Division offices, alongside the destroyer *Ward*, which had fired the first shots of the Pacific war in the early-morning hours of 7 December after spotting a Japanese midget submarine sneaking into the channel entrance. The *Shaw* cast off from the *Ward* at 1352, backed out of the repair basin, and headed for the channel entrance.[16] Out of the harbor she sailed, the first of the Base Force Salvage Organization's severely damaged charges to get out of Pearl, to get back into the war.

A large crowd looks on at Dry Dock 1 as the *Cassin* is righted on 5 February 1942. Behind the destroyers, ready for undocking once the shoring is removed, is the repaired *Raleigh*. Naval Historical Center NH 54564

The work inside the *Utah* was becoming increasingly precarious for both the divers and the men working in the unwatered spaces, and by the end of the first week of February, Stelter was ready to cease all operations on the target ship. The diving officer in charge of the work, Lieutenant Robinson from the Submarine Base, was nervous about sending his men down to the first and second platform decks. He forbade more than one 90-degree turn while descending, lest the divers foul their lines in the wreckage that had shifted about in the overturned hull. The depth of water in the compartments adjacent to the magazines exerted considerable pressure on the doors and hatches where the men were lifting ammunition to the surface, and the bulkheads and coamings leaked badly. The pumps were taking suction through a lift of anywhere from 21 to 24 feet but could lower the water only a few feet in the deepest spaces. Hydrogen sulfide gas was present, forcing the use of respirators, and the concentration of the deadly gas became greater the deeper the men descended into the ship.

The team had recovered all of the useful ammunition and weapons that could be reached through the present openings, and now it was time either to move deeper into the hull or to abandon further recovery operations. If the salvage continued, the divers would have to work their way laterally through flooded compartments to reach the aft group of magazines, or more holes would have to be cut into the hull. Neither could

The ungainly *Shaw*, sporting a temporary bow, a tripod mast, and a lone 5-inch gun taken from the *Cassin*, cruises off Ford Island just prior to leaving for Mare Island Naval Shipyard and a complete rebuild. The hull of the *Oklahoma* is at far right.
Naval Historical Center NH 50005

be accomplished quickly. Finally, Stelter was running into the same difficulty as were other salvage officers and ship superintendents: a lack of resources. In the case of the *Utah*, what was lacking was manpower. In exasperation, Stelter wrote Wallin:

> The lack of personnel to shift hose, break out and load ammunition, etc., was past the stage of annoyance. The original working party of thirty men obtained from the Mobile Repair Unit was recalled and not replaced due to the necessity of their employment elsewhere. The Receiving Station furnished details up to forty men, but, the members of these details were changed from day to day, their reporting for duty could not be depended upon, and, the last one of these parties was recalled on February 4th with no replacements available.

Nevertheless, Stelter considered the whole operation a success. His men had recovered 1,229 rounds of 5-inch/.25 ammunition, 600 rounds of 5-inch/.38 ammunition, and 850 shells for the 5-inch/.51 guns to be taken to the Naval Ammunition Depot.[17] For the next few days the crew worked on recovering the ship's service safe, which was loaded aboard a barge on the eleventh. The hoses, compressors, cutting equipment,

The USS *Utah*, alone and abandoned. In January and February 1942 she was visited by a diving and ordnance crew under F. C. Stelter. Once divers assured Stelter that the ship was stable, holes were cut into the hull to recover ammunition.
Naval Historical Center NH 64498

and other tools were loaded up too and had been removed by the fourteenth. Wallin's *Utah* notation on that day concluded, "No further work to be done for some time."[18] He was correct. It would be a year before the salvors returned to that side of Ford Island.

Early on the morning of 18 February the cables holding the *Nevada* in position were slipped and secured to buoys for later recovery. Tugs came alongside and began the short push across the channel. The pumps were still going, keeping pace with the leaks. The ship drew just 31 feet aft but almost 42 feet forward, the result of the flooded forward compartments equalizing the pressure on the bulkheads open to the sea. Ballast tanks aft were flooded to bring her bow up, and she slid across the sill of Dry Dock 2 just before 1000. The caisson swung closed behind her, and the pumps lowered the water slowly so that she could be properly positioned over the blocks. As the dock emptied, water was pumped out of the *Nevada*'s flooded bow, to reduce her trim and the load on her keel as she settled bow first on the blocks. Nimitz was there to watch. He had looked glumly at her, blackened and flooded, when he first arrived at Pearl back in December. The commander in chief had taken a great interest in the progress of the salvage, and Wallin had briefed him weekly on the status of the work. Nimitz had grown quite fond of Wallin, later calling him the most optimistic man he had ever met.[19] Now, like the officers and men around him, Nimitz watched with a smile on his face as the first ship of the Battle Line to be resurrected from the harbor bottom arrived safely at Navy Yard Pearl.

The day the *Nevada* was secured in Dry Dock 2, the first of the patches was brought out to the *West Virginia*. The patch sections had been designed by Pacific Bridge, again under the direction of Fred Crocker, and were unique in their simplicity and utility. The *California* job involved raising the level of the deck, while that of the *West Virginia* involved building a new shell outboard of the damaged areas. The new shell would consist of a wood, steel, and concrete patch built in sections. As designed they were 48 feet high, 13½ feet wide. Wood sheeting 4 inches thick made up the outer wall of the patch. These sheeting strips, nearly a foot wide, were tied together with horizontal wales, 12-by-12-inch and 12-by-14-inch beams bolted with 7/8-inch bolts to the outer wood sheeting. The bottom of the patch made a 90-degree turn into the ship so that if viewed from the side it was L-shaped and drawn up snugly under the turn of the bilge. The ingenuity of the patch was on the inside. The primary obstacle facing Crocker and his design team was that of shoring the sections against what was left of the hull. The armor belt would provide excellent backing for supporting struts and shores, but much of the hull above and below it was either missing or pushed inboard so far as to be useless for the purpose. To eliminate the need for shoring below the belt, Crocker simply built it into the patch, in the form of huge I-beams 2 feet wide and 20 feet long. These were bolted vertically to the wales with the same 7/8-inch bolts used to secure the wales to the sheeting. The bottom of the I-beam was bolted to the bottom of the patch, while the top would rest against the bottom edge of the armor belt, thus providing firm backing. At the top of each I-beam

Success. The *Nevada*, minus the big patch, makes her way into Dry Dock 2 on 18 February 1942.
U.S. Naval Institute

was welded a bracket of angle iron. This would be drawn up under the bottom of the armor belt, wedged with bits of hardwood, and would take the upward thrust of the patch as it was unwatered and rose. Shoring above the belt would be done on a section-by-section basis, depending on how much of the hull structure remained. That would prove to be a challenge.

The patches were to be butted up against each other and tied together by bolts 1 inch wide and over 2 feet long, spaced vertically every few feet down the outside. The sections were to be brought up tight against the struts and shoring on the hull by four horizontal rows of hook bolts, through holes burned into the shell and secured with butterfly nuts. The bottoms of the patch sections would then be sealed with concrete, using 10-inch tremie pipes placed 40 feet below the surface at the bottom of the patch. Each end section had a 4-foot-wide partition built along its vertical length. Concrete would be poured into this form to seal the ends of the patch. The narrow width of the sections made them much easier to handle than the unwieldy patch built for the *Nevada* and also permitted the patch to follow the curve of the armor belt, which was no longer a solid wall but had been knocked askew by the impact of the torpedoes.

Though the first section had been delivered to the *West Virginia* and was now suspended from the chain falls at frame 52, it was not yet ready to be lowered into place. The *West Virginia* sat on a coral bottom, but the coral had a layer of mud on top that

The inside of a patch. The hatch was for diver access once it had been bolted to the hull. The heavy angle iron atop the I-beams were to be placed under the armor belt.
National Archives

needed to be cleared from the turn of the bilge so that the lower end of the patch could be brought up underneath the hull. A clam dredge was lowered and the mud scooped away; then divers made more measurements between the upper deck and the bilge keel.

The clam dredge proved cumbersome and ineffective, and within days a diving party experienced in using siphons and jets was at work clearing the mud from the bilge. A few more days were spent altering the end sections to clear the bilge keel. As these end sections would be flush against the hull, they would foul the keel, and a notch had to be cut out of each where the keel would pass through. On the afternoon of 23 February the after section of the small patch was successfully lowered into place. It was a good fit, and by the next afternoon the holes for the hook bolts had been burned into the hull and the butterfly nuts tightened. It took a couple of days to get this section into proper position, and on the twenty-sixth the middle section was lifted from its barge, placed on the chain falls, and lowered alongside the first patch. Working in conditions of extremely poor visibility, divers examined the adjoining sections to determine if any alterations were needed to ensure a tight fit. There were none. The design and construction of the patch sections had been precise. Emile Genereaux, who had been assigned by Painter to write a short summary each day for Wallin's noon report to Gillette, wrote, "The middle section of the small patch was placed into position alongside of the after section. It seems to fit very well so operations are being carried out to secure this section of the patch permanently. The forward section of the patch should be ready to be placed in position this afternoon."[20] So

Looking down the length of a patch end section resting on a barge alongside the *West Virginia*. The form built into the right side of the patch was to be filled with tremie concrete to seal it. Note the cutouts for the armor belt. The *Oklahoma* is at upper left.
National Archives

far so good. The third and final section of this small patch was brought out from the yard by lighter, and on 27 February it too was lowered into the water. The small patch covering the forward torpedo damage was not yet complete, but it was in place and bolted to the ship.

The USS *Plunger*, just returned from patrol, had been scheduled for docking on the marine railway on 17 February, the day before the *Nevada* was to be docked. The 300-foot-long submarine was settled on bilge and keel blocks, and the massive chain assembly was bringing the boat and the docking cradle up onto land when the groundways for the pier side of the cradle collapsed. The stern of the sub had just come out of the water when, with a sickening lurch and crash, the *Plunger* rolled off her own blocks and fell against the side of the railway, her conning tower against pier number 1. The frustration in the Navy Yard offices was intense. Just a few weeks after the floating dry dock had been returned to use, another dock was now out of commission. Worse, there appeared to be no quick way to repair it. There were over 1,300 tons of submarine that, for all intents and purposes, had been run hard aground inside.

The disaster further stretched the thin resources of the yard. Pearl Harbor was the only forward shipyard in the war zone, and Gillette needed every inch of repair and docking space. The *Cassin* had finally been removed from Dry Dock 1, and another pair of destroyers, the *Gridley* and *Fanning*, were there for bow repairs and for some top-

The size of the patch sections is apparent as one is lifted clear of the water. The lower wales were spaced closer together than those near the surface, to resist the greater water pressure.
National Archives

side alterations. The *Nevada* was in Dry Dock 2 having her torpedo damage repaired, on two or three days' notice to vacate the dock if necessary. Dry Docks 3 and 4 were under construction. The YFD-2 had been fully repaired, and the submarine *Pompano* was inside for an interim overhaul. The railway was almost always occupied by destroyers, submarines, minesweepers, or other small craft. Now the timetable had been destroyed, and planning officers scrambled to rearrange docking schedules.

The Salvage Office in Building 129 was not far from the railway, and Emile

Genereaux visited the pier not long after the accident. He spoke with the docking officer, asking how the *Plunger* had rolled over. Genereaux had a look for himself under the railway and at the position of the submarine and cradle, then confidently assured the officer that the job of floating the *Plunger* would not be a difficult one. Perhaps to Genereaux, who had observed the *Nevada* being prepared for dry-docking, and who was well acquainted with the complex plans to raise both the *California* and *West Virginia*, the prospect of refloating a slightly damaged submarine just a few yards from the water's edge was a straightforward and relatively uncomplicated undertaking. At any rate he was a sailor, had been all of his life, and this, to him, was a job for a sailor.[21]

Word of Genereaux's positive outlook on the situation reached Homer Wallin, who summoned him to his office. Wallin advised Genereaux that he was temporarily assigning him to the *Plunger* project. Genereaux met with Gillette and with Cdr. Ben Manseau, the shop superintendent, to discuss his idea for righting and refloating the submarine. Luckily the submarine had fallen to starboard, toward the adjacent pier, rather than to port, which had a short stretch of water between the dock and the next pier over. Genereaux planned to use jacks braced on the pier to push the vessel upright in the dock. Once up, she would be secured there with wires and turnbuckles so that the whole assembly, dock, submarine, and all, could be pulled into Southeast Loch. When the *Plunger* was again waterborne she would be floated clear and the dock hauled out of the water again for repair. The *Plunger* would be towed over to YFD-2 to complete her short overhaul.

Riggers set up nine 70-ton jacks on the pier, which would push the submarine upright using timbers inserted into sockets welded to the *Plunger*'s hull. More beams were placed as shoring against the opposite side of the dock, braced from the earth seawall to the railway's port side, to keep the platform from moving laterally when the jacks were used. Long rectangular cleats were welded to the hull every few feet perpendicular to the keel at the point where it met the bottom of the dock. These cleats were positioned to slide between parallel rounded timbers, also perpendicular to the keel, secured to the bottom of the dock. As the sub rolled, the cleats would mortise between the timbers, keeping the cigar-shaped hull from rotating unevenly. Nimitz always made it a point to be present at a major event in the salvage operations, and this was no exception. Along with Furlong and Gillette, he stood on the dock watching as the jacks pushed the *Plunger* nearly upright. Wires were run from the dock catwalks to the sub to keep her there. The next stage was to somehow drag the submarine and docking cradle back into the water.

On 13 February, riggers attached the *California*'s mainmast to lifting tackle on the yard's floating crane, and shipfitters burned away the last of the cage structure a few feet above the deck. Slings had also been rigged on the quarterdeck catapult, and both were removed from the ship on the same day. Another crew was hard at work removing the stud bolts from the top plate of the conning tower. The heavily armored tower was to be removed as part of the overall effort to reduce weight and improve stability, and work had already been proceeding on it for a week.

More carpenters had finally arrived for the cofferdam, and sections were being bolted together at a faster pace. On the seventeenth the first forecastle section to arrive at the ship was set in place and secured to the hull by divers under the supervision of Bill Painter. Pacific Bridge's Les Freeman, the superintendent of salvage operations, and Bert Rice, the rigger foreman, were also there. Rather than eight sections, as originally planned, extending from the superstructure deck to the bow, there would be seven. This first one was placed at the bow. A sandbag wall would run from it across the beam just aft of the anchor chains and would tie in with another sandbag wall comprising the starboard cofferdam.

Anchor chains had to be moved before another section was placed, and number 6 was set two days later. But there was a problem. Yard divers were reporting hydrogen sulfide gas penetrating their suits as they worked inside the ship closing hatches and doors at the third-deck level. The level of gas was low, but the smell was disconcerting, and diving inside the ship was halted until the source of the odor could be discovered. The suits and air compressors were tested, but no sewer gas was found. No one was sure exactly what the divers had smelled. The source of the odor went undiscovered, and the divers went back to work.

Pacific Bridge divers were quite experienced, and they quickly progressed from setting one section per day to setting two. Sections 5 and 4, just forward of turret 1, were placed on a single day, sections 3 and 2 on another. All were weighted down

Left to right: Admiral Nimitz, Admiral Bloch, and Captain Gillette alongside the *Plunger* as she is prepared for righting using the jacks in the background. Emile Genereaux can be seen in the group of officers in the background (*second from left*).
David W. Genereaux

with sandbags. The sections had been prefabricated in the yard, complete with wales and supporting struts to be secured to 6-by-10-inch beams bolted to the deck 10 to 15 feet inboard. The pilings that made up the fence extended 5 to 8 inches below deck level, depending on the location, and rested on the stanchions atop castings interspersed with 4-by-6-inch bearing beams. More beams and blocking spaced the bottom inner edge of the pilings away from the hull plating below the stanchions. Timber lugs, 1-inch bolts $1\frac{1}{2}$ feet long, tied the sections together. The support struts were strengthened with vertical beams, and everywhere sandbags were piled to counteract the buoyancy of the wood. The cofferdam was by no means watertight, and once the pumping began on the forecastle, divers would be kept busy isolating and caulking seams and joints. Pacific Bridge engineers also recommended the novel approach of sealing the leaks from the outside using horse manure, a method that Wallin, rather amused by the idea, had never heard of before.[22] For now, the progress on the ship was very encouraging. Divers continued sealing portholes from the outside using metal covers secured with studs driven directly into the hull.[23] The Salvage Division still planned to wall off the mud from the torpedo damage and seal the holes with tremie concrete. There was a lot left to be done before pumping could begin. The larger and more intricate quarterdeck cofferdam, which would enclose the ship port and starboard, was yet to be secured in place.

The right gun of turret 3 on the *Arizona* was lifted clear on 10 February, as the Salvage Division ordnance group continued to dissemble both after turrets. Turret 3 had been trained 90 degrees to starboard, which cleared the top of turret 4 for work, and now turret 4 was also trained toward Ford Island so that the after catapult could be unbolted from the deck. A cofferdam was needed to make that turret watertight, since the ship had continued to settle into the mud and the quarterdeck was now about 10 feet under water. Within a week all three 14-inch guns had been lifted clear of turret 3.

A fierce wind had kicked up, whipping the waves against the barbette of turret 3 and the rear of turret 4 and grounding the yard's 150-ton crane, which was too difficult to maneuver safely in high wind. The face plate and slide of turret 3 were ready to be removed from the ship, as was the catapult, but it was not until the end of February that the wind died down enough for the derrick to remove them to Waipio Point. The ammunition group had been aboard since midmonth, removing 14-inch shells from turret 3. Those also went to Waipio Point via lighter.

Furlong was still hoping that the *Arizona* could be somehow raised to clear berth F-7, and in mid-February an underwater survey was made of the entire ship, particularly the forward section, so that plans for raising and scrapping her, even in sections, could be studied. That survey was completed by the twenty-third. Similar studies were done on the submerged hulls of the *Oklahoma* and *Utah*. Both fouled badly needed battleship and carrier berths.

Raising any or all of those ships would be work of major proportions. Wallin was already looking to the future, knowing that eventually the disposition of the three would be at the forefront of the salvage effort. "My present feeling," he wrote Gillette on 24 February, "is that the salvage program proper might well be considered completed when the *California*, *West Virginia* and *Oglala* are disposed of. The *Oklahoma*, *Arizona* and *Utah* are long-time jobs which could be handled either by contract or by the Yard." It was hoped that the *Oklahoma* had been damaged no more than the *West Virginia*, perhaps less, and could be returned to service once righted. But Wallin continued:

> My reason for not indicating the *Oklahoma* in the near-term program is that righting her is likely to prove a very extensive job, and I question whether the salvaging of the vessel warrants the diversion of engineering talents, working forces, and material which would be required to do the job. After she is righted there would be a big job of further salvage work and reconditioning to get her into service. I do not question but that this can be done but would require a year or more of time in addition to the talent of working forces mentioned.

The Planning Division was at that time working on a study of righting the ship, and until that was done there was no real way to estimate the time and amount of work that would be involved. Wallin concluded, "Another aspect of the problem is the matter of availability of berths for major vessels in the spaces now occupied by the *Arizona*, *Oklahoma* and *Utah*. It may be that a satisfactory berth can be built outboard of the *Arizona* but not outboard of the *Oklahoma* and *Utah*. In the case of these latter two ships, it might prove entirely practicable to use berths inboard of these two ships."[24]

That would hardly be a satisfactory solution. The *Oklahoma* had rolled far into the channel and was significantly hampering ship movements. Berth F-5 was entirely unusable, not just because of the capsized battleship but because of the *West Virginia* at F-6. Even once the *West Virginia* was removed, it would be a difficult operation to slide a capital ship between the *Oklahoma* and the mooring quays. The bottom of the *Oklahoma* sloped toward the quays, so there was even less room than it appeared. A berth outboard of the *Oklahoma* was out of the question, but the *Utah* had capsized just off the quays. It might be possible to construct a new berth outboard of her.

Wallin suggested that the work might fall to the Pacific Bridge Company, especially the righting of the *Oklahoma*, and that it would have to be arranged by a specific contract like that of the dry docks. Even though the company had drawn up the plans for the cofferdamming of the *California* and the patching of the *West Virginia*, and was doing most of the installation work, he considered Pacific Bridge to be merely assisting in what was a Navy salvage job. "So far as the Pacific Bridge Company's work is concerned on the *California* and *West Virginia*, it is not of a major nature and I would not recommend covering the assistance they are rendering by a contract. As a matter of fact the assistance they are rendering would probably be finished before a contract could be consummated anyhow."[25] Gillette agreed. He believed that Pacific Bridge would need to be contracted only for scrapping the *Arizona*, *Utah*, *Oklahoma*, and *Oglala*.[26]

Jack Graham had quickly and enthusiastically thrown the resources and talent of his company into the salvage effort from the very first, but by mid-February he wanted

The center gun of the *Arizona*'s turret 4 is pulled free on 25 February 1942. The turret had been rotated toward Ford Island to provide clearance for the gun's removal.
National Archives

the role of Pacific Bridge in any subsequent work to be clearly defined. The company was completing Dry Dock 3 and was in the midst of building the massive Dry Dock 4 beyond Hospital Point. So proud were they of this job that their company stationery was headed "Builders Pearl Harbor Dry Dock No. 4. Contract Noy 5049." But the salvage work and the unplanned requests for personnel and equipment were throwing the construction schedule into disarray. Graham wanted the Navy to define exactly what it wanted from Pacific Bridge in the ongoing and future salvage work, particularly in regard to the *Arizona*, *Oklahoma*, and *Utah*, so that the company could be in a better position to plan. No formal contract or modification to the existing contract had been made to cover the work done with the Salvage Organization as yet, but Graham let the Navy know that it was time such alterations were made. Not only did the company wish to get paid, but it wished to help in any way necessary in the months and years ahead. All Graham wanted to know was how, specifically, they were going to be asked to help.[27]

While Graham's men might have been surprised to learn that their work on the refloating of the two battleships was considered to be "not of a major nature," it was in fact probably not a big enough job to warrant a contract. But the *Oklahoma* job would be. The salvage officer also noted that while work on the other two might be covered by a contract, it could also be "considered a backlog of work for the Yard Forces with the idea of recovering as much material as practicable and going ahead with scrap[p]ing of the vessels by cutting up with dynamite or torches as conditions permit."[28] In other words, the yard could handle the demolition of the *Arizona* and *Utah* in its spare time, when wartime conditions permitted, perhaps even waiting for the end of the war.

The new plan for righting the *Oglala* was delivered by Holtzworth's Design Section on 24 February. Ten submarine salvage pontoons secured to chains girdling the hull and held by stoppers on the starboard side would be used to flip the *Oglala* upright. Divers from the *Ortolan* went down that same day to explore the harbor bottom between the ship and Ten Ten Dock. What they found was a clutter of debris and wreckage, including some sections of hull, masts, and rigging that had been cut away during the earlier plan to raise the *Oglala* by barge. All of this would need to be cleared away so that the pontoons could be properly placed next to the deck. The divers began by lifting to the surface the 8-inch Manila lines that had been used to moor her to Ten Ten Dock. It would be days before a derrick, probably the *Gaylord*, would be available to lift the debris. In the meantime, McClung and his assistants briefed the crew of the *Ortolan* on the plan and what would be needed from the diving team.

It was the *Haviside*, not the *Gaylord*, that arrived on the first day of March to hoist the heaviest of the wreckage to the surface. The *Ortolan* crew had given up on recovering the ship's safes. They were too far inside the ship, too heavy to maneuver safely, and there was no clear path for a derrick to make the lift. So a pair of divers continued to attach lines to the wreckage in the darkness 40 feet down and swam clear as it was brought up.

On 3 March another diving team went down with the first pilot cables. Six hundred feet of 7/8-inch wire rope had been retrieved from the *Oglala*'s forward winch, and this rope was run by the divers under the bow. In the meantime the *Haviside* had been replaced by the *Gaylord*, which lifted the aviation booms and blocks. A week after pilot cables had been run under the bow, the *Gaylord*'s crew dragged a 1-inch cable with a large shackle back and forth under the hull to clear a path through the mud for the pontoon chains being prepared.

The progress was slower than expected, and the *Oglala*'s salvage team requested permission to work all daylight hours, not just the normal working day that ended at 1700. Permission was granted. The first chain stoppers had arrived at Ten Ten Dock, and welders walked over the makeshift gangway to the hull and began attaching them to the side of the ship. Stern pilot cables were run next, and on 12 March the first chain for the lifting pontoons was reeved under the *Oglala*. In order to aid the rolling motion of the minelayer when the pontoons were blown, it was expected that a small channel would be dredged outboard of the hull. The *Oklahoma* had pushed up a tremendous amount of soil from the bottom when she had capsized, but her berth had been located over some exceedingly soft mud. The bottom beneath Ten Ten Dock was firm, and an investigation along the *Oglala* port bilge showed that little in the way of a berm had been created by her rolling over. There was good news reported on 13 March: very little, if any, dredging would have to be done.

Delivery of the chain stoppers had ceased after the first two had been welded in place. The work had no priority, and other welding orders were being completed first. Yet by mid-March a few more had been turned out, and these were welded to the *Oglala*'s starboard side as chains continued to be run under the hull. The innermost chains were pulled under first, attached at both ends to the derrick on the surface, which then slid them slowly back and forth up the ship until divers, following the progress as best they could through the swirling silt and listening to the links rattle and scrape against the hull, reported them to be in position. By the nineteenth the midship set of chains was in place, and four days later the last of the stern set was run under the old ship's hull. Over in the Pacific Bridge Company offices in the Navy Yard, Fred Crocker's men were working on the plans for the fence cofferdam to be used in unwatering the ship once she was righted. Happily, they had concluded that some of the sections used on the *California* could be adapted for use on the *Oglala*. By the time they were ready for them to be placed, perhaps the *California* would be resting in dry dock.

A few weeks after Wallin's memo to Gillette about the *Arizona*, *Oklahoma*, and *Utah*, Admiral Furlong expanded on these ideas in a letter to BuShips.[29] The February diving survey had convinced him that floating the *Arizona* as she now lay was not practical. The "whole area forward of the smoke stack is badly wrecked and burned, and the hull appears to be generally opened up below the present waterline." Limited visibility and the nature of the wreckage had prevented the divers from obtaining a complete picture of the hull forward of the superstructure. One of the original ideas for salvaging the *California*, that of driving a cellular sheet-piling cofferdam around the entire ship, was a possibility. The material that had been ordered for the *California* had arrived but was still in storage. Furlong optimistically wrote, "This would permit uncovering of the damage, removal of wreckage and temporary repairs possibly sufficient to regain enough buoyancy forward to permit floatation."[30] If that would not work, perhaps the forward part of the ship could be severed while she was dry within the cofferdam. The after part could then be floated to shallow water for scrapping while the forward section was broken up in place. The need for scrap metal was great, as the home-front drives would soon show. Furlong estimated the cost as perhaps $500,000. Alternatively, he suggested a much simpler approach: cut off all visible structure above the waterline, build a battleship berth outboard of her, and leave the wreck as it was.

A similar diving survey on the *Oklahoma* had shown four large holes in the port side, though the extent of the damage was impossible to determine exactly because of the amount of mud and coral that had been pushed up. There was one hole at frame 38, just aft of turret 1, about 5 feet in diameter, that was apparently a bomb near miss. There were two torpedo holes at frames 47–51 and 61–67, between turret 2 and the stack, and more damage, mostly still covered by mud, at frames 90–98, under turret 3.

By this time the preliminary study of righting the ship had been nearly completed by the Design Section, and the quantity of material and labor that would be required was considerable. Material requirements would include twenty to thirty winches or hydraulic rams, an equal number of multiple-sheave tackles, 8,000 feet of 3-inch wire, 75,000 feet of 1-inch steel wire, and 20 tons of steel forgings, to name but a few items. Two hundred specially qualified men would be required, along with temporary living quarters nearby. The estimate Furlong had been given was one year, at a cost of about $1.5 million.

Furlong then described a second option to "clear the *Oklahoma* from her present berth": utilizing "the method employed in salvaging for scrap the German vessels scuttled at Scapa Flow."[31] This method, he wrote BuShips,

> consists essentially of removing masts, turrets, and other topside weights by
> mechanical means or by blasting and then to float the vessel upside down by blow-
> ing out water with compressed air. It may be found that the depth of water is not
> adequate for this method, but if it is then this is probably the cheapest and quickest
> method of getting the *Oklahoma* cleared. Following flotation, the vessel could be
> towed out to sea and sunk, or as in the case of the German vessels she could be
> placed in a dry dock, if one were available, for scrapping. If upon docking it is found
> that the vessel is in good enough condition to recondition, arrangements could be
> made to right the vessel. This would also permit removal of valuable material in case
> reconditioning is not worthwhile.

An underwater inspection of the *Utah* had also been completed at the same time. Three large holes had been located, all centered roughly amidships. There were torpedo hits above the bilge keel at frames 55–61 and at frames 77–82, and a torpedo hit or near-miss bomb damage at frames 69–72. In his letter to BuShips Furlong noted that "salvage operations in the *Utah* would parallel very closely those outlined above for the *Oklahoma* except that the task is of less magnitude. As yet no detailed study or approximate computations have been made as to forces required to right the vessel."

Furlong, like Nimitz, was concerned about the lack of carrier and battleship berths. The *New Mexico*, *Idaho*, and *Mississippi* had returned from the Atlantic to reinforce the *Tennessee*, *Pennsylvania*, and *Maryland*. The *Nevada* had been raised and docked and in a month or so would be on her way to the West Coast for complete repair. It was hoped that before the year was out, new-construction *North Carolina–* and *South Dakota*–class battleships would be joining the fight in the Pacific. The *Yorktown* had returned from the Atlantic, and the *Hornet* had sailed from Norfolk to the Pacific on 4 March.[32] Furlong needed as many berths around Ford Island as possible. F-8, the *Nevada*'s berth on 7 December, could be adapted as a carrier berth, as could F-13. Dolphins were to be driven just outboard the *Arizona* for a battleship berth, and Ten Ten Dock, F-3, and F-6 would be cleared by midsummer. But it wasn't enough.

As much as he needed the space, Furlong was realistic: "The labor and material necessary to float these vessels would constitute a diversion from the war effort that should be concentrated on new and vital construction and repair. The manufacture of enormous quantities of special steel cable, blocks, steel forgings, and winches required for this work and the employment of labor and skilled engineers for a year or more to raise and rehabilitate these three vessels is not warranted at this time. They are much better left as a post war employment of labor." Except for the recovery of accessible scrap metal and ammunition, Furlong recommended that the active salvage operations end with the raising of the *Oglala*, sometime in July.

SEVEN

No Time to Be Concerned with Personal Comfort

By 23 February, five days after the *Plunger* tumbled off her keel and bilge blocks, the last section of the *California's* forecastle cofferdam had been erected and secured to the boat-deck bulkhead. Divers from the Navy Yard were inside the battleship, closing and checking the covers on the manholes on the third deck that led to the voids below. According to the divers, six port covers had been missing and another dozen had been found with the tightening nuts slacked off. Three of those had the sealing gaskets blown out. Unfortunately for subsequent investigations, the precise location of seventeen of these eighteen covers was not specified. All had been replaced by arduous and dangerous dives deep inside the ship, and what had been reported to Wallin was that the eighteen were above damaged or flooded voids on the port side. A few manhole covers had also been replaced on the starboard side.[1]

Work on the top conning tower continued too, with nearly all the bolts and tap rivets holding it in place removed by the time the forecastle fence had been completed. Pacific Bridge brought a cement barge and sections of tremie pipe alongside, and some of the larger openings in the cofferdam, where the sections did not fit flush with the deck, were plugged with concrete. A pair of gasoline-driven pumps were brought aboard on 23 February and set up on scaffolding over the forecastle. Other pumps, some electric-powered, were placed on the boat deck. A fuel barge, the *Juicy Lucy*, was brought alongside the ship so that 5,400 gallons of fuel oil trapped in the uptakes of the number 2 funnel could be pumped out. In the forward superstructure, jacks and blocks were set to break the conning tower free from its foundation.

The forecastle pumps were started up on the twenty-fifth as Painter and Garland tested the watertight integrity of the fence. Twenty thousand gallons a minute were pumped through the two units, but the water level dropped very slowly. Obviously much work needed to be done to seal the joints of the fence and plug gaps between the bearing beams and stanchions. The indispensable divers located leaks by feel or by observing the current of water as it pushed oil and debris along its path.

Unwatering the forecastle of the *California* on 27 February 1942. Sandbags help counteract the buoyancy of the wood shoring.
National Archives

For several days the exploratory pumping continued as the conning tower was finally broken free and as more fuel oil was removed from the stack uptakes. Diving teams were kept busy caulking seams with rags, pieces of hose, and sandbags. The pumps were keeping ahead of the leaks, which were being reduced with every dive, so that within two days the forecastle deck had been cleared of water. There was no intention of unwatering the main deck until the quarterdeck cofferdam had been set in place, and that was expected to take a couple of weeks. If for some reason the main deck had to be unwatered first, the openings in the bulkheads cutting off the quarterdeck from the rest of the ship would have to be closed off.

Once the stern crane was removed, the *Haviside* lowered the first of the quarterdeck sections. This was the U-shaped stern section, which was bolted to the deck on the twenty-eighth. The conning tower was still in place, its removal delayed first by the high wind that had grounded the 150-ton crane, and then by the crane removing

The stern section of the *California*'s quarterdeck cofferdam will be placed just in front of the stern crane. Battleship Row lies in the distance.
National Archives

the face plate and slide from the *Arizona*'s number 4 turret. A working party of men awaiting assignment were sent out from the receiving station to begin the long process of cleaning the *California*, now that parts of the ship were being reclaimed from Pearl's oily water.

Both the Design Section and the Pacific Bridge Company had made studies of the requirements to float the ship, and they had drawn the same conclusions: hold off patching the two torpedo holes with concrete; hold off patching them altogether. Enough pumps had been brought aboard, and were of such high capacity, that Wallin, Holtzman, and Graham believed they could keep ahead of any incidental flooding once the major leaks had been stopped from inside the ship. The torpedo bulkheads were intact, and the manhole covers were in the process of being secured. As on the *Nevada*, once the pumping began, the head of water against the compartments inboard of the damage would increase, and those compartments would have to remain flooded. This would restrict the draft that could be reached and would initiate a balancing act between getting the ship over the sill in Dry Dock 2 and avoiding a collapse of the torpedo bulkheads. If the *California* could not be raised sufficiently to get her safely over the blocks, then some sort of temporary patches would have to be installed at frames 52 and 101 so that enough water could be pumped out of the ship to dock her.[2]

Farther down Battleship Row, one set of divers went into the armory of the *West Virginia* on 1 March, recovering small arms and ammunition, while another, armed with cutting torches, crawled inside the hatch built into the patch sections. Holes were burned into the shell, and one diver outside the patch fed long hook bolts into the space between the patch and the hull while another worked the end of the bolts into the holes in the shell. Once they were inside they were wedged into place and the butterfly nuts tightened. All of the bolts were secured within a few days. Meanwhile work had ceased topside on preparations for the long patch. There was water over the main deck port side aft, and this had to be walled off with a small cofferdam from the break of the upper deck to turret 3, to provide a dry area for working on the aft end of the long patch and for equipment. The carpenters of the Mobile Repair Unit started bolting this cofferdam together on the fifth.

While that work progressed, Emile Genereaux, George Ankers, and Levi Knight surveyed the upper and main decks on 8 March to determine the best location for the compressors, boilers, pumps, and air, power, and water lines that would soon be delivered. Four compressors, with a combined capacity of 950 cubic feet per minute, were lifted aboard the following day. These were placed between turret 3 and the mainmast while inside the mast a work party took down the "spud locker." A boiler delivered a few days later was set up on the starboard side of turret 3, with the oil tank that fueled it atop turret 4.

Dives on the small patch had ceased so that the teams could concentrate on closing scuppers, portholes, and drain lines. There was apprehension over the extent of the damage from the stern torpedo hit. Wallin, McNally, Genereaux, Ankers, Liedstrand, Knight, and White met at Building 129 on the ninth to discuss whether the damage could be isolated. One 6-inch pump was set up on the stern to try to pump down the after steering compartment. This exploratory pumping, like that on the forecastle of the *California*, would provide an indication of how badly the compartment leaked. The water would be pumped out as far down as the third deck and a careful watch maintained by divers on the water level. To their dismay, the pumps had no impact on the waterline. The leaks must be enormous. Another investigation confirmed these fears. The damage was extensive and the compartment essentially open to the sea. A survey would be needed to determine the situation in adjacent compartments. Perhaps the flooding could be limited by undamaged watertight fittings forward and inboard. Perhaps there would be no need for another time-consuming and laborious underwater patch job.

Wallin's meeting with his *West Virginia* team also addressed the issue of the availability of electrical power from Ford Island for the big Pomona pumps and the need to begin gathering cleaning gear. "The time is now ripe," he noted to the assembled officers, "to start building up the facilities and services preparatory to floating the USS *West Virginia*." Long gone was the pessimism of mid-December, when some, perhaps many, had doubted that the *West Virginia* would ever be floated from her berth. She was alive with activity now, and Wallin was estimating that she would be afloat sometime between May and July. His optimism certainly did not gloss over the massive damage inflicted on her or the unknowns that lay ahead. But he was upbeat, as was her captain, who wrote to him on the seventeenth that "the plan for refloating the *West Virginia* seems to present no difficulties which can be foreseen at present."[3] One had only to look aft to the battleship that would never sail again, or forward to another whose fate was still to be determined, to realize just how far the Salvage Unit had progressed on BB-48.

Meanwhile, divers placed strongbacks over the portholes that were too badly warped or bent to close. The strongbacks consisted of metal bars straddling the portholes and welded to the hull. A steel cover was placed beneath the strongback and secured by hammering wedges between the two. Starboard portholes, those near and above the normal waterline, were similarly secured. A number of these had been badly warped by the fires that had burned on the surface during and after the attack. Drain lines and scuppers were closed, as on the *Nevada* and *California*, by driving wooden plugs into them. The patches would keep most of the water out, but it was vital to reduce the flow from additional sources to an absolute minimum.

One disturbing aspect of the *California* job was the anticipated shortage of personnel to work on her once the decks were unwatered. Many more men would be needed to clean the ship than were being supplied. Lieutenant Commander Peterson, the *California*'s acting captain, and Garland, her ship superintendent, were constantly frustrated by the inadequacy of the help being sent out to F-3 each morning and afternoon. Peterson complained often to Homer Wallin that he was unable to properly organize his makeshift complement to handle the reconditioning.

The receiving station at Pearl, where newly arrived recruits were billeted, was sending out dozens of men twice a day for work parties, but many times that number were required. Thirty-eight sailors were shipped over by boat on 3 March, fifty-three on the fourth, thirty-five on the fifth. By the second week of March parties of one hundred and more were being dispatched, and it looked as though the ship might finally get enough men, but within days the numbers had fallen to half that. The daily shortfall of working men would continue.

As captain, Peterson, not the Salvage Unit, had the responsibility for the cleaning of the ship and the reconditioning of her machinery and equipment. The work often required special ratings, and he requested, through McNally, the use of some of the men from the Mobile Repair Unit. McNally forwarded the request. But Peterson was in a difficult spot. To request specific ratings from the ranks of the Mobile Repair Unit, he needed to know what work was to be performed on a specific day. Yet Horne's personnel were available only on a day-to-day basis, depending on where they were needed in the harbor, which rendered any advance planning by the captain impossible. The unit was extremely busy. At one point in mid-January specialists were involved with the *Cassin*, *Downes*, *Shaw*, *Arizona*, and YFD-2 as well as refurbishing the ex-tug *Navajo* for duty as a floating boiler. Some worked with Public Works on the construction of new barracks near F-6 for the salvage groups. Others were overhauling torpedoes for Patrol Wing 2. There were crews at the engineering reclaiming shop and the radio laboratory, and there was even a party analyzing the cleaning solution being used.[4] The *California* would need priority over the multiple requests for Horne's men, and that Peterson did not have.

Peterson was equally concerned about assembling a new crew for the battleship once she had been docked, repaired, and made ready to sail to Bremerton. He would need men familiar with the operation of electric-drive machinery. The *Nevada*, he had pointed out to Nimitz, had on board 341 rated men two weeks before she was raised. These men knew the ship and were part of an existing organization, and even with those advantages they found the job of preparing the *Nevada* for sea again a difficult one. A similar requirement for experienced personnel awaited the *West Virginia* when she was ready to leave Oahu, for the question of the ship's returning to duty had long ago become a matter of "when" rather than "if." It might even be necessary to return a portion of the *California*'s electric-drive personnel to Hawaii after the ship reached Puget Sound, so that these same men could bring the *West Virginia* back, too.

Peterson took charge of a draft of one hundred apprentice seamen who reported to his crew on 12 March, but these novices, fresh from boot camp, were of little use initially and required much direction and training. A few of the *California*'s former crew were even returned to her in an effort to provide needed experience. Fifteen petty officers who had been manning antiaircraft shore batteries were sent back, as was a boatswain assigned to the Navy Yard after the attack. New construction had taken four officers, but the orders for two of them were changed so that they would not report to their new commands until the *California* had reached the West Coast.

Showers and head for the salvage crew on the forward quay of F-3. The anchor chain securing the ship still girdles the quay. The causeway leads to "Tent City," where the crew lived during the salvage.
National Archives

Peterson went so far as to suggest that rated men be transferred from Horne's out-fit. A few were moved on a temporary basis, but as the Bureau of Navigation had directed that the unit remain intact for the salvage operations that were sure to follow, Peterson's request was denied. He butted heads with Wallin occasionally. His need for a crew to take his ship home sometimes ran contrary to the salvage officer's focus on his own mission of husbanding the scarce resources of men and material available to those necessary to deliver the *California* from F-3 to dry dock. Peterson requested from Nimitz a clarification as to who exactly was responsible for the salvage, preservation, and reconditioning of the *California*. If those duties were to be divided between himself and the Salvage Unit of the Industrial Department, then what defined the limits of the responsibility and how would he be able to carry out his duties?[5]

Nimitz deferred to Furlong on these questions, and Furlong weighed in on the side of Wallin, mildly chiding Peterson by reminding him of the excellent cooperation that had been maintained between the salvage team under George Ankers and Emile Genereaux and the crew of the *Nevada*. The comparison wasn't quite fair. Ankers and Carpenter Mahan had since been transferred over to the *California* project, and both could see that this was a situation unlike that of the beached *Nevada*. That crew had been reduced significantly less by transfer, since her salvage had initially been esti-mated to take only a month or so. But the commandant of the Navy Yard made it plain to Peterson that salvage, not the assembly of a new crew, was the primary job here. "Satisfactory progress of salvage operations in the *California*," he wrote in a letter to Nimitz with a copy to the *California*'s skipper, "will be made only if it is clearly under-stood that the Salvage Officer is in charge of the work and that all ship's personnel must cooperate in every way possible." If it interfered with getting the ship to dry dock, the formation of Peterson's crew would have to wait.[6]

It took until 23 March to place the last of the stern chains underneath the *Oglala*'s hull, but finally the *Ortolan*'s divers reported that they had finished the job.[7] The submarine rescue ship was moved away from the *Oglala* so that soundings could be made where the ship would settle when she was righted. Stoppers were still being welded to the *Oglala*'s starboard hull while the *Ortolan* divers awaited the delivery of the pontoons. On the twenty-eighth the first set were sunk into position.

There were ten pontoons in all: a single one at the bow, three single ones aft, and six others, rigged in three pairs, amidships. Numbers 6 and 7, one of the amidships pairs, were the first placed. Another pair, 4 and 5, were sunk on the thirtieth while divers hooked up air hoses to 6 and 7. Two of the three aft pontoons, 9 and 10, were sunk next. The chains for these were secured to the propeller shaft rather than to stop-pers. Number 8 was placed on Saturday, 4 April, and was pulled underneath the king-post. The third pair, 2 and 3, were next. Only the single pontoon at the bow remained to be sunk into position.

The chains used were destroyer anchor chains. A single length of chain ran from each stopper (or the shaft) underneath the vessel to a bridle on the pontoons. From each bridle ran two more lengths, one to each end of the pontoon. The plan worked

Ortolan divers prepare to sink pontoons alongside the *Oglala* on 5 April 1942.
U.S. Naval Institute

out by the Design Section called for the pontoons to be blown in a specific sequence so as to avoid putting too much strain on the hull and to break the adhesion of the hull to the mud gradually. The *Gaylord* was to be anchored off Ten Ten Dock with two lines to the *Oglala* and would pull once the pontoons had been blown and the ship was beginning to roll. For additional buoyancy, air was to be pumped into the hull—not much, less than 4 pounds per square inch, but adequate to blow out 3 or 4 feet of water. If all of that failed to get the *Oglala* free of the mud, two 75-ton hydraulic jacks would be placed on the dock and push against her bow to help. The next few days were spent rigging the bow pontoons and checking air compressors and hoses, chains, bridles, and stoppers. Saturday, 11 April, was to be the big day.

Reclaiming the electric-drive machinery of the *California* and *West Virginia* would present a new challenge to the ingenuity of Wallin's salvage team and ultimately Gillette's specialists in the Navy Yard. Unless the ships were going to be towed back to the mainland, at least some propulsion equipment would have to be put in running order. On those two battleships that meant reconditioning the electric motors and wiring that had been submerged in salt water, mud, and oil for months.

Some experience had been acquired, and a measure of confidence gained, by the work done on the wiring and electrical equipment aboard the *Nevada*. But Wallin acknowledged that "electric motors are the worst problem in view of the large number that must be reconditioned and the limited facilities now available."[8] In most cases, small motors were removed from the *Nevada* and sent to the electrical shop. But that was a far cry from the huge electric motors and generators of the *California* and *West Virginia*.

The *Nevada, Arizona, Pennsylvania,* and *Oklahoma* were propelled by steam-driven turbines turning the propeller shafts, while the *California* and *West Virginia* (along with the *Maryland, Tennessee,* and *Colorado*) were turbo-electric drive. That is, the steam produced by the eight boilers was directed to General Electric or Westinghouse geared turbines that generated electricity for a quartet of massive 62-ton alternating-current motors, one for each shaft.[9] The main generators also supplied electricity to six auxiliary turbo-generators for turrets, the refrigeration plant, ammunition hoists, lighting, communications, and all electrical equipment. This was the machinery now sitting at the bottom of Pearl, possibly corroding in the salt water.

After many conversations with electrical specialists and representatives from General Electric and Westinghouse, McNally had developed a procedure, or at least an outline, for reconditioning machinery once the engineering spaces were unwatered. Most important was to clean and preserve the motors immediately, the instant the water level had receded. Motors and generators were to have a four-hour continuous shower from fresh hot water from boilers atop the ship piped through the fire mains. Once the salt water had been thoroughly rinsed out, the equipment had to be completely dried. The compartments had to be wiped down completely so that no puddles remained. Moisture anywhere in the equipment or compartment would saturate the air and delay the drying. Delay in flushing the equipment with fresh water and contact with the air would result in rapid deterioration. Insufficient drying procedures were equally detrimental. "It cannot be too strongly emphasized," wrote Wallin about the control rooms, "that after the first fresh water wash-down these spaces and equipment must be thoroughly dried down and Cargoaire units installed" (these were dehumidifier units 4 feet long and 3 feet high, weighing about 400 pounds, with two silica gel absorbers for removing moisture from the air at a rate of 36 cubic feet per minute).[10] With careful planning and attention to detail, the electric-drive and auxiliary machinery of both ships might be salvaged for use.

The initial scope of Steele's Base Force Salvage Organization had shifted. No longer were the engineers and ship superintendents solely focused on "delivering the ships to the Navy Yard for disposition" and limiting their work to achieving that narrow but clearly defined goal. In mid-February, Nimitz wrote to the Bureau of Ships, regarding the *California* and *West Virginia,* "The minimum which must be accomplished at Pearl Harbor is the cleaning and preservation of the machinery and equipment upon unwatering to prevent further deterioration."[11] He didn't specifically state it, but that job would fall on the Salvage Division, since the ships would be unwatered before reaching dry dock. Wallin had complained that too much equipment had been unnecessarily removed or dismantled on the *Nevada,* complicating and delaying her repair. An engineer and Naval Academy graduate, Lt. Cdr. Charles Rhodes, had been assigned to the *California* and *West Virginia* in early March to oversee the rehabilitation of her remaining electrical equipment. The more repair work that could be done in place, without complicating the number one goal of docking the ship, the faster she could be returned to duty. That was precisely why McNally had been assigned as the salvage planning officer at the yard. The more input the Design and Production

Sections had in the salvage of the ships, the less work might be necessary when the vessels were docked. The Salvage Division had been a part of the Navy Yard for months, but as the work proceeded on the battleships at F-3 and F-6 and concern mounted for the state of their propulsion systems, it had become very clear just how intertwined the two organizations really were.

Placing the *West Virginia*'s galley back in operation, with lights and stoves going, the sounds of pots and pans and the smell of cooking food filling the air, would bring some measure of life back to this dead vessel. But the advantage was more than symbolic. Time was lost every day when working parties walked over the gangway back to Ford Island or when the noon meal was brought out to them. Once the galley was functioning, the ship could once again take care of feeding her own.

Just aft of the galley, the *Haviside*'s crane raised two lifting rings to the mainmast so that they could be fastened and a strain taken on the cable. The 50,000-pound mast would be cut off and lifted clear, as on the *California*. Though work had halted temporarily on installing the patches, the *West Virginia* was still a beehive of activity. Divers were going into the ship, methodically opening doors and hatches so that she would drain completely when the deep-well pumps began taking suction from the hold. The Mobile Repair Unit was connecting up the boiler and the attendant feed pumps while another knot of men connected an air-driven auxiliary training motor to the gears of turret 4. To clear space for a pump, Genereaux wanted to train the turret to starboard.

Sparks flew from the ring at the base of the mainmast as it was cut away, and on 23 March the badly scorched cage mast was lifted clear. Two days later turret 4's training motor was powered up, but the turret wouldn't budge. Shells in the handling room had broken free and were fouling the gears, so divers now went below to close off the hatches to the area so that the handling room could be pumped dry and the shells removed.

By the end of March, five air compressors had been hooked up together in one continuous bank, with one air line running from turret 1 all the way back to turret 4, furnishing air for all of the pumps and divers. Electricians were running power leads from Ford Island to the ship, and the ex-tug *Navajo* had tied up alongside to starboard between the stacks to furnish steam. There was a hatch at frame 125, just aft of turret 4 and on the centerline directly under the guns, and an electric deep-well pump would be installed there once the turret was rotated. Directly below, divers were cutting holes in the first and second platform decks so that the pump could take suction as low in the ship as possible. Carpenters had resumed work on the A-frames for the long patch but were quickly halted. The *California* job was about to reach a critical point, and Genereaux was temporarily away from the *West Virginia*. He had been given another chance to refloat the *Plunger*.

The starboard quarterdeck cofferdam was now being placed on the *California*, although progress was slower than Wallin had anticipated. He had wanted to use one derrick on

The *California*'s port quarterdeck cofferdam under construction on 10 March 1942. Pacific Bridge carpenters shore the latest section as divers bolt it to the ship.
National Archives

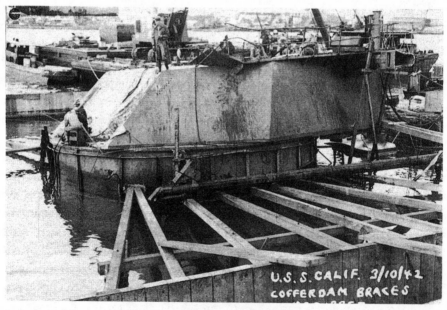

A close-up of the massive shoring secured to the *California*'s turret 3. Canvas covers the missing face plate.
National Archives

each side of the ship, installing a port and a starboard section each day, beginning at the stern. But it was too much. The derricks weren't always available, and about one section a day was all that could be handled. But by 4 March there were four 30-foot sections along the starboard gunwale, with three of them bolted into place. They were placed by Pacific Bridge civilian divers, with James Greely offering assistance and advice from the Salvage Division. Strands of oakum (loose rope fibers bound together with tar and held in place by canvas) had been run along the bottom edge of each section where it met the stanchions and hull for a watertight seal. The fourth section had to be notched so that it could clear the barrels of turret 4, and divers cleared away the starboard gangway and mooring wires that were in the way of the fifth section. There was still an anchor chain around the barbette of turret 3, and that too had to go.

The first of the port sections went by derrick out to the *California* from the coaling dock assembly area on 5 March, as divers from the Salvage Unit brought one of the fleet paymaster's safes to the surface from the main deck. On shore, men from the receiving station and the ship's force were setting up tents for temporary quarters. Having the men berthed close to the ship would extend the workday. Three days later, on 8 March, the last of the starboard sections were being secured. Five sections had been placed on the port side. Hundreds of sandbags were transported to the ships, and ultimately over a million pounds of sand would be used to weigh down the lumber on the quarterdeck.[12] The forecastle deck was dry, the pumps there silent, as Painter waited for the quarterdeck to be sealed off, but gasoline pumps were still removing water from the port casemates. There were electric-driven pumps too, but the power supply from Ford Island was tenuous and frequently shorted out. The gasoline pumps could not handle the volume of water alone, and the port casemates often reflooded. It was 12 March before the quarterdeck cofferdam was completely in place. Despite working only one side of the ship at a time, the divers were three days ahead of Wallin's initial estimate.

Two more 10-inch Jaeger gasoline pumps were started up on the quarterdeck, making three in all, and they were pumping at full capacity. This was exploratory pumping, as had been done on the forecastle, so that divers could plug and caulk leaks in the cofferdam. There were plenty, but the inflow of water was controlled with just half of the pumping capacity available. Both conning towers were ready to be removed, after weeks of work removing bolts and rivets and using jacks to break them free from their foundations. The weight savings would be a great help in reducing the ship's draft. But riggers to attach lines to the towers and cranes to lift them were not available. There was no need to remove them now, anyway. Their presence aboard would not affect flotation, just the ship's final draft as she approached dry dock.

With the forecastle dry, the pumps lowered the water on the main deck until the starboard side became dry on the seventeenth, St. Patrick's Day. The wood of the quarterdeck cofferdam had increased the buoyancy of the ship by about 5,000 tons and helped to raise the stern first, breaking the suction of the mud. Inside the vessel careful steps were in place to ensure that there would be no repetition of the fatal accidents that had occurred on the *Nevada*. A party of men from the Mobile Repair Unit

This view of the *California*'s unwatered quarterdeck shows the extent of the shoring necessary to keep the cofferdam from collapsing from the exterior water pressure as the deck was pumped down. One starboard section had to be altered for the guns of turret 4. The base of the mainmast is visible at lower right.
U.S. Naval Institute

immediately ran electricity on the main deck for lights and blowers to circulate fresh air. Dr. Parker came out to test the air and pools of water for hydrogen sulfide gas. The ventilation lines were efficient, and Parker pronounced the starboard compartments safe. The port side of the main deck was still submerged, still untested, and that slowed the work of the parties, which now began the immense job of cleaning the *California* deck by deck, compartment by compartment.

Wheeler units had been at work removing the layer of oil that floated on or near the ship. Some 31,000 gallons of the sludge had been removed by 15 March, the same day the *Nevada* was removed from Dry Dock 2 and towed to the repair basin.[13] Kerrick hydro-steam cleaners had been taken from the ready-storage locker at berth 5 to hose down the bulkheads, decks, and overheads. These were compact devices, weighing only 28 pounds, and were connected to tanks of Turko or Tectyl and to steam and freshwater lines. The cleaning guns delivered the mixture under pressure and were very effective. Small pumps collected the water and oil from low spots in the compartments and pumped them overboard. But the work of cleaning the interior was progressing very slowly. It was awful work, accomplished in large part by men living in

Sailors clean lockers and other equipment removed from the *California* with a high-pressure "jenny" on 10 March 1942. Items such as lockers, chairs, and tableware were needed by other ships with increased wartime complements.
National Archives

tents across the causeway built from the quays to Ford Island and with no connection to the vessel other than the fact they had been ordered out to her, given a pair of overalls (called a tank suit), and pointed in the direction of the compartment to be cleaned. Lockers, chairs, light fixtures, even plates and silverware were cleaned for reuse aboard other ships. The salvage was proceeding on schedule, but it looked as though it would take months, perhaps a year, to clean the ship to the point that she could sail to the West Coast. Wallin acknowledged the appalling conditions the men worked under but exhorted them to press ahead. "The work required to clean up and recondition these ships [the *California* and *West Virginia*] is a dirty messy job," he wrote on the sixteenth, "but it is A JOB OF UTMOST IMPORTANCE, and it is the job which has been assigned to us, whether we like it or not!" Wallin was stretching the division of labor a bit, as it was Peterson, not him, who was responsible for the task. Nevertheless, he presented a united front to the men: "Every man engaged in this work is expected to 'TURN TO,'—to regard it as his current contribution to the national war effort and to see to it that his contribution is of real value to the cause. This is no time to be concerned with PERSONAL COMFORT or the CONVENIENCE of individuals or groups. What is required is that every individual do his UTMOST to increase the output of WORK,— TO PRODUCE, TO WORK OVERTIME,—and above all to do it whole heartedly and IN THE NAVY SPIRIT." He continued his exhortation: "*REMEMBER THIS:* OUR ENEMIES are recognized for their industry, toil and perseverance,—let them not SURPASS US!"[14]

Looking aft through a berthing area of the *California* on the main deck portside, near turret 1, showing the extent of the cleaning that faced Garland's crew when the ship came afloat. This photograph was taken on 19 March 1942. Two days later the crews began finding bodies. National Archives

Overall, Wallin was optimistic about the progress of salvage operations throughout the harbor. "Things are going along pretty well here, especially in salvage matters," he wrote his friend Capt. Edward "Ned" Cochrane at the Bureau of Ships on 5 March. He told Cochrane with some pride that the *Nevada* had been floated "without the big patch they were building while you were here" and that the *California* and *West Virginia* would both be afloat in a matter of months. He hinted to Cochrane that Claude Gillette was not happy about the prospect of the two battleships spending months in dry dock having their main propulsion machinery repaired. The Navy Yard manager would have preferred that that job be done at a mainland yard. Wallin could have used his old friend as a sounding board for the many tough decisions he was faced with every day. "Lots of things going on which I would like to have a chance to talk over with you; maybe Charlotte could send you out again, especially if we can arrange to have a raid or something," he wrote, tongue in cheek.[15]

Forty-five *California* personnel were unaccounted for in the days after the attack, and it was assumed that most, if not all, had gone down with the ship. Although it was possible that remains could be found anywhere within the hull, the majority were expected to be found on the starboard second deck, where the bomb hit had killed a number of men, and in the third-deck crew spaces, where those who had been overcome by fuel fumes in the darkness had drowned.

Hospital corpsmen from the *Solace* stood ready to recover bodies as the water receded. By 20 March the water was below the second-deck centerline hatches, while some standing water remained on the port side of the forecastle and main decks. The ship had regained enough buoyancy that the stern had floated free. The following day, sailors wading through the foul shallow water on the second deck noticed a small round object floating in the muck and water. To their horror, it was a human head. The first of the *California*'s missing in action had been found. Corpsmen were called in, and they gently removed the head and took it to Aeia landing.

Two days later the water had been lowered at the centerline to just 2 feet above the third deck. It was maintained there because fifteen more bodies had been found on that deck. The pumping now continued only to maintain the current depth of water. The corpses were complete but badly decomposed after more than three months' submergence, and hospital personnel quietly went to work. They carried canvas bags, open at one end and large enough for a body. The bags were closed with a drawstring to keep the contents and odors inside. Each body was gently floated into a bag, then it was sealed and carried topside to a boat tied up amidships. With the constant movement of men carrying all manner of equipment, trash, and debris, the bags were hardly noticed. There was no fanfare, no ceremony. To the majority of the dirty, tired men in the work gangs, these objects were just more wreckage being removed. But to the men carrying these awkward, cumbersome loads up ladders and out onto the weather decks, it was a solemn duty, performed with quiet dignity and great care.

The next day, 24 March, one body was removed and, more disturbing, part of another was found floating in the oily, stagnant water. Eight more bodies were recovered the following day, and Garland noted in his daily log that there were twenty-two shipmates still unaccounted for. The ship was now afloat, having broken completely free from the suction of the mud, and the water level continued to be held where it was, a few feet above the third deck. It would be maintained there by careful pumping for more than a week so that the search could go on. A sandbag cofferdam had been erected on the starboard bow because it had been anticipated that when the ship came afloat she would try to right herself, possibly dipping the unprotected starboard side of the forecastle under water. Pumping was carefully organized and tightly controlled by Lieutenant Ankers and Gunner Mahan. They were in direct charge of the pumping operations and were also responsible for ensuring that all of the forecastle deck hatches were closed and dogged tight. A sudden onrush of water down those hatches could be catastrophic.

Three complete bodies and parts of another were located and removed on the twenty-sixth, reducing the total number of missing to eighteen. In the crew spaces, ammunition passageways, and workshops and around the immense barbettes, flashlight beams pierced the darkness and nauseating sewer gas permeated the air. One or two narrow tubes of light would stop on a dark mass breaking the surface of the oil and water, swaying slowly on the small waves created by the men wading through water over their knees. There would be a closer, tentative look before gloved hands reached for the shreds of decaying clothing. With a few awkward movements another canvas bag would be brought topside and taken to the Naval Hospital. If the body could be identified, another family would be notified that their son or husband or brother, missing since that dreadful day, was dead. The progress of the salvage operation might well have been measured in terms of patches completed, pumps placed in operation, draft readings, and weight reduction, but the cost of that Sunday morning in December was still being added up.

No bodies were found over the next two days, and it wasn't until the twenty-ninth that the remains of two more were removed from the third deck. There were still sixteen men unaccounted for, but no more bodies were found. After another day of searching, Painter ordered the pumping increased. It was time to finish the job, to dock the ship.

The divers opening hatches and doors and plugging washbasin, shower, and toilet drain lines inside the *West Virginia* were under the able direction of John M. Ephland of the *Widgeon*. Ephland's rating was chief shipfitter, but his title was master diver, and by now he was one of the most experienced of the salvage divers. He had supervised many of the dives in the interiors of the *Nevada* and *California* and now was in direct charge of nearly all the diving inside the Weevee.

The salvage team studies blueprints aboard the *California. Left to right:* Master Diver John Ephland, Lt. Wilfred Painter, an unidentified officer behind Painter, Cdr. John Warris, Capt. Homer Wallin, Lt. Jim Greely, Lt. Wilbert Bjork, and Lt. James Darroch.
Naval Historical Center NH 64486

Diving in the black, unfamiliar world inside a submerged battleship was extremely hazardous. Lights were of little use in the murky water, and the men had to feel their way carefully through passageways, hatches, machinery, and floating debris sometimes many yards from where they entered the ship. Face plates could be smashed if the diver collided with a beam or projection. They often had to go up and down ladders, complicating their route back. Pressure differentials caused by pumping or large leaks could suck an unwary diver into a jagged hole. Telephone cables and air hoses were frequently fouled by debris, bulkheads, and hatches. Air hoses or diving suits could be punctured by sharp pieces of wreckage. This was a constant worry when diving in areas of the ship that had been damaged. And even if a clear path was maintained for the air hose, there was no guarantee that the pumps and compressors would not break down.

Diving in the inverted *Oklahoma, Utah,* and *Oglala* presented the additional hazard of machinery, furniture, shells, or other objects falling from the deck to the overhead below. Heavy items that fell could sever or cut off the air hoses or even block the return path. That particular danger wasn't limited to the capsized ships. One of Haynes's divers became trapped inside the *California* by a toppled ventilation motor. It was many hours, and several rescue dives later, before the man was finally pulled to safety.[16] Another diver, one from the Mobile Repair Unit, fell through a gaping hole above the *West Virginia's* armor belt while examining the aftermost point of the torpedo damage amidships. He fell some 20 feet but miraculously was unhurt.[17]

The danger from hydrogen sulfide gas was ever present, the lesson learned the hard way aboard the *Nevada* never forgotten. Whenever an air bubble was established inside a ship, divers were required to wear air-supplied face plates. Any leakage of seawater into the suit could also result in the concentrated gas killing a man within seconds. Explosive gas, often present in pockets of air or released from solution in the water by the flame of underwater torches, could be ignited, and small explosions were an all too common occurrence.[18]

Ephland was familiar with all of this. On the *California* he frequently made the most hazardous dives himself, and he made many others to check the work of the men under his supervision. He worked closely with Garland Suggs on the *West Virginia* and with two other diving groups, led by a metalsmith named Rutledge and a warrant bosun named Aubra Calhoun. It was Ephland who was in direct charge of the men opening the watertight closures and hatches to permit water to flow freely throughout the ship when pumping commenced.

By the beginning of April much had been learned and much experience gained diving on the sunken ships. A total of 406 recorded dives had been made altogether on the *Nevada,* about fifteen hundred hours. Over 250 had been made thus far on the *California,* about half of them by the Pacific Bridge Company, with nearly nine hundred hours spent underwater. Well over two hundred had been made through the end of March on the *West Virginia,*[19] and scores more had been made on the *Oglala, Arizona, Utah, Oklahoma, Raleigh, Maryland, Vestal,* and *Shaw.*

A diver in typical equipment. Although shallow-water facemasks were also used, this was the suit normally worn for extensive diving, particularly within the ship. This photograph shows the diver placing the air hose inside the cuff of his suit, the emergency procedure should the air inlet become fouled or jammed shut.
National Archives

Many methods to minimize the inherent hazards had been devised through trial and error. Ship plans were carefully studied to route divers away from heavy machinery that might have become unstable. Wherever possible, diving groups were assigned a particular section of the vessel, so that they might become familiar with the passageways they would be navigating in the darkness. The dives were carefully planned, the nature and extent of the work given strict parameters, and each dive was discussed in detail beforehand by the entire group involved.

One and sometimes more divers were stationed between the working diver and topside, ready to provide rapid assistance should something go wrong. Supervisors, tenders, and divers were given instruction on how to get emergency air into a diver's suit, either by inserting the hose into a cuff or by slitting the suit above the waist line with a knife and snaking a line inside. Occasionally a diver's air supply valve jammed and he was unable to free it by hand. A special wrench was developed that would fit over the valve and could even fit over the stem should the valve come off. The air supply itself was now piped to the divers from multiple sources, so that a failure of a single compressor was no longer life-threatening. Large accumulators stored a reservoir of air in case of power failure. Even compressed air that was being used for other purposes was bypassed first into the divers' system so that another emergency source was available. A pair of compressed-air bottles, about eight minutes' worth, was issued to each man before his descent. Small strips of cloth were tied to the divers' wrists to give an indication, where visibility permitted, of a strong current toward any openings in the hull that might suck in an arm or leg or head. Holes were drilled through bulkheads to be burned, to ensure that there was water, and not gas, on the other side. But no satisfactory solution had been devised for the problem of the explosive gas released from solution and ignited. These small explosions were annoying and frightening and caused a few minor injuries, yet they were one of the hazards that had to be endured.

Experience was essential. Older divers, those averaging twenty-seven years of age, were consistently rated higher than younger ones. A doctor examined each man every eighth day, and those constantly exposed to hydrogen sulfide gas, particularly near the openings in the hulls where they entered and exited the ships, were given fresh milk daily to act as an absorbent. Careful records were kept of each dive, the daily log recording the diver, the work to be performed, the work accomplished, and the time spent under water, with a minute-by-minute account of the dive. The work was arduous, and liberty was granted during daylight hours every fourth day.[20] Thanks to their precautions, planning, training, and ingenuity, all the diving teams—from the Navy Yard, the Submarine Base, the *Widgeon* and *Ortolan*, the Mobile Repair Unit, the Pacific Bridge Company, and the ships themselves—had been extraordinarily successful in learning this new craft of salvage. There had been no fatalities, no serious casualties of any kind, among the divers to this point. It was a superb safety record under difficult circumstances, and men like John Ephland and Pappy Haynes, Gunner Arnold Larson of the *Ortolan*, and Carpenter E. L. Urbaniak of the *Arizona* were largely responsible.

With the cofferdams in place and the leaking under control, and with the recovery of bodies complete, the *California* was unwatered again in earnest on 30 March. Damage from the bomb hit had been examined and wreckage cleared away. By the next day the forward engine room, motor rooms, and port firerooms had been pumped dry via a deep-well pump taking suction from the shaft alley after divers burned an access hole through the overhead. Because fuel oil had entered the ship at the third-deck level and

A Pomona deep-well power pump on the *California*'s fantail. Divers not only placed the cofferdam and shoring underwater but also secured scaffolding to the deck for the pumps.
National Archives

then floated on the water as it rose inside the ship, the cleanup crews were spared the grimy task of scouring the two platform decks and hold. Oil skimmers had removed virtually all of the oil before the water level receded below the third deck, and while the boilers, generators, and turbines all suffered from some degree of oil contamination, they were not mired in the thick sludge that coated the compartments above. The ship was on practically an even keel, with just a slight list to port, and was drawing just over 43 feet.

The torpedo bulkheads inboard of the damaged areas were holding up well under the increasing head of water. There was minor leakage from the patch on the port bow and from a few popped rivets caused by another near miss to starboard. Had there been time on 7 December to set Watertight Condition Zed, had the manholes on the third deck been properly in place, the big ship would have shrugged off her two torpedo hits and the near miss and stayed afloat long enough to get safely to dry dock.

Cdr. John Warris, Steele's former *Utah* executive officer, had by now relieved Peterson as captain of the *California*. He would take the ship into dry dock and oversee her repair. By 3 April the *California* was ready for docking, but the two large graving docks were full. The *Lexington* had entered Dry Dock 2 that day to have her heavy 8-inch turrets removed from her flight deck, and Dry Dock 1 held the cruiser *Minneapolis* and the destroyers *Maury* and *Phelps*. On the eighth the *Lexington* would be undocked and moved to the repair basin before departing for the Coral Sea, and the *California* would replace her in Dry Dock 2. Dry Dock 3 had been ready for emergency dockings since the middle of March but was too small for a battleship. Shuffling the ships in and out of the yard and preparing to dock salvaged ships continued to be a constant juggling act.

Each day Gillette held a "Commandant's Conference on the Status of Work on Vessels under Repair" with members of Nimitz's staff and with the commanding officers (or their representatives) of the ships in the yard for overhaul or restricted availability. After the attack he had suspended the weekly report, not wishing to require officers to leave their ships to meet with him. But he reinstated the conferences on 9 March as activity in the yard resumed a normal, though accelerated, pace. The requirement to dock ships damaged on 7 December for extended periods was a severe complication. By the time the *California* was ready to dock, Gillette had thirteen destroyers, three submarines, the cruisers *San Francisco, Minneapolis,* and *Indianapolis,* and the *Lexington* and *Nevada* under his care. There were also tugs, minesweepers, minelayers, a covered lighter, a floating workshop, the Army's SS *Hawaii,* and a floating derrick under repair or construction. Many required docking. Horne's unit was assisting with the *Cassin, Downes, Sotoyomo,* and *Nevada,* some construction work, and the installation of 20-mm guns on a few heavy cruisers, but Gillette continued to have a shortage of men and resources.[21]

Especially resources. Gillette was fighting a constant battle against waste. Rubber hoses and gaskets and Manila line in particular were in short supply, and the yard manager wanted substitutes used whenever possible. The war was only four months old, and it was going to be a long uphill battle to defeat the Axis. Gillette reminded his men:

> Every last one of the 130,000,000 of us is in this war up to his neck. Have no illusions about it—we are fighting for self-existence. All our resources are needed for this purpose and it is especially necessary to prevent wasteful expenditure of material and money. New materials of all sorts—wire, cable, nuts, bolts, washers, fuses, lights, paints, welding supplies, pipe, valves, etc., have been left carelessly about by

the employees, eventually ending up in the rubbish bins. You can produce replacements only with man power, raw materials and machines. Wastage of material requires curtailing of national output of the instruments of total war.[22]

As Gillette decried that wastage had reached a "critical stage," the salvage of the *California* had, too. The anchor chain around turret 1 was removed, and floating cranes carefully removed the forecastle cofferdam as it was unbolted from the ship. The sections were taken to the coaling dock to be stored, and the shutters that had sealed off the port casemates were removed. There was still a considerable amount of water in the ship, especially on the port side, and the removal of the cofferdam and shutters increased the vulnerability of the ship to sudden or unexpected flooding. The fuel oil relay tank near the hole at frame 102 was giving the divers a particularly hard time. The ruptured pipes leading into the tank were difficult to seal off. As on the *Nevada*, bounding compartments had been left unwatered so as to reduce the outside pressure on the last of the holding bulkheads and to provide a backup for the patch over the near-miss hole. By Saturday, 4 April, the *California* was drawing 41½ feet and still rising slowly. Wallin estimated that she would draw something less than 38 feet by the time the *Lexington* had been undocked and blocks prepared for the *California's* arrival on 9 April. Over the weekend of 4–5 April, Warris, Garland, and Painter planned to oversee the removal of the remainder of the forecastle cofferdam, the pumping down of the second platform deck and hold, and the cleaning of the engine and motor rooms. On Monday the quarterdeck cofferdam would be removed, beginning with the starboard sections, while the ship's force ensured that all hatches and skylights on the deck were ready to be quickly closed should the ship settle again and take water over the side. Once a crane became available, main battery powder and shells would be lifted off. The remainder of the week would be devoted to the onerous job of opening the ship's cold storage and removing the several tons of meat that had been rotting for four months.[23] It was a job that everyone was dreading, but if all went well the *California* would be nudged into dry dock on Thursday, 9 April.

It was on the ninth that the last of the pontoons was secured to the bow of the *Oglala*. On Saturday morning, 11 April, a large crowd including Nimitz and Furlong had assembled on Ten Ten Dock to watch the wreck rolled upright. The signal was given, and compressors blew charged air through the connecting hoses into six of the ten pontoons. Two sets of double-rigged pontoons were being held in reserve so that their force could be applied once the *Oglala* had started to rise. The ship began to roll slightly to starboard as the water roiled and frothed between the hull and Ten Ten Dock. Then there was an unexpected and most disheartening sight: pontoons popping to the surface. They had broken loose. The ship settled back down. The attempt had failed. Disappointed, Nimitz and Furlong returned to their offices while Wallin and McClung assembled a diving crew to inspect the pontoons and the hull to see what had happened.

The first attempt to right the *Oglala* fails on 11 April 1942 as the pontoons break free of their chains.
National Archives

The answer was quickly forthcoming. Two-and-a-quarter-inch forged rings had been used as bridles and had parted where the ends were welded together. The stopper for the forward chain had carried away, too. This stopper had not been welded to the hull but was attached by rivets. The Design Section now recommended that single chains be used in place of the bridle arrangement, but this plan was quickly revised to a double-chain setup. Larson's *Ortolan* divers went back to work running a second set of the heavy chains under the hull for each of the ten pontoons. With any luck, in less than two weeks McClung would try it again.

The *Oglala* setback came less than a week after Painter and his salvage team had experienced an unfortunate and potentially dangerous incident on the *California*. Early in the afternoon on 5 April, Easter Sunday, the battleship was rocked by a violent explosion as members of the crew returned from church services. Those who had been aboard on 7 December likened the blast to the impact of the bomb and torpedoes.[24] Four sailors suffered first- and second-degree burns, and another was wounded by splinters. The large patch that had been placed there in January was blown off, and four of its 10-by-12-inch vertical timbers were severed. The patch was located in the mud by a diver and hauled to the surface by derrick, but was so distorted that it was unusable.

The exact cause of the blast was a mystery. About 3,000 gallons of aviation gasoline for the spotter planes was normally stored nearby, and the ship's force had been

Her forecastle crowded with pumps, hoses, sandbags, and lumber, the
California floats free on 30 March 1942.
National Archives

directed by Wallin to remove this hazard by the time the vessel was docked. The regular hydraulic system was wrecked, so the crew tried air-driven skimming pumps.
These pumped mostly water instead of gas, but the gasoline hold was later reported
clear. Warris and his men assumed that most of the gas had been pumped overboard
by the deep-well pump in the nearby trunk, but they maintained a careful watch for
more. Smoking was forbidden. Small pockets of gas might still be present.

When the patch blew off, water rushed in as it had nearly four months earlier. The
boatswain's stores, canteen stores, awning locker, paint-mixing room, and chief petty

officers' quarters were all flooded. Within two hours the bow was down 5 feet and the stern had risen 3 feet, but the situation was quickly brought under control. Divers isolated the damaged area, and by 1700 a 10-inch gasoline pump was taking suction in the trunk. Within a day the bow was rising again, the draft forward reaching 43 feet 10 inches by Monday afternoon.[25] Though it was assumed that lingering gasoline vapors had somehow accumulated and been ignited, sabotage was also considered a real possibility. Many were still convinced that Japanese fifth-column agents had had a direct hand in the sneak attack in December.

The explosion, while shocking and certainly disturbing, affected the docking schedule not at all. More 14-inch shells were removed from the forward magazines the next day, as was the rotted meat in the cold-storage lockers. Almost 200,000 gallons of loose oil had been skimmed from the interior and the waters surrounding the ship, and more was being pumped out of the remaining fuel tanks. The flooding caused by the explosion was keeping the draft below acceptable limits for docking, so the upper conning tower was removed by derrick, as were hundreds of cans of main battery powder from the forward magazines. It still wasn't enough to get the *California* safely over the blocks, and the after peak tank and a few oil tanks aft were flooded to bring up her bow. Early on the morning of the ninth, four tugs came alongside and gently guided the water-stained battleship across the water to Dry Dock 2, where a crowd numbering in the hundreds awaited her arrival. Her crew and men from the Salvage Unit were perched everywhere on her superstructure for the ride everyone had been waiting for.

The *California*'s stern crosses the sill of Dry Dock 2 on 9 April 1942, just four months after she was sunk.
National Archives

Ahead of the *California* in Dry Dock 2 is the *Sotoyomo*, undergoing repair by a detail from Horne's Mobile Salvage Unit on 19 May 1942.
National Archives

By 1100 she was inside the dock and eased over the blocks with ropes and shores. Just ahead of her was the little *Sotoyomo*, dry-docked for more repair work. The caisson doors closed, and pumps emptied the dock in a matter of hours. The Mobile Repair Unit would continue work on the tug on the floor of the big graving dock, while Navy Yard Pearl would take the first steps to get the "Prune Barge" back into the war. Some of the first electric motors removed from the battleship would soon be on their way to the West Coast for repair aboard the *Nevada*, which was at berth B-18 in the repair basin, preparing to sail for Puget Sound on 22 April. Fifty-eight men from General Electric had been assembled from all over the United States and rushed to the West Coast for the trip to Hawaii. Some had even been sped across country by train in a special Pullman. They arrived at Pearl Harbor on 18 April to clean and rewind the huge main motors. The civilians were assisted by eighty-nine men from Horne's Mobile Repair Unit, and by an officer from the Electrical Section of the Bureau of Ships named Hyman G. Rickover. These men began working three shifts a day, seven days a week, to repair two main propulsion generators and two motors to get the ship back to the mainland. When the *West Virginia* finally made it to dry dock, they would tackle that job, too.[26]

Throughout the end of February and into March the ordnance group and a diving team aboard the *Arizona* continued dismantling turrets 3 and 4 and removing 14-inch shells from them. One of the yard's seaplane wrecking cranes, YSD-19, removed 5-inch/.51 broadside guns 7, 8, 9, and 10 in early March. All had been submerged and were badly burned, and all were delivered to the yard for stripping. The holding-down clips, rollers, training racks, and stands for the four guns also were cut away and removed by divers in the following days. Part of the boat deck was cut away for better access to guns 5 and 6, and work continued to remove them as well as 5-inch/.25 gun 1 on the starboard side. The 5-inch/.25s were secured to the boat deck by thirty-two threaded nuts and bolts, each 2 inches thick. Sometimes a pneumatic impact wrench could be used on the less damaged foundations, but those that had been distorted by fire had to be cut off. More cutting was done beneath turrets 3 and 4 to gain access to the powder and shells in the handling rooms. While the *California* was towed to dry dock and while the first patches and pumps were placed aboard the *West Virginia*, the *Arizona* was slowly and ignobly cannibalized.

No attempt was being made now to recover the nine hundred bodies aboard. A final tally showed 1,177 *Arizona* sailors and Marines either dead or missing and pre-sumed dead. Many of the dead had been pulled out of the water in the days after the attack. Others had been found crumpled on deck. Some had been reduced to piles of ashes and bone. All that had been found of Admiral Isaac Kidd, commanding officer of Battleship Division 1, was his Naval Academy ring. Late in January, responding to pressure from Washington, divers from the Mobile Repair Unit were sent down to recover bodies for identification and burial. Army and Navy medical personnel went in boats to collect any bodies that could be brought to the surface. Previous dives had revealed a cluster of corpses in the shop area, and one of the unit's veteran divers sug-gested that they be floated to the surface via a nearby access trunk.

The resulting scene was horrifying. The bodies had disintegrated, and what little clothing remained had rotted away. They floated to the surface, bloated, headless, their extremities reduced to bone. The medical personnel wrestled with them, hoist-ing them aboard and stuffing them into canvas bags. The odor in the hot tropical air was so foul that gas masks had to be used. Many of the medics grew sick and vomited. Forty-five corpses were removed, according to one diver, but that was the last attempt at recovering the crew. The dead men could not be identified, nor could a description of what was removed from the vessel be divulged to anxious families. The *Arizona* dead would stay where they were.[27]

By April no decision had been made on what to do with the ship other than to con-tinue with the recovery of salvageable material and the removal of wreckage above the waterline. The most visible parts of the ship, her masts, were to come down as soon as the 150-ton crane could be spared for a few days. When divers became available an extensive survey could be made that would either modify or confirm the recommenda-tions Furlong had made to BuShips in March. The war, now into its fourth month and going badly for the United States and its allies, demanded that only work that could reverse the tide of Japanese victory be undertaken. The *Arizona* did not fit that criterion, not since her forward magazines had exploded shortly after 0800 on 7 December.

When Ben Manseau, Genereaux's commanding officer for the *Plunger* project, had been transferred, his place had been taken by another officer, one far less enamored of

Genereaux's scheme for pulling the submarine and dock into deeper water. Work was suspended while he ordered a review of the entire situation. Frustrated, Genereaux advised Wallin that the whole scheme was on hold, and that he was ready to report back to the Salvage Division. The *Plunger* and the marine railway stayed where they were, causing a bottleneck in the scheduling of repair work and reducing the submarine counteroffensive against Japan by one badly needed boat.

The officer who had taken over work on the *Plunger* had not been up to the task. Several weeks went by before Gillette, Furlong, and Adm. Thomas Withers (Commander, Submarines, Pacific Fleet) had had enough. Gillette and Furlong needed the dock, and Withers needed the submarine. Gillette called for Genereaux, who explained to him how he had been replaced on the *Plunger* job and had gone back to the Salvage Division and his work on the *West Virginia* and *California*. After several meetings with Furlong and Withers, Emile Genereaux was back on the job, promising to have the *Plunger* back in the water within days. He was true to his word. The starboard catwalk was cut away; winches were set up on the pier and cables run to the dock. The *Haviside* anchored astern of the railway and ran lines to the cradle as well. Lead ballast was removed from the sub to lighten her, and at 1400 on 10 April both the sub and the dock were pulled into the water some 40 feet, until the *Plunger* was nearly afloat. Over the next two days she was reballasted and the supports and shores to the dock removed. On 12 April, nearly two months after she had immobilized the railway, the *Plunger* was pulled into the water of Southeast Loch. The railway was in need of significant repair and was not ready for use again until August. But the Salvage Division, and in particular Genereaux, could chalk up one more success.[28]

EIGHT

A Monotonous, Backbreaking Job

It took weeks of diving inside the *West Virginia* to open doors and hatches so that water could drain to the lower spaces for removal by deep-well pumps. While Salvage Division divers carefully maneuvered their way through the unlit passageways and down ladders, Pacific Bridge men continued shoring, sealing, and bolting together the three sections of the forward patch. There was a slight pause in early April when a few carpenters were sent to the *California* to remove the cofferdam before she docked. They quickly returned to tackle the first sections of the long patch arriving via barge alongside the *West Virginia.*

The galley was nearly ready to begin preparing meals for the crew, and a 500-gallon oil tank was set up to furnish fuel for the stoves and ovens. A clam dredge removed mud and coral beneath the long patch as the yard's Public Works Section continued to try, unsuccessfully, to run electrical leads to the ship. Somewhere along the line there was a short, and electricians could not locate it. The next day the first section of the long patch was lowered into place. The same Wheeler system used aboard the *California* began removing oil on the water inside and alongside the ship. A body, the first one recovered on the *West Virginia*, was found by divers on 19 April. It had been floating between the main and second decks forward and was recovered by medical teams using the same method as on the *California.*

The first three sections of the long patch were rapidly put in place, and the diving team working on the forward patch reported it securely attached to the hull. The key plates from the tops of all four turrets had been cast loose and all but one removed so that ammunition in the turrets could be unloaded. Turret 3 still had a water tank atop it, and the removal of the key plate would have to wait until the tank had been relocated.

The power cable from Ford Island finally went into operation on 16 April, and a deep-well electric pump was started up between the forward turrets to circulate toxic water out of the ship. Four patch sections were in place by 23 April, and another deep-well pump was set up at frame 13 to take suction all the way down to the hold. To make room for the pump and attending equipment, an auxiliary training unit was rigged to turret 1, and it was slowly rotated toward Ford Island. As the seventh patch section was bolted to the hull and to section 6 next to it, another pump was set up at frame 125 after turret 4 was also trained abeam to permit access to a centerline hatch. There were now four electric pumps in operation, sending four thick streams of polluted water cascading over the side of the ship. Water continued to flood the vessel through the gaping holes in her port side, but this was of little consequence at the moment. The purpose of the pumping was not to unwater but to rid the interior of as much stagnant, hydrogen-sulfide-contaminated water as possible.

On 1 May the eleventh and last patch section was fitted to the hull. All of the diving work on the sunken vessels had been difficult and arduous, but none more so than the fitting of these massive wood and steel patches. To counteract the buoyancy of the wood, each section had a cradle built into the bottom in which a lead weight was placed. The bridle was transferred from the derrick to the chain falls on the A-frames so that the patch could be more carefully controlled as it was lowered. Once it had been maneuvered under the turn of the bilge and brought up against the adjacent section, divers went through a door in the patch to burn holes into the hull for the hook bolts. Others bolted the sections together. The iron brackets at the tops of the I-beams were wedged tight against the underside of the armor belt to prevent any movement as the ship rose.

Because the patch was snug against the underside of the ship, and hard against the armor belt, the need for shoring below the belt was minimal since the water pressure would be taken up by the I-beams and the wales. Above the belt was a more difficult situation. Where the hull was intact, blocks could be wedged between the patch and shell. But much of the shell above the belt was missing, so 10-inch H-beams were set vertically on end atop the armor belt, spaced about every 8 feet. An iron bar was welded to the bottom of the beam, extending beyond it so that it overlapped the outside of the armor belt and kept the H-beam flush with the outside of the belt plates. The top of the beam was secured in place by struts welded between the beam, the deck, and the adjoining bulkheads. The beams were also tied together with more braces against which the patch sections could be shored.

The scrapping of the *Arizona* continued just a few hundred feet away. At one time McNally had recommended five different options for her disposition, including bracketing the ship with two sides of a floating dry dock or a newly designed salvage ship; building a permanent graving dock around her; pouring concrete around the hull and making a fort out of it; and making a dock out of the ship and using her boilers and electrical facilities for power. He was quite an optimist. "I strongly believe that the salvage of the whole ship [should] be done as easiest and [most] practicable," he wrote. "In regard to the possibility of the ship having a broken back, I believe that subsequent investigation will show that this is not as serious as preliminary work indicates. My belief is based on faith in the inherent strength of battleship construction. I am optimistic enough to believe that submergence prevented the fire from doing as much damage as is anticipated forward and that below the third deck there is still a lot of

Another section of the *West Virginia*'s long patch goes into place on 24 April 1942. The patch will be transferred from the derrick's hook to the chain fall pulley and lowered into position. Divers prepare to go into the water on the small float alongside.
National Archives

good hull remaining."[1] Not many shared the salvage planning officer's confidence. None of the proposals was given serious consideration, and divers continued to close off ports and hatches so that ammunition removal and dismantling could continue.

At the *Oglala*, rigging the new chains to the pontoons and to the stoppers was completed on 22 April. Lines were again run from the *Gaylord* to the *Oglala* so that the derrick could help with the initial righting. Hoses were again run from compressors on

The H-beams placed on top of the armor belt for shoring are visible in this photograph taken after the docking of the *West Virginia*. Parts of the patches have already been cut away. The iron bars welded to the bottom of the beams kept them flush with the outside of the belt, and struts secured them to the deck and superstructure above. Note the displacement of the armor belt and the corresponding curvature of the patch bottoms. Constructing the patch in 13-foot-wide segments allowed the sections to be molded to the battered hull.
Naval Historical Center NH 64488

the pier to fittings on the hull and to the pontoons. On the morning of 23 April, everything was in readiness for another attempt. Once again Ten Ten Dock was crowded with onlookers eager to see if the Lalie could be rolled upright.

At 0800 air was pumped into the hull until the pressure slightly exceeded 2 pounds per square inch. At 0845 the three single pontoons aft were blown, lifting the stern slightly and helping to break the adhesion to the mud. Forty-five minutes

The *Oglala* is righted alongside Ten Ten Dock, 23 April 1942. Some of the pontoons have already come to the surface.
National Archives

later the bow pontoon was blown and one of each of the pairs placed amidships. A pair of jacks had again been set up near the bow to give the ship an initial impetus off the bottom, but they weren't needed. The *Oglala* was slowly, gradually, coming upright. What was left of her topside structure and the heavy vent ducts were breaking water. The lines from the *Gaylord* drew taut as the barge pulled slowly away from the pier and added to the righting moment. By 0940 the seven blown pontoons had come to the surface and bobbed in the unsettled water between the ship and the dock. The *Oglala* came to rest with a list of just over 20 degrees to port. The last three pontoons, the second of each of the midships pairs, were then slowly blown to relieve the list.[2] By the next morning it had been reduced to 8 degrees. Some of the pontoons were detached, partially sunk, and new hitches taken on the chain stops. The pontoons were then blown again, and the list was soon reduced to 6 degrees. Over the next few days a siphon was lowered from the *Gaylord* to remove mud from beneath the starboard bilge, and the pontoons continued to be rerigged by Larson's divers. The ship settled toward the pier, then came upright again as the mud was removed, finally settling with a 6-degree list to port. It was good enough. Now McClung's men, and over a dozen divers from the *Ortolan* and Pacific Bridge, would prepare her to be refloated.

Two days after the last patch section had been placed on the *West Virginia*, and as six electric pumps hummed along circulating water in and out of the ship, a crew from Pacific Bridge sealed the ends and bottom of the small patch with concrete. It was a rich mixture, one part cement to three and a half parts aggregate, to aid in maintaining

Pacific Bridge workmen pour concrete through tremie pipes to seal the
bottom of the *West Virginia's* forward patch on 2 May 1942. The hopper
was filled from a barge alongside and lifted by derrick to the pipes. The
tremie pipe on the left was used to seal the end patch section from the bottom to the waterline.
National Archives

cohesion as it disappeared from the hopper down the 10-inch tremie pipes placed
inside the patch. Four days later the barge was moved aft, tremie pipes were installed
at 10-foot intervals, and concrete was poured into the eleven sections of the long
patch, which had by now been bolted to the hull and to each other. Some 100 cubic
yards had sealed the forward patch and another 225 cubic yards the long patch, form-
ing a seal 4 feet thick at the bottom and 4 feet wide inside the partition that sealed the

ends. Where the end sections of the patch did not come up flush against the buckled hull, wood shoring was placed to help hold the concrete in place. Beneath the turn of the bilge, where it was difficult to get the thick concrete to flow, divers wedged sandbags between the patch and the hull.

Concrete had also been poured on the deck of the scullery and officers' galley, to provide better footing and to improve sanitation. By now the galley was serving three

Captain Wallin (*left*) with Lt. Cdr. William White, the *West Virginia*'s commanding officer throughout her salvage. Both are wearing "tank suits," issued to the majority of the salvage crew each morning for the day's work in the oil-soaked interior of the vessel.
Naval Historical Center NH 64490

meals a day, and had been since 27 April. The daunting and seemingly endless cleanup on the *California* had eroded morale aboard that vessel, and William White was determined that this would be avoided aboard his ship. "The *West Virginia* had always possessed a fine ship's spirit," he wrote after the war, "so to foster this, a decision was made to spare no effort to conserve the men's energy and to make the crew as comfortable as possible during this difficult oil soaked job. This decision was vigorously pursued during the entire salvage operation." His crew, which would never exceed 370 while the salvage was under way, greatly appreciated the effort. They filed aboard each morning at 0745 via the catwalk they had built from Ford Island, exchanged their uniforms at a check room and received a pair of overalls (called a tank or "goon" suit), as well as boots, socks, and hats, for the day's work. Equipment came from stores on the boat deck, in the casemates, and in various shops. The men had previously returned to Ford Island to clean up and change for the midday dinner, but now they ate aboard their ship, under an awning that had been spread over the boat deck. Tables and benches had been brought out, and the men were given the chance to wash face and hands before sitting down in their soiled overalls to eat. No longer did they waste time and energy going from ship to shore each noon. At 1600 the tired men, dirty from their cleanup work, were able to wash in makeshift showers set up in a pair of gun sponsons before exchanging their grimy overalls for uniforms and returning to their quarters on the island for supper. The overalls and rags used that day were then shipped to a contract industrial laundry for cleaning and reuse.[3]

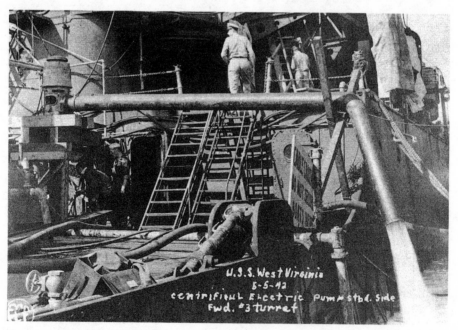

Pumping out the *West Virginia* with a centrifugal electric pump on the starboard side of turret 3 on 5 May 1942
National Archives

Once the cement barge had been towed away, divers from the Salvage Division resumed their work of shoring and wedging patches, opening interior hatches, and plugging scuppers and other drain lines on the exposed portions of the hull, especially on the starboard side. There were now nine electric and gasoline-driven 10-inch pumps aboard, and at 1030 on 12 May, Painter ordered them all switched on. Almost immediately the water level dropped, and by midday Lt. Earl Liedstrand, one of Painter's assistant salvage engineers, noted in his daily report to the Salvage Division office that the water level had fallen to just above the second deck. The extensive ventilation lines that had been run throughout the length of the ship meant that respirators could be discarded within a few days, making working conditions much more tolerable.

As the decks were pumped dry, the removal of debris continued. Months before, Wallin had anticipated the cleanup that would be required once the *California* and *West Virginia* had been pumped out. With his usual optimism he had written, "Anyone who has ever watched a coaling ship using small buckets will realize that large quantities of material can be handled quickly using small containers and a chain of passers."[4] Now the men of the *West Virginia*, like those of the *California* before them, were learning the harsh reality of cleaning a salvaged battleship. It was a "monotonous, backbreaking job," White later wrote. Wheelbarrows were lowered below and rotted bedding, clothing, furniture, books, paper, electrical fixtures, and sludge shoveled into them by work crews. The wheelbarrows were then hauled topside via slings and emptied into a barge. Once the compartments and passageways were cleared, they were sprayed with a mixture of Turko and steam from the ex-*Navajo*. The solution was applied under pressure with spray nozzles and was very effective at removing not only the oil but paint from the bulkheads. Smaller sump pumps then removed the accumulated water and muck.[5]

Most of the crew's personal effects were still on board, and as the decks were unwatered White issued orders for the recovery of those items. Twelve teams of sailors, each under a junior officer, were responsible for collecting valuables and other items from the enlisted berthing, the chiefs' quarters, and the officer staterooms. The Marine Detachment patrolled the crew's quarters to ensure that there was no repetition of the looting that had been reported in the days following the attack.[6] Items that could be identified were returned to their owners, if possible. Anything that remained unclaimed was to be auctioned off later, with the money going to the crew's emergency fund.

As had been anticipated, bodies were found floating in the stagnant water. Most of these were in even worse condition than those found two months earlier on the *California*. There were seventy *West Virginia* personnel unaccounted for, and an equal number of canvas body bags had been prepared. Recovery was accomplished in the same manner as had been used on the *California*, and by 17 May forty-nine bodies, mostly dismembered and unidentifiable, had been located and removed.[7]

Once the *Oglala* had been righted, divers got their first look at the ruptured port side. The damage, Wallin wrote, "consisted of a pressure wave in-buckle from about frame 65

Weighted with sandbags, another cofferdam section is placed aboard the *Oglala* on 12 May 1942.
National Archives

to about frame 75. The divers found three vertical splits in this area varying from five feet to nine feet in length and from nine inches to thirteen inches in width."[8] Battens were applied to the damaged hull to ascertain the shape of the patch needed. At the coal dock, carpenters continued to modify the *California* cofferdam sections for use on the *Oglala*. On Monday morning, 11 May, two completed sections arrived at the ship via barge. The next day the first of what would total twenty-nine sections was put in place, weighted down with sandbags and bolted to the hull beneath the deck coaming. By the fifteenth there were four secured to the deck edge, and more woodworkers and caulkers were dispatched by the yard to help erect, secure, and seal them. Work quickly progressed on placing the 30-foot-long starboard sections, held up only briefly on the twentieth by a poorly fitting section at the bow. This was quickly remedied, and the barge, loaded with more segments, moved inboard so that Pacific Bridge crews could work on the port side. This meant that the pontoons, still attached by chains to the hull, had to be cleared away. There was concern that once the pontoons were removed the ship might roll back to port, but she rested firmly in the mud. There was no movement.

An 18-foot high, 20-foot-long patch for the hull rupture was constructed on Ten Ten Dock and lowered into place on 17 May. After enough mud and coral had been removed from beneath the bilge, several days were spent attaching the patch, but the result was worth it. The fit, reported *Ortolan* divers, was perfect. Very little water would enter the hull here.

For weeks the cofferdam continued to grow, extending the outline of the *Oglala's* hull above water in an ever-growing rectangle. Each section had an outrigger brace built into the inboard side that was fastened to the deck wherever there was no obstruction. Finally on 7 June the last section was lowered into place at the stern and bolted to the deck and to the adjacent segments. Like the cofferdam on the *California*, the vertical wood planks that made up the walls of the cofferdam varied in size according to the depth of water in which they were placed and the corresponding head of water they were expected to withstand. The deck at the bow was 6 feet below the surface, and 4-inch-thick planks were used on those sections. The water at the port quarter was 25 feet deep, and 10-inch-thick planks were used there. The 10-by-12-inch lower wales, which would be under enormous water pressure once the water level within the cofferdam was lowered, were supported by steel tie rods secured directly to the *Oglala*. For some reason, perhaps in the rush to complete the job, the Pacific Bridge crew working on the stern section failed to install those tie rods there. That failure to follow the careful designs of Fred Crocker and his design team would soon come back to haunt Marshall McClung and the rest of the salvage crew on the *Oglala*.

Wallin's daily report to Furlong on 18 May relayed to the Navy Yard commandant the welcome news from Liedstrand that the *West Virginia* had come afloat the previous day after five and a half months on the bottom at F-6. While on the bottom she had drawn 50 feet 6 inches forward and 40 feet 10 inches aft. She maintained that trim as she rose, her list fluctuating as various compartments were drained and the hull shook itself loose from the grip of the mud. She heeled slightly to port, then steadied and slowly came upright. By the morning of 19 May she drew just over 48 feet at the bow and 39 feet 7 inches at the stern. Five days later the difference between bow and stern draft would be reduced to just 12 inches as additional water was pumped from her forward spaces.[9]

Rather than move the ship to the quays of berth F-6 and risk snagging the bottom of a patch on undiscovered wreckage, the ship had been moored in place since 12 May by four 6,000-pound anchors and lengths of $1^{7}/_{8}$-inch chain. The anchors had been dropped about 120 feet from the ship, off both sides of the bow and off the starboard and port quarters. One-and-five-eighths-inch galvanized wire had been run from the stern to the wreckage of the bow of the *Arizona* as a preventer. The wire lay on the bottom but could be made taut if a high wind from astern kicked up.[10] On 26 May a wind from abeam caused the bow to drift toward Ford Island, so another cable was run through the bullnose to the *Oklahoma*.

That same day the air flask of a Japanese torpedo was found in the wreckage of the second deck, near the barbershop. It was graphic evidence that torpedoes had caused at least some of the damage above the armor belt. Several days later that theory was reinforced by the discovery of a dud bomb at frame 63, between the main and second decks. The bomb, believed to be a 1,700-pound armor-piercing type, was removed by the Bomb and Mine Disposal Squad. At least one such heavy bomb was reported to have hit the ship in this location. There had possibly been more. Yet here was one of them, and it had failed to explode. Perhaps the ship had been hit by more torpedoes than originally believed.[11]

The damage to the stern had been patched with wood planks, and the steering room had been pumped out. The battleship was now ready to be dry-docked, but the water over the blocks of Dry Dock 1 was too shallow to take her with her present draft. Dry Dock 2 was occupied by the *California*, still completing repairs. Both Furlong and Nimitz wanted the repair work on the *West Virginia* to be handled in Dry Dock 1, to keep the deeper and larger Dry Dock 2 available for emergency dockings. There were two options open to Wallin and Painter. One was to remove as much ammunition, oil, water, and stores as would be necessary to get the draft down to about 32 feet, sufficient to clear the blocks in Dry Dock 1. The other was to seal up the *California*, tow her out of Dry Dock 2, bring the *West Virginia* in, and "drain out as much free water as possible and make quick repairs to the patch cofferdams and to underwater hull plating to limit the inflow of water to an amount which will insure a draft below 32 feet when the dock is reflooded. The time in Dry Dock #2 should not exceed three days."[12] The ultimate goal was still to land the ship in Dry Dock 1 for the several months it would probably take to repair her port-side damage.

The war raging in the South Pacific further complicated the climax of this most difficult salvage operation. The Battle of the Coral Sea had been fought in early May, and a Japanese attempt to take Port Moresby in New Guinea had been thwarted. But the beloved *Lexington* had been sunk and the *Yorktown* heavily damaged. She had arrived for repair at Pearl on the twenty-seventh and been tied up at the repair basin's berth 16 that afternoon. But she needed a dry dock. Early the next morning tugs eased her out of the basin, past the divers installing the nineteenth cofferdam section on the *Oglala*, and placed her in Dry Dock 1. Immediately she was swarming with shipfitters, welders, and machinists. Months of work had to be completed in days. The Japanese were coming. Intelligence gleaned from the broken Japanese naval codes had indicated that the Japanese fleet was headed for Midway and the Aleutians, to capture those strategic American outposts and to draw the remnants of the Pacific Fleet, particularly the carriers missed at Pearl Harbor, into battle. Nimitz, gambling that the information was correct and that the Japanese fleet was not actually heading for Hawaii or even the West Coast, ordered all three of his carriers northeast of Midway to set an ambush. He needed the *Yorktown* back at sea by the thirtieth. The *Enterprise* and *Hornet* had arrived back at Pearl the day before the *Yorktown* and had been refueling and reprovisioning. The *Hornet* tied up at berth F-10, astern of the hulk of the *Utah*, while the Big E moored at F-2. On the twenty-seventh, with the *Arizona*, *West Virginia*, and *Oklahoma* visible along Battleship Row, Nimitz had come board the carrier to present medals to some of the men of the Pacific Fleet, including survivors of the attack on 7 December.

The *Enterprise* and *Hornet* sailed on 28 May under Ray Spruance, who had replaced an ailing Bill Halsey. Five heavy cruisers left the harbor with the carriers. The *Yorktown*, with only the most rudimentary of repairs but able to put to sea, sailed on the thirtieth, her crew given a bird's-eye view of the *West Virginia* alongside Ford Island, the great square patches on her side, streams of water cascading from the pumps. It would not be long, they could tell, before the battleship was dry-docked and under repair as their own ship had just been. The repair effort on the *Yorktown* had been miraculous, a tribute to Gillette's men, but he was not there to see it. He had been ordered to Washington, and Capt. R. W. Paine had taken over as manager on 24 May.

Just two cruisers went with the *Yorktown*. One, the *Astoria*, was captained by a man all too familiar with the ravages inflicted on the fleet back in December: Capt. Francis Scanland, former skipper of the *Nevada*. Far out to sea, in a position to pursue the Japanese fleet no matter which way they came, was the *Plunger*, fully repaired after Genereaux's salvage work and back in the war at this most critical hour.

The possibility of an air raid on Hawaii was ever present, but never so much as now. Ten .50-caliber machine guns were installed on the *West Virginia*, two on the fantail and eight in the superstructure. Water tanks for cooling the guns, along with piping, were placed in the foretop.[13] A crew of five to seven was assigned to each gun. They were for close-range defense only, the crews having been ordered to hold their fire until targets had come within 600 to 800 yards. Only the yard signal tower or the ship's battery control officer could give the order to fire. Given the crowded conditions of the harbor, the gunners were cautioned to "use the utmost care to prevent firing into buildings, shore installations and ships."[14]

Painter drew up assignments for the salvage officers aboard ship to keep the pumps, compressors, and electric power going in the event of an air raid. Four fire watches were established, each with a wheelbarrow full of sand, two shovels, and a pair of fire extinguishers. Civilian yard workers and enlisted men without antiaircraft or firefighting stations were to cross the bridge to Ford Island in the event of a raid and get into plane revetments for cover. Painter had no authority over the Pacific Bridge men, merely noting that they could stay on board if they wished. Since a bomb or torpedo hit, or even a near miss, could have a catastrophic effect on the patches, the salvage team was ready to place a collision mat over any hole in the sections and to counterflood starboard voids and empty fuel tanks to keep the ship on an even keel if the patches gave way.[15]

While the battle of Midway raged in early June, ammunition was unloaded from the *West Virginia*. An empty Dry Dock 1 awaited; all that was needed was to lighten the ship. The sixty-seventh and last body had been removed on 27 May, and as ghastly as the discoveries had been on the *California* and on White's ship, the salvage crews were shocked in a different way when the *West Virginia* was unwatered.[16] Several bodies were found lying atop steam pipes in the after engine rooms. Apparently there had been an air bubble, and the men had crawled to the high point in the compartment only to suffocate when the oxygen ran out. Three more men, wearing blues and jerseys, were found in storeroom A-111, which had just 3 feet of water in it when opened. The men were lying on the lower shelf of the storeroom. Manholes to nearby freshwater tanks had been opened, and the men had consumed their emergency battle rations. They wore watches, and a calendar was found with the days between 7 and 23 December marked off.[17] Stunned, the salvage crew realized that at least some of the men had been alive more than two weeks after the attack. They were still clinging to life when Horne's men had made their first inspection of the ship back in December.

Working on the quarterdeck in tank suits, members of the *West Virginia*'s crew wet down powder bags removed from the magazines on 21 May 1942.
National Archives

Mobile Repair Unit divers who had sounded the hull and reported hearing no reply were devastated by the news.[18]

By the evening of 1 June, the *West Virginia* was drawing just 34 feet 4 inches forward, 36 feet 2 inches aft—nearly enough to get her into Dry Dock 1. The engine rooms had been unwatered on 25 May and the motor rooms six days later. Yard machinists had entered the engine rooms as soon as decontamination crews declared them safe, to flush the alternators and motors with hot water and Tectyl. All of the main battery ammunition had been removed, as well as the powder, and 5-inch shells and powder cans were now being taken off, too. Nearly all of the fuel oil had been pumped out, some 900,000 gallons of it. There was "considerable apprehension" over the question of how to unload the 70 tons of meat and dairy stores that had been decomposing for six months. The first plan was to use a 10-inch gasoline pump to flood the refrigerated compartments while an electric pump sent the water and meat overboard. But the thought of all that decomposed meat in the harbor, with its attendant stench, prompted a reevaluation. The plan was modified to allow the meat to be carried from the ship in 10-gallon cans and placed in a garbage lighter for dumping at sea. Once shredded by the high-pressure 10-inch hose, the rotted meat resembled ashes and its odor was much reduced. Within a few days the provisions had been successfully removed, to the relief of all concerned.[19]

By 6 June all of the ammunition had been unloaded, and the blocks were being set in Dry Dock 1. They had been cut down to just 33 inches in height and been set so that the ship would be 5 feet to starboard of the centerline of the dock, leaving greater clearance for the patches and as much room as possible for removing them. An additional set of blocks had been placed to take their weight. Preparations were also under way for undocking the ship if an emergency arose and Dry Dock 1 was needed for another vessel. A 1927 inclining experiment on the ship had been studied, and the Design Section concluded that seventeen starboard compartments would have to be flooded to counteract the list caused by the damage to her port side once the patches were gone.[20]

The following day, as the yard prepared to receive one battleship, it undocked another. The *California*, along with the *Sotoyomo*, was removed from Dry Dock 2. The tug went to the repair basin and the *California* to berth 22, along the seawall between the basin and Merry Point. Here she would complete repairs that would enable her to sail for Puget Sound.

At F-6, the *West Virginia's* crew had carefully run a line under the ship to check for protrusions below the docking keels and patch ends. They found nothing, and neither did a second examination. Trash, unneeded pumps, dry stores, scrap metal, and the Wheeler system were taken off over the next few days. By now the only pumps in operation were a pair of diesels in the two patches. Water that had leaked into voids had been blown out with compressed air, but the ship continued to alternate between a slight port and starboard list.

No emergency dockings arose to delay the *West Virginia's* arrival on Tuesday, 9 June. Everything that could have been accomplished in preparation had been done, yet there was still considerable trepidation. A patch might have been weakened by teredos (shipworms). A structural failure might cause a patch to spring a large leak or even collapse in the middle of the tow. A tug might accidentally collide with a patch section and tear it loose. White had attended a conference the day before with the assistant captain of the yard, yard pilots, and the docking officer to go over all the details and possible problems.

The tugs came alongside at 1230, maneuvering carefully to avoid contact with the patches. Within an hour and a half the ship had completed her trip across the harbor and was eased into Dry Dock 1. Lines were run to the sides of the dock, shoring placed against the hull, and the caissons swung closed. The battleship settled, her six-month voyage across the waters of Pearl Harbor complete.

The previous day the submarine tender *Fulton* had arrived in Pearl with hundreds of survivors from the *Yorktown*, which had gone down at Midway. White welcomed 232 of them aboard as new *West Virginia* crewmen. He was happy to have the help for the long repair and refit to follow. When dry-docked, his crew had numbered just 155 officers and men. Now he had close to four hundred—still far short of a battleship complement, but a start on the long road back to service.[21]

Off her starboard bow was the *Downes*. The *West Virginia* was expected to have a lengthy stay in dry dock, and this afforded a good opportunity for the Mobile Repair Unit to scrap the destroyer. On 8 May the *Downes* and *Cassin* had been towed from the repair basin to the newly completed Dry Dock 3, their fate still undecided. Wallin was

Hugging the starboard side of the dock to avoid bumping the patches, the *West Virginia* arrives in Dry Dock 1 on 9 June 1942. Just ahead of her is the hulk of the *Downes*, placed there for scrapping.
U.S. Naval Institute

of the opinion that the ships could be rebuilt at Pearl. He saw them as projects the shipyard could fall back on when the heavy salvage workload ended. In the first few months of 1942 the yard's workforce had been increased by thirty-three hundred men, and they were on a six-day workweek. About twenty-five hundred of Furlong's men were in the shipfitting trades and could work on the destroyers, perhaps in Dry Dock 3, when the present hectic pace slowed, thus keeping the highly trained force occupied and employed.[22]

The weekly "Conference on the Status of Work on Vessels under Repair" reflected the confusion over what to do with the destroyers. On 4 May Furlong had noted, "[Navy] Department has directed that the vessel(s) be prepared to return to Mainland on own power. Repairs to battle damage being made by Pearl Harbor Repair & Salvage Unit." One week later the ships had been removed from Dry Dock 3, and he wrote to King, "Department has directed work held in abeyance pending consideration of Yard's recommendation that new hull(s) be built on Mainland and machinery shipped back." Finally, on 25 May, a decision had been reached: "Buships has directed Mare Island to build new hull(s). Yard to ship recovered machinery and fittings."[23] The pair would be scrapped, the machinery used in a new *Downes* and *Cassin*.

Within weeks huge sections of the *Downes*'s deck had been removed to facilitate

Once the patches were removed, Paine's yard workers began cutting away the damaged bulk-heads and deck of the *West Virginia*.
U.S. Naval Institute

The *West Virginia*'s rudder, knocked off by the torpedo hit in the stern, is recovered on 11 June 1942.
National Archives

the removal of equipment and machinery. She would be completely broken up by 26 August. The *Cassin* was scrapped in the repair basin and placed in Dry Dock 2 on 15 September, along with the battleship *Mississippi* and the destroyer *Ellet*, to complete the job.[24] Between June and December, crates carrying the salvaged parts of the two ships were sent to Mare Island, where keels for the new ships had already been laid down.[25]

That lay in the future. For now, in early June, work on the *Oglala* proceeded. Some of the carpenters were startled by sharp explosions from down the dock until they were told that small dynamite charges were being used to remove some of the concrete adhering to the *West Virginia*'s hull as the patches were removed. They bolted beams to the top wales of each of the *Oglala*'s cofferdam sections, extending them across the width of the ship. Scaffolding planks were run fore and aft atop these beams and pumps placed on platforms built on the shoring timbers and scaffolding. More shoring ran between the cofferdam and what remained of the deck structures.

By 17 June, ten days after completing the cofferdam, divers were sealing visible gaps within it. Five electric and three gasoline pumps had been installed on top of the platforms, as well as a trio of siphons, and all were at work circulating water to dissipate the sewer gas. The Design Section was constantly reviewing the ship's stability characteristics, which were complicated by the cofferdam's shifting her center of gravity. The critical unknown was how far the water could be lowered before the top weight and remaining free surface water combined to destabilize the ship to the point that she could not safely be towed to Dry Dock 2.

On the eighteenth, discharge pipes were trained over the sides of the cofferdam; the water was no longer being circulated but removed. As always, the pumping was slow and deliberate so that the sections could be monitored for leaks and signs of collapse. Two sections on the starboard side did show signs of weakening, and the cofferdam was reflooded to permit their repair. Two days later they had been replaced, and pumping began again. At 0900 on the twenty-third, the *Oglala* lifted from the bottom on a fairly even keel. McClung and Wallin had decided that the ship would not be cleared of trash and equipment, nor would fuel and ammunition be removed, before she was docked. There was no time. With over 600 tons of cofferdam and sand on her deck, she was too unstable to be left floating alongside Ten Ten Dock any longer than necessary. A draft of 42 feet was the initial goal, then word was received from the Navy Yard that the *Oglala* was to be placed in the dock with the *Northampton*, which meant that the little minelayer had to clear the blocks set for the cruiser at $37\frac{1}{2}$ feet.[26]

The pumping continued to decrease her draft, and now trouble began. When the draft reached 40 feet and the water level aft was 2 feet below the mine deck, the ship began to list to port. Soon the list reached 7 degrees. Several hundred tons of sand were removed, but still the *Oglala* wallowed to port. The wind was strong and pushed hard against the high sides of the cofferdam. There was no guarantee that the *Oglala* could make the trip to the dock entrance, and Wallin regrettably had to order her docking postponed until Dry Dock 2 could take her with a draft of at least 40 feet. For now, the *Oglala* would stay at Ten Ten Dock.

With the *Oglala* cofferdam in place and the pumps lowering the water, Pacific Bridge men check the sections for leaks as the water level drops.
National Archives

After sinking because of the failure of several pumps on the night of 25 June 1942, the *Oglala* is pumped out again. At upper left in Dry Dock 1 is the *West Virginia*. The cruiser *Northampton* is in Dry Dock 2.
National Archives

The cofferdam could not be removed to save weight and improve stability without raising the deck farther above water. It had originally been intended to remove the cofferdam when the waterline was 4 feet below the lowest point of the deck edge.[27] But this would reduce the free surface water inside to the level of the open mine deck, where it would negatively impact the ship's stability because of a lack of longitudinal subdivision. The volume of water that could flow unrestricted from port to starboard could easily capsize her. The answer, at least for the time being, was to remove sand and shoring and pump out as much water as possible on and above the mine deck while waiting for Dry Dock 2 to become available. The longer the salvage team was forced to wait, the more potential there was for trouble. And there was trouble to come.

Long after dusk on 25 June a gasoline pump was removing water at the bow when it stalled and shut down. There was an electric pump on standby, but its intake hose had been placed higher than that of the gasoline pump, too high to take suction, and as water flowed into the ship, the Oglala went down by the bow. Water on the mine deck rushed forward, and floating rags and clothing flowed into the suction heads of both pumps. The gasoline pump was restarted, and the electric pump was finally able to take suction, but debris clogged the intake strainers. The ship continued to sink, the bow coming to rest on the bottom in 48 feet of water. The cofferdam, which had been out of the water for days, had shrunk and was no longer watertight. It flooded too, with the remaining pumps merely serving to keep the Oglala on an even keel as she went down.[28] Wallin, asleep at his quarters at Makalapa, was awakened by a steward with the news that the minelayer had gone to the bottom again.[29]

It was a setback, but not an overwhelming one. The ship had an 8-degree list to starboard, the cofferdam was still in place, and the pumps were still functioning. Neither McClung nor Wallin was concerned. They reported to Paine that the Oglala would shortly be refloated. The pump intake lines were cleared, the shoring was reinforced, the cofferdam was again unwatered, and the ship came afloat for the second time on the twenty-ninth. That success too was to be short-lived. Wallin inspected the Oglala that afternoon, and while he was walking atop the stern cofferdam section the wood suddenly shifted beneath him. The lower wale was giving way. The joints to the adjoining sections parted, and water flooded the cofferdam in a torrent. There was no stopping it. The Oglala settled stern first, and as the top of the cofferdam disappeared below the water, the tired old ship went down for the third time alongside Ten Ten Dock.[30] The missing tie rods had indeed been necessary.

The section was immediately removed and repaired. The next day it was lowered into position, divers made the familiar connections, and on 1 July the pumps started up yet again. The unstable vessel came afloat quickly, but problems struck the troubled Oglala once more. Shortly after 1815 a gasoline pump at the bow ran out of fuel. While filling the gas tank, the pump watch crew spilled some of it onto the hot exhaust manifold. The gas caught fire, slightly burning the two men and igniting the remaining gas in the jerry can. Frantic, the men threw it into the water, where the flames quickly spread to oil on the surface inside the cofferdam and to the oil-soaked cofferdam itself. The *Ortolan* crew quickly broke out a fire hose, and yard tugs were dispatched to the scene as the fire burned out of control. More hoses were brought to the scene, and the fire was finally put out after a half-hour, the yard Fire Department having laid down a blanket of foam on the blaze. Fortunately the damage was limited to the charring of the inside of the forward cofferdam and the destruction of several pumps and hoses.[31]

The sooner the *Oglala* was in dry dock, the better, before another disaster struck. Pumping continued all day on the second while the cofferdam was given a last bit of shoring for the trip to Dry Dock 2. Divers searched the bottom for projections, noting the patch as the only obstruction. This information was relayed to the docking officer so that the blocks could be positioned to avoid it. The ship was now drawing 40 feet 6 inches, and only the bow section of the vessel itself was above water. The wind was calm, and it was hoped that it would remain so on the third when the minelayer, along with the submarines *Trout* and *Pollack*, would be docked.

By 0900 the next day the *Oglala* was under way from B-3 to Dry Dock 2. Because so much of her was still submerged, there were only a few places from which to run lines to the tugs and to the handlers in the dock. There was almost no wind. One tug pulled with a bow line, another had run a line to a pendant attached to a submerged stern chock. More tugs were on either side of the bow. Given her history and poor stability, nerves were understandably tense as the *Oglala* slowly made her way. She was kept away from the entrance to Dry Dock 1, and just before 1000, spring lines were

With the *Saratoga* in the background at Ford Island, the *Oglala* gingerly makes her way into Dry Dock 2 on 3 July 1942 as pumps try to keep ahead of the flooding. The 600 tons of cofferdam on her deck made handling the ship difficult, but the tugs were aided by a lack of wind that morning.
National Archives

cast to the docking crews. They brought her to a gradual halt, lest the water inside her surge forward as she stopped. But there were no problems. The most troublesome of Steele and Wallin's charges was safe.

It was several days before a crane was available to begin removal of the *Oglala*'s coffer-dam, and then her crew spent two and a half weeks draining the remaining water and removing equipment and ammunition. The Salvage Division men left on 10 July, yard workers took over, and ten days later, patched and watertight, the ship was undocked for completion of her temporary repairs prior to sailing for the mainland. Pacific Bridge presented the Navy with a bill for $107,500 for its part in her salvage, including $30,900 in labor and $31,000 in material, with direct and indirect overhead account-ing for another $45,600.[32] The charges for work on the *California* and *West Virginia* had already been submitted; $153,650 on the former, $138,700 on the latter.[33] All of these charges were supplemental to the contract between the company and the Navy for the construction of Dry Dock 4. Now a larger and far more complicated and costly job lay ahead for both the company and the Salvage Division.

In March, Admiral Furlong had recommended that the salvage operation come to a close when the *Oglala* was in dry dock, and that work on the *Oklahoma*, *Arizona*, and *Utah* be undertaken at a future date, possibly after the war. But three weeks later, the vice chief of naval operations, impressed by the progress and success of the salvage so far and buoyed by the dry-docking of the *California*, asked for a review of the situation with respect to the *Arizona* and *Oklahoma*. Furlong ordered that the survey of the *Oklahoma* be made and a plan drawn up for her salvage. A month later he reported to the Navy Department that the salvage of the capsized battleship was feasible, and that he was prepared to go ahead if so ordered. The Pacific Bridge Company was con-tracted for righting the ship using winches and cables and the subsequent patching of her port side. The Navy would handle the installation of the proposed lift pontoons, the interior diving to close watertight boundaries, any necessary dredging, and the removal of ammunition, oil, and stores. Now, in mid-July, the Salvage Division was ready to proceed. At the same time, Furlong cautioned Washington that the salvage of the *Oglala* did not mean that the recovery from the disaster of 7 December was com-plete. As he reminded Secretary Knox, Admiral King, and others, "There is still much to be done in the *California*, *West Virginia* and *Oglala* to prepare them for service. This is a part of salvage that may be lost sight of in the joy of seeing the vessels brought afloat."[34] He also cautioned the Bureau of Naval Personnel that requests for transfer of enlisted men from the Salvage Division should be made through him, since much work remained to be done on the *Oklahoma* and he needed as many experienced enlisted men as he could retain.[35]

Wallin's assignment as salvage officer was at an end, and he would shortly report to Calhoun's Service Force (formerly the Base Force) as fleet maintenance officer. Rhodes, McClung, Beauchamp-Nobbs, and other officers had orders to report to the fleet or had reported for duty at the yard. Some of the familiar faces of the early days of the salvage were gone. Curtis had gone to Calhoun's Service Force in February as mobile salvage engineer. Stelter had departed on 27 February to take command of the destroyer *Beatty*, under construction in Charleston. Horne had been relieved as commander of the Mobile Repair Unit on 19 April by his executive officer, Lt. Cdr. C. P. Altland. Genereaux was soon to take command of a salvage tug. Gillette, who had received orders back in November 1941 detaching him for duty in Washington, D.C., had finally been relieved as the manager in late May.[36] Others had been assigned temporary duty elsewhere. Lindstrom, Bjork, Ankers, and Beauchamp-Nobbs had spent time off Canton Island in April, working on refloating the grounded transport *President Taylor* under the command of Jim Steele. Steele had since moved to Nimitz's staff. After the *Oglala* was docked, Liedstrand had gone to the salvage tug *Seminole*, to Guadalcanal, and to the USS *Portland* until the *Oklahoma* project was to begin. Additional officers had been requested by Furlong as far back as March, but Washington had denied his request. Wallin had also been plagued with a shortage of enlisted men and had been hampered by the transfer from his unit of experienced men needed for duty with the expanding fleet or for salvage work elsewhere. Six officers and 135 highly experienced men had been transferred from the Mobile Repair Unit to San Diego in April to form a new unit. In May more men were sent to Iceland.

But there was still an experienced team of officers and engineers with the Salvage Unit, and they would shortly begin work on the daunting task of raising the *Oklahoma*. Lindstrom had worked closely with the Pacific Bridge Company on the righting calculations and the proposed air bubble since returning from Canton Island in late May. Pappy Haynes would still be in charge of all the diving operations, with Jim Greely in direct charge of all work on the ship itself. Greely had arrived in Pearl Harbor as a highly educated engineer, but with no salvage experience. He would go to work on the *Oklahoma* project with the *California* and *Oglala* jobs behind him as a newly promoted lieutenant commander.

While the work of removing ammunition from the turrets of the *Arizona* continued and the *California*'s anchor was dredged out of 18 feet of mud, operations began on the *Oklahoma*. As Calhoun had noted back in December, "To turn such a mass back through 150 degrees is an engineering feat of considerable magnitude which will require careful planning and thorough preparation. . . . This is a job which appears to fall within the scope of civilian heavy contractors' experience and could well be let to them for accomplishment."[37] Pacific Bridge had indeed been called upon, and the job would live up to Furlong's prediction.

On 12 July, Wallin's daily report listed the ship for the first time since 3 January, noting that a work platform was being constructed at frame 90 and that holes to the fuel tanks had been marked off on the hull.[38] The next day men under Jim Greely began cutting access holes into the *Oklahoma*'s bottom and blister so that the starboard fuel tanks could be emptied to the barge *Intrepid*. Covers for the holes had already been made and delivered to the ship. They would be bolted closed once the oil had been removed.[39] Based on Bode's report of the attack and the limited survey conducted by divers of the port side, Wallin was optimistic about the chances of raising the ship without patches. He hoped that the damage had been limited to her fuel tanks and voids and did not extend to her inner bulkheads. Perhaps the cofferdam used on the *California* and *Oglala,* now stored at Waipio Point, might be used to raise her. He expected that it would take three to five months to right her, another three to raise her. By March 1943, she should be in dry dock.[40]

The dead weight of the *Oklahoma* was calculated to be about 27,200 tons, and to aid in initiating the turning movement, as much water as possible would be removed from the interior. This could best be accomplished by the use of compressed air if the hull could be subdivided and sealed so that the loss of pressure in one damaged compartment or hatch would not compromise the entire air bubble. From dives made above the mud line on the inshore side of the ship, divers had previously located four areas of significant damage extending 260 feet along the port side. There had been no extensive diving inside the ship as yet, and it was not known how many of the watertight boundaries were intact.

There was considerable trepidation among the officers of the Salvage Division and the engineers of Pacific Bridge that the *Oklahoma* would slide rather than rotate when pulled upright. Coupled with the removal of the fuel oil, introducing an air bubble would have the advantage of aiding in the righting moment of the battleship without contributing to any movement toward Ford Island. But many questions remained. Would the bow and stern turn equally? Would the ship pivot about her center of gravity if the pulling force could not be made constant and consistent along her 583-foot length? Would she sink further into the mud as her port bilge rotated down and dug into the soft bottom? How much pulling force would be required to pull 27,000 tons of battleship through a 151-degree arc? Should a trench be dredged inshore of the ship for the mud wave that would be pushed up, so as not to impede the rolling motion of the hull?

To help provide an answer and determine the best method for righting her, divers from Pacific Bridge drilled thirty-eight soil test borings next to the hull and as far away as 200 feet all around it. The bores were deep, anywhere from 65 to 80 feet below the surface of the water. The samples were sent to San Francisco, to Mr. Charles H. Lee, a well-known and well-respected soils and hydraulics engineer, who analyzed them for unit weight in air and water, moisture content, and cohesion.

Lee divided the soil into two broad groups: soft material, consisting of silt and soft gray clay; and firmer material below, made up of layers of hard and soft clay, stiff mud, shell, and coral. The moisture content was high for both: 84 percent for the soft material, 75 percent for the firmer soil beneath. The depth of the soft material over the firmer varied and grew dramatically deeper down the channel toward F-3. Near the bow it was over 50 feet deep, and it was into this kind of soft silt that the *California* had settled. As far back as frame 60, almost the entire hull of the *Oklahoma* and most of the superstructure were suspended in almost 20 feet of liquid mud. From frame 70 aft, though, the port side sat atop the firmer mud, clay, and coral bottom. Lee determined that overall, the soil cohesion of the bottom, coupled with the pressure of the ship's hull on the soil, would cause the ship to roll rather than slide when pulled.

The extreme fluidity of the mud at the bow, and the knowledge that this condition persisted down the channel, raised the concern that the *Oklahoma* might slide forward if the bow dipped more than 5 degrees below the keel line during righting. This would not be a hazard during the early stages of the pull, when the superstructure and masts were still embedded in the mud. But once the ship reached a 90-degree position, lying on her side with 12,000 square feet of mostly smooth steel plates in contact with the firm mud and with a layer of silt acting as a lubricant, any rocking motion could set her on a forward, downward slide into the deepening silt of the lagoon.

The test borings were completed by 14 August, and by that time there was a new superintendent in charge of the Salvage Division. Wallin had been relieved on 21 July by Solomon Isquith, and for a week Isquith, who was also in command of vessels-in-ordinary of the Service Force, oversaw work on the *Arizona* and *Oklahoma* as acting superintendent. On 28 July, Isquith was relieved by Cdr. Francis Whitaker. The forty-three-year-old Whitaker was a 1922 graduate of the Naval Academy and a 1926 graduate of the Massachusetts Institute of Technology, where he had earned a master's degree in naval construction. The tall, good-looking Texan had been the hull superintendent of the Navy Yard and was involved in much of the early salvage operation. He was very familiar with the Salvage Division and its personnel.

Whitaker knew that one of the most difficult elements of righting the *Oklahoma* would be gaining sufficient impetus at the outset of the pull to overcome the weight of the ship and the water inside and the grip of the mud on the masts, stack, and superstructure still attached to the ship. The use of submarine salvage pontoons had been considered, to increase the initial lift. They were to be secured with chains to masts, kingposts, and turrets. The salvage team hoped to use up to twenty: the ten used to right the *Oglala*, plus an additional ten sent from the West Coast. But the Bureau of Ships in Washington had denied the request to borrow them from the mainland. The Salvage Division would have to either manufacture ten more or resort to some other means of augmenting the lift, perhaps by the use of Army gasoline tanks.[41]

Using pontoons would be difficult. Locating them on the *Oklahoma* and securing them to the ship might pose serious problems. But there was no question about the need for an air bubble. The last half of August was spent cutting access holes in the hull for Mobile Repair Unit divers to enter the ship and begin the long, tedious process of closing hatches to create air bubble boundaries. Initially it was thought that five subdivisions would be adequate. This figure was later changed to seven: from the bow to frame 20; frames 20 to 30; frames 30 to 60; frames 60 to 83; frames 83 to 98; frames 98 to 110; and frame 110 to the stern. Eight holes were cut into the bottom, starboard of centerline, and every day for months five groups of divers descended into this dark, upside-down world to open hatches below the second deck while closing hatches along the boundaries. They also plugged drains and other openings to the hull wherever possible. The fireroom uptakes were concreted lest the air escape through them when the ship was righted. Whitaker acknowledged the complexity of the work: "The position of the ship, the derangement of material inside of the vessel, the saturation of the water with hydrogen sulfide gas, and the complete absence of light made this interior diving both hazardous and difficult."

A diver prepares to enter the *Oklahoma* on 22 September 1942 to continue the job of isolating various compartments into separate air bubbles within the hull.
National Archives

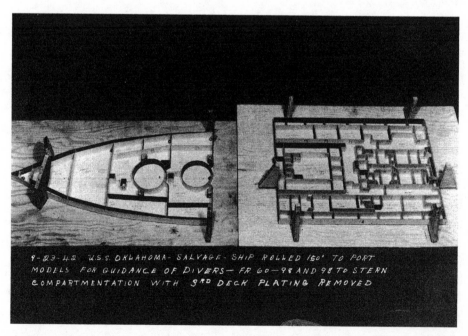

A portion of the model built to familiarize and train divers for the hazardous work inside the *Oklahoma*
National Archives

The dives were carefully planned, using a model of each deck to familiarize the men with the compartments, ladders, hatches, and potential obstacles. Because of the distance they sometimes had to travel inside the vessel, a second diver would be stationed halfway along the route to provide immediate assistance if needed. It was pitch black down there, and furniture and equipment had been thrown about when the ship capsized. Occasionally the men had to dive beneath the ship to the main or upper deck, locate a hatch, and ascend into the ship from below to reach a compartment, particularly those on the second deck. They were subject to considerable physical and mental strain as they picked their way carefully and slowly along the chosen routes, accomplishing their limited and specific tasks. The dives went on for months, and by the time the job had been completed the total number came to 4,188, with 10,279 hours spent underwater.[42]

Ashore, several buildings that held enlisted men's quarters along the Ford Island shoreline had been removed to make way for the concrete deadmen that would hold the winches and anchor assemblies for the righting tackles. This was the job of workers from Pacific Bridge, and they began excavations on 23 August. In a little over a month they were done and began pouring 8,000 tons of concrete into the anchor foundations. The construction of the winch foundations atop them followed. Much of the activity surrounding the *Oklahoma* was recorded by a team of photographers from the Fleet Camera Party, which came out to the scene on 22 September to shoot dozens of pictures.

When the winch foundations were completed in November, there were two lines of them: thirteen in a line 575 feet from the *Oklahoma*'s keel, and another line of eight,

Construction of the winch foundations on Ford Island on 28 October 1942
National Archives

36 feet closer. Forty-five feet ahead of and attached to each foundation was the anchor rod assembly for each of the fixed tackle blocks. Two 1-inch wires led from each block through a compound pulley system. The sixteen sheaves of the fixed block combined with seventeen sheaves of an outer, moving block, returning the 1-inch wires to a winch with a pair of 24-inch drums. This thirty-four-part block-and-tackle arrangement gave the winches a mechanical advantage of seventeen. The strain on the wires as they were winched in was seventeen times less than would otherwise have been the case if the winches had been pulling directly on the hull. It was this mechanical advantage that would enable the twenty-one winches, working in tandem and under careful control, to pull the dead ship upright. The disadvantage of this setup was that the 1-inch wire, reeved through so many sheaves, would have to be extraordinarily lengthy. Excess wire would rapidly accumulate on the winches, and the pulling would frequently have to stop for it to be removed.

The outer block assembly was attached to two 3-inch wires that would actually be attached to the ship. For leverage, the 3-inch wires were run to lugs on the starboard side over the top of timber headframes, or "bents." Each of the lines was divided into four "cattails" at the apex of the 40-foot-tall triangular headframes, and the ends of the cattails were secured to connections tack-welded onto the hull. Intercostal spreaders were welded between the connections to prevent movement. Each headframe was made up of four thrust timbers, or compression members, to take the strain of the pulling wires. These were secured to the inshore side of the bottom against the centerline keel and docking keel, since these structures were built to take the great loads associated with dry-docking. The headframes were supported on the offshore side against the pulling force by eight backstay wires run from the top of the headframe to pads welded directly to the starboard blister. In order to secure the lowest portion of the headframes to the hull below the waterline, a cofferdam was built on the bottom of the ship. Another, smaller cofferdam was constructed on the starboard blister forward to allow the fitting of some of the backstay wires. Three diagonal rows of planks spliced the headframes together to form a single unit.

Air locks were needed to hold air pressure within the bubbles while work continued. By the end of September, work was under way on the first of six of them. These large cylinders were placed under awnings atop the diving holes in November, and by early December water in each of the air bubble sections was being blown down with air from two air control barges, one forward and one aft, using 1 1/4-inch hose. The water escaped through the damaged sections of the hull and was held below much of the second deck, about 25 feet below the outside water surface. Smaller bubbles were blown into the starboard sides of the forward main and even upper decks, partly in an effort to keep the bow raised sufficiently to prevent sliding forward into the deep silt.

The *Oklahoma* work site was a beehive of activity. Eleanor Roosevelt visited the ship late that fall on her way to the South Pacific for a tour of the front and was given a brief but firsthand look at the salvage. Correspondents were also given tours. Power and control stations for operating the winches were under construction by November, and

Pacific Bridge riggers reeved 1-inch wire through the sheaves of the fixed and moving blocks to the winch assemblies. The winches were aligned and fixed in place atop their foundations. On the hull the air locks were installed and tested. Divers descended into the ship, discovering just how badly the torpedoes had wrecked the hull. There were now five, rather than four, main areas of damage that had been plotted.

Throughout November and into December, as the first anniversary of the attack passed, the winches were readied. They were equipped with variable-voltage drives,

The *Haviside* crew placing the righting "bents" or headframes on the hull of the *Oklahoma* on 8 January 1943. There would be twenty-one in all, braced against the docking and centerline keels.
National Archives

assembled from General Electric factories and warehouses on the mainland and shipped to San Francisco for modification before being sent on to Hawaii.[43] The drives would enable each winch to be controlled separately by varying the voltage. Controlling the speed of each individual winch was vital to ensure that the strain on the cables could be instantly equalized should there be a problem. Calculations had shown that as the ship came upright, the righting cables would not clear F-5, so the tops of the quays were chipped away. The construction of the headframes was completed ashore, and the *Haviside* brought the first of them (actually the number 2 in sequence) out to the *Oklahoma* on 8 January 1943.

Five days earlier, as heavy rains pelted Oahu, preliminary work to right the *Utah* had begun on the other side of Ford Island. Work on the ship would proceed slowly as long as the *Oklahoma* project was under way. She was to be raised solely in order to clear her berth and for the scrap value of her hull. Little planning had been done during 1942 for her removal, but now that the *Oklahoma* job was approaching the righting phase, it was decided to right and refloat the *Utah* using the same methods.

An exterior survey was made to close all accessible portholes and scuppers. The topside was also surveyed, to record the location of wreckage that had broken loose and that which was still attached to the ship but embedded in the mud. The cones from the propellers were taken off so that the propellers themselves could be removed. Frame marks were painted on the hull for reference, and a floating walkway was constructed from the hull to quay F-11-N. For the first time, the *Utah*'s position was accurately fixed. She had capsized farther than the *Oklahoma*, 165 degrees, in 43 feet of water. Her bow was 19½ feet higher than her stern.

Most of the work duplicated that carried on aboard the *Oklahoma*. Survivors of the ship still attached to the Salvage Division helped construct a model of the *Utah*'s interior, and divers familiarized themselves with it before entering the hull to establish the air bubble boundaries. In April, Pacific Bridge construction crews began to lay out and excavate the anchorages for seventeen winches. Inasmuch as that corner of Ford Island housed several thousand men, the contractor was asked to minimize nighttime work and to use electric machinery, rather than noisier gasoline-powered equipment, whenever possible. With an eye to the future, the commander of the Naval Air Station had requested that the concrete winch foundations be placed below ground level, so that the area could be returned to normal use one day.[44] As on the *Oklahoma*, work would continue for months.

While the first steps were being taken to right the *Utah*, the final preparations were under way on the *Oklahoma*. The starboard blister was strengthened by welding stiffeners and braces to take the strain of the backstays. A bridle had been attached to the rudder to keep it centered while the ship turned, and the screws had been removed on 11 December to prevent them from being damaged. On 22 January, 4,500 cubic yards of coral soil were dumped on the inshore side from the bow to frame 55 to check any sliding toward Ford Island or forward into the silt. All of the headframes were installed between 8 and 20 January, and aircraft-warning lights were placed atop them.

The pace increased when Pacific Bridge went on a two-shift schedule on the twenty-eighth. Floodlights were installed for night work, the threat of an air raid being not nearly so imminent as a year earlier. By 4 February the 3-inch wires were being run from the apex of the headframes to the moving tackles while divers located the broken or badly bent masts by the position of the tops in the mud. One month later all the righting tackles had been rigged and strain gauges installed on all lines. After eight months of preparation, Whitaker's men were ready.

At 0841 on 8 March 1943, the winches were started under the first of three round-the-clock watches. Two officers and twenty men, including some transit men from Pacific Bridge, comprised each watch. There were men stationed in the central control station and at two air-control barges, one forward and one aft, to regulate the airflow into the bubbles. Others were positioned to record the ship's rotation and the strain on the winches. A diving group was standing by.[45] Once again Admiral Nimitz took time out from his busy schedule to come to Ford Island and watch the first efforts to right the ship.

For over thirteen and a half hours the winches ground away while all about the harbor, eyes watched the almost imperceptible movement of 1.4 degrees per hour. Rolling was halted for a day to repair the 3-inch wire connection to the eyebolts of headframe 11, then resumed again on the tenth for a few hours until more eyebolts failed. All were reinforced while a dredge removed some of the mud pushed up from frame 60 aft. Pulling started again on the seventeenth and went on for fourteen and a

Reeving the tackles with 1-inch wires on 13 February 1943
National Archives

Commencement of righting operations, 8 March 1943. The twin drums of the winches reeled in the 1-inch wires of the fixed and moving tackles, which were connected to the 3-inch wires run over the tops of the headframes to the starboard side of the *Oklahoma*.
National Archives

Left to right: Pacific Bridge's Jack Graham, Adm. William Furlong, commandant of the Pearl Harbor Navy Yard, and Capt. Francis Whitaker, superintendent of salvage, on the shore of Ford Island, 31 March 1943. The headframes have been removed from the *Oklahoma*'s hull, and the 3-inch wires have been attached to turret barbettes and kingposts.
National Archives

half hours until the ship had reached a list of 109 degrees. The accumulated 1-inch wire on the winches was cleared away and the wire reconnected before pulling resumed the next evening at 2027. Eighteen hours and forty-three minutes later the ship had rolled past the 90-degree position and settled at 70 degrees. A tug cruised noisily back and forth along the offshore side of the ship, washing mud off the superstructure, turrets, and deck with fire hoses. The next day the winches were started up for just twenty-five minutes. The headframes had now dipped so low that the 3-inch wires and cattails had lifted clear of them. The bents were removed and floated off in a long pile astern until they resembled a timber breakwater. The cables were run across the flattened quay tops and barges to keep them above water.

With the 3-inch lines running directly from the outer tackle to the starboard blister, the winches were run for another seven hours and sixteen minutes on 20 March. When that pull was completed the *Oklahoma* had a list of just 40 degrees. Nine sets of wires were wrapped around the barbettes, conning tower, and starboard kingpost, and pulling resumed, continuing off and on for the next seven weeks. More wires were shifted from the starboard blister connections to the barbettes and to the stumps of the foremast and mainmast legs. Deep-well pumps were placed on deck to unwater intact areas of the bow and stern, and a pendulum clinometer was installed on the superstructure deck. The anchors were removed, as was most of the chain, and accumulated soil under the starboard side was dredged and jetted away.

The winches were being subjected to excessive loads, and they were started up

Lt. Cdr. Solomon Isquith, commanding officer of vessels-in-ordinary, pulls himself up the sloping forecastle of the *Oklahoma* on 6 April 1943. A smiling Captain Whitaker is second from the right, next to Assistant Secretary of the Navy Ralph Bard.
National Archives

A splendid view of the *Oklahoma's* quarterdeck and the wires around the barbettes of turrets 3 and 4. The more the ship was righted, the less leverage there was, and the wires and winches soon began to fail under the stress. Not much of the *Arizona* remained visible in the background when this photograph was taken on 6 May 1943.
National Archives

only five times between 7 April and 16 June. Assistant Secretary of the Navy Ralph Bard was on an inspection trip of Pearl Harbor in April, and he watched one of those pulls from a viewing stand in back of the winches. The shipyard that Bard could see beyond the *Oklahoma's* hull across South Channel was much larger than that which had existed when the battleship capsized sixteen months before. Three graving docks were in use, with Dry Dock 4 scheduled for completion later in the year. Another marine railway was under construction, this one adjacent to the floating dry dock, and would be completed by May. Auxiliary shipfitting, electrical, and machine shops were being built, as well as a service shop for the dry docks and a bombproof twenty-thousand-kilowatt electrical plant. There were over twenty-three thousand employees at the shipyard, nearly five times the number on 7 December 1941.[46] They had repaired the *West Virginia* and *California* sufficiently to get them to the West Coast under their own power. The *West Virginia* departed on 7 May 1943 and sailed for Puget Sound as the *Oklahoma* was being righted. The *California* was already there, having arrived on 20 October 1942.

The longest continuous pulling period during the next nine weeks lasted just two hours and forty-eight minutes, but by the end of the last one on the afternoon of 16 June the wires surrounding barbette 3 were snapping under the strain. The list had been reduced to just 2 degrees 10 minutes. That was good enough. The ship was upright. Now she had to be patched and floated. Even before the pulling had stopped, divers were examining the shattered port side, taking measurements for the patches. The torpedo damage was tremendous. One 48-foot armor plate had been blown off. Others had 4- and 5-inch cracks. The upper deck was missing altogether along the port side amidships.

Supports were placed for the main patch, and the first section was delivered alongside and set in place on 4 August. These patches were similar in concept to the *West Virginia's*, in that they would be closed on the bottom and ends by tremie-poured concrete. But they were substantially strengthened by steel girders on the outboard side. There were five sections, 56 feet high and extending 132 feet along the hull. They were set and concreted by 14 September. Sixteen cubic yards sealed the forward end, 22 cubic yards the aft section, and 340 cubic yards the bottom. More concrete was poured into five smaller patches. Four were between frames 74 and 85. A fifth, 16 feet high and 52 feet long, was set beneath turret 1. That one and another beneath the mainmast were at the main- and second-deck levels, indicating that torpedoes had still been striking the ship when her main and upper decks dipped below the water while capsizing.

The main deck was submerged, so a small cofferdam was built from frame 85 to frame 115 (the break of the upper deck to just aft of turret 4) to improve stability and

With a list of just over 2 degrees to port, patching of the *Oklahoma* begins. A cofferdam was later built from the break of the quarterdeck forward of turret 3 to just aft of turret 4, increasing the water-plane area of the ship. Wallin's initial hope that cofferdamming alone would be enough to raise the ship was quickly dashed by the terrific damage discovered along the ship's port side.
National Archives

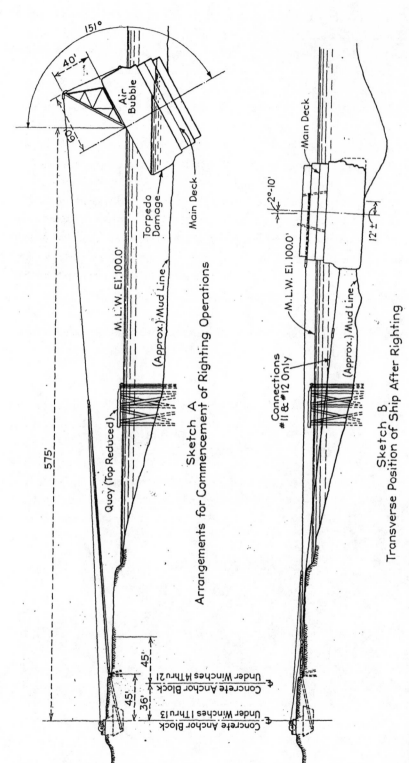

Sketch A

Arrangements for Commencement of Righting Operations

Sketch B

Transverse Position of Ship After Righting

A diagram of the righting operations on the *Oklahoma*.
Transactions of the Society of Naval Architects and Marine Engineers

The heavily reinforced main patch for the *Oklahoma* on 21 August 1943. The form built into the end of the patch for tremie concrete is visible.
National Archives

increase the water-plane area of the hull. Pumping to refloat the *Oklahoma* began on 20 September. As the water level lowered, ventilation lines were set up and Salvage Unit personnel cleared mud and debris from the passageways. There was no need to clean the compartments as thoroughly as on the *Nevada, California,* and *West Virginia,* but they were cleared of sludge and oil by pumps and skimming equipment. Unlike the *California* and *West Virginia,* there were no bodies to be floated into bags. The four hundred crewmen had long since decomposed into bone and teeth. Fragments, sometimes with rotted clothing, were picked out of the mud by medical personnel for burial in a common grave. None could be identified.

A careful and continuous watch was maintained on the ship's attitude. A clinometer was installed to show her list and a trim indicator for longitudinal trim. A scale was placed on turrets 2 and 3, attached by wire to the quays, to indicate any movement toward or away from the shore. Four sets of raised numerals were placed on the bow and stern, on the starboard side of the hull, and on the patch to indicate draft. Readings were taken of each indicator every hour. In addition, deck plans were updated frequently with crayons indicating watertight boundaries and pump locations, and another set of plans was used to track the air quality in each compartment.

Refloating the *Oklahoma* was a balancing act, a combination of the patches used on the *West Virginia,* the cofferdam used on the *California* and *Oglala,* pumping, and careful counterflooding. There were twenty-eight 10- and 12-inch electric and diesel deep-well pumps aboard, though not all were in use at the same time, and they pumped out the ship in stages. By 15 October the water was below the third-deck level, $21\frac{1}{2}$ feet below the waterline, and divers under Haynes and Aubra Calhoun worked to plug leaks. Most troublesome were the cracks in the bottom hull plating, caused, it was thought, by the stress of righting the ship. Dye was released under the ship and tracked as it was pumped out, to help locate the leaks. Kapok was stuffed into the openings, held there by the immense suction of the pumps.[47] It worked. On the evening of 3 November, the ship came afloat. She handled gingerly, and the stability calculations took into account the flooded compartments, the missing armor, the weight of the patches and mud, and the shifting of main battery shells to port when she rolled over. All of this affected buoyancy, trim, and list.

Then, unexpectedly, tragedy struck. An explosion rocked the ship shortly after she came afloat, killing three sailors who had been cutting wreckage inside a poorly ventilated area that contained explosive vapor. The three, Robert Norton, Joseph Finney, and Irvin Tessmer, were buried at Halawa Naval Cemetery on Friday, 12 November. Many of their shipmates, the officers and chiefs in khaki, the enlisted men in undress whites, attended. Whitaker, now promoted to captain, wrote letters of condolence to Finney's wife and to Norton's and Tessmer's parents.

Salvage work remained extremely dangerous and had claimed another life on the *Utah* a few months before. A diver from Altland's unit, a shipfitter named Tom Cary, was deep inside the ship on 22 June 1943, removing the dogs from a hatch as the work of establishing the air bubble boundaries continued. Without warning he reported to his talker that the valve controlling his air supply had jammed closed. Then all communication ceased. Another diver, stationed at the halfway point for just this type of emergency, went to his aid. Others followed, but it was an hour and forty minutes before Cary was brought to the surface, dead. Altland wrote a letter to Cary's mother in Bellingham, Washington, the letter that every commanding officer hated, the letter that every mother waiting at home dreaded. A few weeks later she wrote him back: 'The news of his [Cary's] death was dumbfounding although I have had a gone-feeling in the pit of my stomach ever since he wrote that he was diving; the news all but paralyzed me."[48] The agony that Cary's mother endured had been repeated, and would continue to be repeated, in hundreds of thousands of families anxiously awaiting the safe return of a loved one from a war that had no end yet in sight.

The death of Cary and the three men on the *Oklahoma* cast a pall over the otherwise fine progress, but after a brief pause for the funeral in November, the Salvage Unit got back to work. The key plates of all turrets were removed, the breeches of the guns jacked open, and the barrels painted with zinc-chromate as a preservative. When the ship came afloat, barges were placed between her and the quays to prevent her from drifting toward shore and catching the patches on the bottom or on some obstruction. She was anchored forward and aft, and lines were run to the quays. The last ten righting wires were removed on 10 November, having been left in place to counteract any tendency to roll back into the hole her hull had created. With the ship afloat and stable, they were not needed. After some debate, pontoons were secured to the patch to give the ship a slight list to starboard, allowing more clearance for the bottom of the vulnerable patches as she was towed to dry dock. The difficulty in securing them to the fragile patches had to be weighed against the added buoyancy they provided. Whitaker decided that it was worth the trouble to raise the bottom of the patches. There would not be much clearance over the harbor bottom, and it was a long tow to the newly completed Dry Dock 4, down the channel from Hospital Point.

It was while securing the pontoons that disaster struck again. One of the Pacific Bridge divers, attempting to secure a pontoon, fell upside down into the water. Either his air hose became pinched between the pontoon and the hull, or the small amount of water in his suit filled up his helmet while he was inverted and he drowned. It was just the seventh death in two years of salvage work, and the second death of a diver—a remarkable record, considering the hazards from toxic gas, explosives, fuel oil, and jagged metal that the men braved each day.[49]

Careful preparations were made for docking the *Oklahoma*, for she was in a tenuous condition. The damage to her was extreme, and a failure of any of the numerous patches would rapidly cause her to capsize in the channel, destroying eighteen months of hard work and immeasurably complicating another righting attempt. The fear of blocking the South Channel or the entrance was as great as when the *Nevada* had made her short-lived sortie more than two years before. The Public Works Section sounded and swept the path to ensure that there was a minimum depth of 42 feet at mean low water. The entrance fenders and access ladders were removed from the dry dock to eliminate the chance of their catching on the patches. A six-hundred-kilowatt generator was installed on deck to power the pumps on the journey, and a tug was assigned to carry a 460-volt land line to the ship if the generator failed. Firefighting equipment was placed aboard, and the floats and barges were removed from alongside to make way for the tugs. A crane barge, with spare pumps and pump motors, was to follow the *Oklahoma* down the channel.[50]

Before dawn on 28 December, 751 days after she had been ripped open by Japanese torpedoes, the *Oklahoma* started on her way to Dry Dock 4, a dock that had not been built when she capsized.[51] A full detail of Salvage Unit and Pacific Bridge personnel had been aboard since 0330 getting her ready. Her trip coincided with the morning high tide, and she was eased straight ahead by a trio of tugs, avoiding the wreckage on the bottom off her port side. She crept along past the new marine railway, past the hospital where so many victims of the attack had been treated. Her hull was a mere 2½ feet above the bottom, but fortunately no obstructions caught on the patches. It was nearly two hours before the sodden hulk was finally landed on the blocks. There was no rebuild awaiting her, no swarm of shipfitters, electricians, and hull experts determining the best way to get her back into action.

In January, divers would return to F-5 to rig the *Oklahoma*'s stack for lifting and use explosives to blast the wreckage lying partially submerged in the silt so that it could be removed. The thin metal of the stack ripped under the strain of the lifting cables, and it too had to be blasted apart and lifted in pieces. In Dry Dock 4, the hull was patched for towing to the yard. Under the hammerhead crane the turrets and upperworks would be removed under the guidance of the Design Section, and the ship would be towed away to West Loch, where she would await the highest scrap metal bidder.[52]

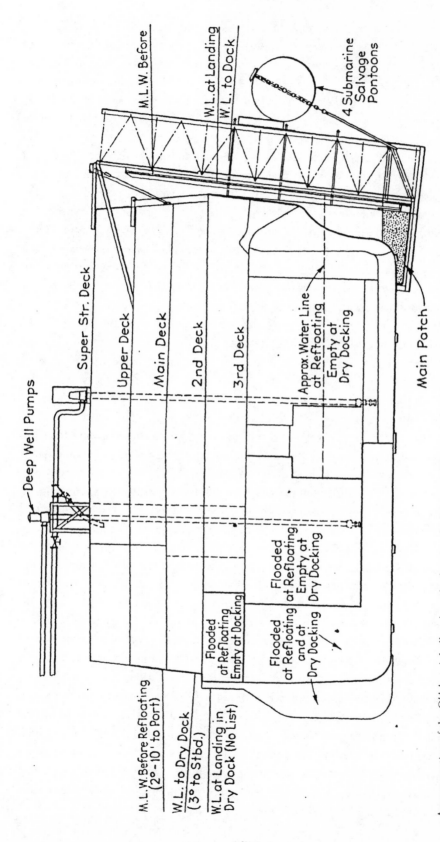

Deep Well Pumps

M.L.W. Before

W.L. at Landing
W.L. to Dock

Super Str. Deck

Upper Deck

Main Deck

2nd Deck

3rd Deck

Approx. Water Line at Refloating

Empty at Dry Docking

4 Submarine Salvage Pontoons

Main Patch

Flooded at Refloating Empty at Docking

Flooded at Refloating Empty at Dry Docking

Flooded at Refloating and at Dry Docking

M.L.W. Before Refloating (2° - 10' to Port)

W.L. to Dry Dock (3° to Stbd.)

W.L. at Landing in Dry Dock (No List)

A cross-section of the *Oklahoma's* hull and patch, showing the location of the pontoons. The complete destruction of the port blister and hull is evident.
Transactions of the Society of Naval Architects and Marine Engineers

After a long, precarious tow around Hospital Point, the *Oklahoma* reaches Dry Dock 4 on 28 December 1943, two years and three weeks after she was sunk. Her dry-docking was more a relief than a triumph. By this time there was no thought of repairing her.
National Archives

For the *Oklahoma*, the war had ended two years before. It had ended then for the *Utah*, too. On the *Utah*, airlocks were installed to facilitate the partitioning of the hull. A cofferdam was built to unwater the area where the cable backstays were attached. Engineers again filled page after page of ruled notebook paper with buoyancy, weight, and displacement calculations, center-of-gravity analyses, oil, ammunition, and water estimations. Pacific Bridge had installed righting tackle and headframes to her hull throughout the last months of 1943. The pace of work increased as men and equipment became available from the *Oklahoma* job, but even as late as February 1944, the enlisted complement under Whitaker was twenty-one men short.[53] With the war effort growing and the shipyard and fleet increasing in size, the *Utah* job simply had little priority.

Many of the Salvage Unit's enlisted men were asked if they wished to transfer to duty elsewhere once the *Utah* was righted. Nearly all said they did. Salvage duty was hard, monotonous work in the backwater of the war, and many had been at it since the attack. Some wanted to get into the war. Some wanted to go anywhere as long as it wasn't Pearl Harbor. Motor Machinist Second Class William Bailey wrote on his request form, "Diesel school or any other ship or station other than the 14th Naval District desired." Others wanted diving school. One chief motor machinist, James Reddy, was nearly alone in wanting to see the job through to the end. He merely wished for thirty days' mainland leave before returning to the *Utah* salvage. He had been with the Salvage Unit, without a break, since 28 December 1941.[54]

The air bubbles were supporting more than 75 percent of the *Utah*'s weight now and would substantially aid in her righting. The soil under her was softer than that under the *Oklahoma*, and the buoyancy created by the bubbles would reduce the tendency of the ship to sink into the mud as she rolled. Seventeen headframes had been installed on the 521-foot *Utah*. Backstay connections were attached to the hull and amidships to longitudinal bulkheads after the blister plating had been cut away. The two quays at F-11 had been removed, not because they would interfere with the cables but because the ship would probably slide enough to strike them when righted.

Preparations for righting took thirteen months—five months longer than for the *Oklahoma*, mostly because of the need to wait for equipment. The Bureau of Ships had recommended in January that work on the ship cease, but Furlong had persuaded Washington to reconsider, and King had agreed. The commandant of the Fourteenth Naval District, Adm. Robert Ghormley, had chimed in with the recommendation that the ship be towed to sea and sunk, given the fact that all the necessary personnel and equipment were on hand.[55] Others estimated that within the year, and certainly by the beginning of 1945, the *Utah* would be upright, patched, and dry-docked for scrapping, though it was often contemplated that she would be better left where she was after righting.[56] The salvage was in constant limbo and subject to change whenever conditions indicated that the cost outweighed the benefit.

Finally, at 0800 on 9 February 1944, the rolling commenced. "The ship rolled easily and with no interruptions," wrote Furlong in a later report.[57] By the afternoon of the eleventh she had reached a position of just over 68 degrees to port. But there was a problem, and it was becoming more apparent with each hour the winches turned: the ship was settling into the mud rather than rolling on top of it. Her center of gravity was sinking. The soil under the *Utah* did not have the strength to support the increased pressure brought against it. The hull had rotated so far, and sunk so deep, that the headframes had been pushed up by the bottom against the cable assembly righting pins, and the 3-inch cables could not lift clear of the frames. In fact, the headframes were so embedded in the mud and pressed so hard against the cables that they could not be removed. They had to be blasted off with dynamite.

The 3-inch connections were removed from the side of the ship and rewelded to the main deck, barbettes, and kingposts. The cables were reattached, and on the morning of 3 March, pulling was resumed. The ship continued to right but continued to settle, too. Whitaker and Pacific Bridge were fighting a losing battle to get her upright before she sank so far as to make further pulling impossible because of the excessive loads on the winches. She was now at 37 degrees 45 minutes but would go no further. She had sunk too far into the mud. The winches would not take the strain. As Furlong noted, the *Utah* "had sunk to such an extent that it was not feasible to continue without taking further steps. As a result of discussion it was decided that the cost and time involved in further action would not warrant the continuance of righting operations since for practical purposes the ship was in as favorable a position as would be needed."[58] In other words, the *Utah* was out of the way. Nimitz had already indicated his desire that the salvage end when she was dragged upright close to F-11.[59]

On 10 February 1944, after a day of righting by seventeen sets of winches and cables, the *Utah* has reached a 90-degree position. By the next afternoon she had rolled so far to starboard that the head-frames had become embedded on the bottom. They would be blasted free with dynamite, but already the ship was beginning to sink into the mud rather than roll on top of it.
Naval Historical Center NH 83059

The tackles were slackened off to see if the ship would slide away from Ford Island or rotate back to port. She moved about a foot and stopped. A watch was maintained for a couple of days, but the old battleship-turned-target-turned-hulk didn't budge. The cables were removed. For a few days divers looked for the mast and stack in the mud. The mast had previously been marked with a buoy, but it had carried away. They couldn't locate either. On 15 March, all diving ceased. The salvage operation following the day of infamy was over.

Epilogue

On 6 May 1942 the toppled, blackened foremast of the *Arizona*—one of the most enduring images of the attack—was cut down and placed on a barge. The disturbing yet distinct outline of Battleship Row, defined at least in part for the past five months by the sad sight of that mast bowed forward over the *Arizona*'s smashed bridge, had been changed. Reminders of the attack were systematically being removed as victims were resurrected to fight again.

The mainmast was cut away on 23 August, and turrets 3 and 4 were removed and turned over to the Army as shore batteries. Ammunition continued to be recovered by divers, and the guns of turret 2 were also lifted away in September 1943. Since the turret could not be trained abeam to make room to work, this necessitated removal of the conning tower, considerable wreckage, and the top, front, and rear armor so that the guns could be lifted straight up. The boat cranes and kingposts were taken away. The wrecked superstructure was cut down. In time only the boat deck remained above water. Over the years the hull settled gradually into the mud so that only the barbette of turret 3 remained visible. The *Arizona* was stricken from the Naval Vessel Register on 1 December 1942, and all work on her ultimately ceased on 11 October 1943. There she lay, alone at F-7, while the war went on around her.

The captain of the yard, Capt. Francis Craven, was ordered by Furlong to form a "Board for the Inspection of the *Oklahoma*" on 7 July 1944. There was little to inspect, and the board was a mere formality. She was not worth the money it would take to repair her. Two months later she was decommissioned and stricken. Towed to the repair basin, she was stripped of her guns and superstructure and moored alone, in silence, in West Loch for the remainder of the war. She was sold for scrap, but the damage suffered on 7 December had weakened her greatly. She sank under tow to California on 17 May 1947.

The *Utah* was placed out of commission on 5 September 1944, four days after the *Oklahoma*, and she was stricken on 13 November. Her hulk rendered F-11 useless, but

The toppled, blackened foremast of the *Arizona* lies on a barge, 6 May 1942. The foremast, surrounded by dense black smoke, would be one of the enduring images of the attack. But in the spring of 1942 it was just so much scrap metal to be removed.
National Archives

she had been pulled far enough inshore to permit the use of F-10 and F-12. There she stayed, rusting and nearly forgotten, on the far side of Ford Island. In the 1950s some thought was given to raising her to clear F-11, but the righting equipment had long since been sold off. She was left where she was. The *Utah*, like the *Arizona*, was more than a derelict and an obstruction. She was a war grave.

The other ships damaged or sunk in the attack returned to duty one by one. The *West Virginia*, thought by some to be a total loss on 7 December 1941, was repaired at Puget Sound, served in the Pacific theater, and was present in Tokyo Bay on 2 September 1945 when the Japanese surrendered aboard the USS *Missouri*. The *West Virginia*'s story, and that of the others, could, and do, fill books, and all owed their war careers at least in part to the men of the Base Force, of the Salvage Unit, of Navy Yard Pearl Harbor. Those men had a job that was dirty, backbreaking, and dangerous, yet they carried on in the dark days after 7 December 1941 to give their navy, and their country, a fighting chance. For much of that time they were on the front lines, expecting another attack at any time. Each ship that lived to fight again was one more to defeat Japan. Victory was far from certain in 1942, defeat a definite possibility.

Little glory came the salvors' way. Their reward was in the damaged ships reaching the repair basin, the sunken ships limping into dry dock. They received little national recognition and few medals. Yet their job was as vital to the war effort as any other. Upon hearing of the death of her son while engaged in salvage work at Pearl, Mrs. Lela Norton wrote to Captain Whitaker in January 1944 about her beloved

Robert: "I hope he was the brave, courageous man I would want him to be, and I feel that those boys who go daily in to dangerous work are just as great heroes as any who give their lives on the battlefields, altho I doubt if they are recognized as such."[1] She was correct. They were not recognized as heroes. But they should have been. The men she referred to, "those boys," resurrected a fleet that had suffered a humiliating defeat in one of their nation's darkest hours and set it on the road to victory.

Notes

CHAPTER 1. 8 DECEMBER 1941

1. Commander, Battleships, Battle Force, "Report of Damage, Battleships," 7 December 1941, Naval Historical Center (hereafter NHC), Wallin Papers. Hereafter "Report of Damage, Battleships," 7 December.

2. Commander, Battleships, Battle Force, "Report of Damage, Battleships," 8 December 1941, NHC, Wallin Papers. Hereafter "Report of Damage, Battleships," 8 December.

3. "Summary of Damage Reported to the Planning Section, December 7, 1941," NHC, Wallin Papers.

4. "Report of Damage, Battleships," 7 December.

5. "Report of Damage, Battleships," 8 December.

6. H. N. Wallin, "USS *Raleigh*—Flooding in Way of Bomb Hit Aft. Behavior of Damage Control Facilities," 5 January 1942, NHC, Wallin Papers.

7. R. B. Simons, "War Damage Report," 14 January 1942, NHC, Wallin Papers.

8. Some students of the battle have now put the number at nine.

9. Commanding officer, "USS *Oklahoma*. Damage Sustained during the Action at Pearl Harbor, December 7, 1941. Preliminary Report," 20 December 1941, NHC, Wallin Papers.

10. W. H. Hobby, "Rescue and Salvage Work, USS *Oklahoma*," 12 December 1941, National Archives, Record Group 181 (hereafter NA, RG 181).

11. "USS *Pennsylvania* Bomb Damage," war damage report no. 14, 1 June 1942, NA, RG 181. Hereafter *Pennsylvania* war damage report.

12. H. E. Kimmel, "Report of Action of 7 December 1941, Enclosure: Partial Narrative of Events," 21 December 1941, NA, RG 181.

13. Log of *Shaw*, NHC, Wallin Papers.

14. Commanding officer, USS *Shaw*, "War Damage Report," 29 January 1942, NA, RG 181. Hereafter *Shaw* war damage report.

15. Eric C. Caren, *Pearl Harbor Extra: A Newspaper Account of the United States Entry into World War II* (Edison, N.J.: Castle Books, 2001).

16. "USS *Nevada* Torpedo and Bomb Damage," war damage report no. 17, 18 September 1942, NA, RG 181. Hereafter *Nevada* war damage report.

17. Lt. Cdr. Francis Thomas had been in temporary command when the ship initially ran aground near the *Shaw*. The commanding officer, Capt. Francis W. Scanland, boarded a few moments later and

directed her final beaching at Waipio Point. Thomas later received the Navy Cross for the action, and Scanland believed it was partly because he was thought to have been in command when the ship beached at Waipio Point, thus saving her from sinking. Months later, upon hearing that Thomas had received the decoration, Scanland wrote to the chief of naval personnel to correct that impression. F. W. Scanland, "USS *Nevada*, Grounding of, December 7, 1941," 2 September 1942, NA, RG 181.

18. Commanding officer, "USS *Nevada*, Report of December 7, 1941 Raid," 15 December 1941, NHC, Wallin Papers.

19. Ibid.; *Nevada* war damage report.

20. "Report of Damage, Battleships," 8 December.

21. USS *Nevada* situation report, 8 December 1941, NHC, Wallin Papers.

22. Edward C. Raymer, *Descent into Darkness: Pearl Harbor, 1941: A Navy Diver's Memoir* (Novato, Calif.: Presidio Press, 1996), p. 23.

23. Commanding officer, "USS *California*. Report of Raid (Revised), Dec. 7, 1941," 22 December 1941, NHC, Wallin Papers. Hereafter "*California* Report of Raid (Revised)."

24. "Report of Damage, Battleships," 7 December.

25. Log of *California*, NA, RG 24.

26. Ibid.

27. "USS *California* Torpedo and Bomb Damage," war damage report no. 21, 28 November 1942, NA, RG 181. Hereafter *California* war damage report. There are discrepancies between the war damage report, which is partly based on later diver reports submitted during salvage operations, and the initial damage reports submitted by the *California*, as to how many manholes were off or were loosened.

28. "*California* Report of Raid (Revised)."

29. Ibid.

30. H. N. Wallin, memorandum no. 4 , "Visit to *California* at 2300," 7 December 1941, NHC, Wallin Papers.

31. Log of *California*, NA, RG 24.

32. Commanding officer, USS *California*, "Information on Damage Control," 26 January 1942, NHC, Wallin Papers.

33. Ibid.

CHAPTER 2. BIRTH OF THE SALVAGE ORGANIZATION

1. Thomas Buell, *The Quiet Warrior: A Biography of Admiral Raymond A. Spruance* (Boston: Little, Brown and Co., 1974), p. 97.

2. Log of *Enterprise*, NA, RG 24.

3. H. N. Wallin, "Memorandum Covering Apparent Damage to Vessels in Pearl as of 1600 This Date," 7 December 1941, NHC, Wallin Papers.

4. H. N. Wallin, "Memorandum Covering Apparent Damage to Vessels in Pearl as of 1345 This Date," 7 December 1941, NHC, Wallin Papers.

5. H. N. Wallin, memorandum no. 5, "Report of Damage to Vessels Not Previously Reported," 0200, 8 December 1941, NHC, Wallin Papers.

6. "Report of the Repair & Salvage of Naval Vessels Damaged at Pearl Harbor, T.H. on December 7, 1941, by the Salvage Officer," 13 July 1942, NA, RG 181.

7. D. H. Clark, "Battleship Condition as Reported by Commander Kranzfelter and Lieutenant Mandelkorn at 1000," 7 December 1941, NHC, Wallin Papers.

8. H. N. Wallin, memorandum no. 7, "Check up of the Situation on the Battleships as of 1600 This Date," 9 December 1941, NHC, Wallin Papers.

9. United States Congress, *Pearl Harbor Attack: Hearings before the Joint Committee on the Investigation of the Pearl Harbor Attack*, 39 vols., 79th Cong. (Washington, D.C.: U.S. Government Printing Office, 1946) (hereafter PHA), part 24, pp. 1368–69.

10. Stark's nickname.

11. Commanding officer, "Supplementary Report of Damage Attendant to Bomb Near-Hit, USS *Honolulu*," undated, NHC, Wallin Papers.

12. "Report of Damage, Battleships," 7 December.

13. Planning officer, memorandum for the manager, 8 December 1941; commanding officer, USS *Maryland*, "Damage Sustained in Action December 7, 1941," 19 December 1941, NHC, Wallin Papers.

14. Planning officer, memorandum for the manager, "Drydock No. 2 Dimensions," 8 December 1941, NHC, Wallin Papers.

15. Log of *Case*, NA, RG 24.

16. PHA, part 37, p. 1286.

17. Later examination of the captured submarine showed that it would have been nearly impossible to sneak under the net without being detected.

18. PHA, part 24, p. 1649.

19. Log of *Enterprise*, NA, RG 24.

20. William F. Halsey and J. Bryan III, *Admiral Halsey's Story* (New York: McGraw-Hill, 1947), p. 83

21. PHA, part 24, p. 1373.

22. Ibid., p. 1496.

23. PHA, part 37, p. 1287.

24. Ibid., p. 1275.

25. PHA, part 24, p. 1501.

26. Ibid., p. 1500.

27. Signal log of *Antares*, NA, RG 24.

28. PHA, part 24, pp. 1650–52.

29. Various action reports, http://www.history.navy.mil.

30. Base Force salvage memorandum (hereafter BFSM) 17 December 1941. All Base Force salvage memoranda cited here are from NA, RG 181.

31. BFSM 14 December 1941.

32. "Pearl Harbor Navy Medical Activities," http://www.history.navy.mil/faqs/faq66-5.htm.

33. PHA, part 37, p. 1271.

34. Commanding officer, USS *California*, "Report of Raid, December 7, 1941," 13 December 1941, NHC, Wallin Papers.

35. "*California* Report of Raid (Revised)."

36. W. H. Hobby, "Rescue and Salvage Work, USS *Oklahoma*," 12 December 1941, NA, RG 181.

37. Commander, Battleships, Battle Force, "Attack at Pearl Harbor by Japanese Planes on December 7, 1941," 19 December 1941, NHC, Wallin Papers.

38. Edward C. Raymer, *Descent into Darkness: Pearl Harbor, 1941: A Navy Diver's Memoir* (Novato, Calif.: Presidio Press, 1996), pp. 26–27.

39. Paul Stillwell, *Air Raid Pearl Harbor!* (Annapolis: Naval Institute Press, 1981), p. 252.

40. http://ussutah.org/.

41. C. A. Bartholomew, *Mud, Muscles, and Miracles: Marine Salvage in the United States Navy* (Washington, D.C.: Naval Historical Center and Naval Sea Systems Command, 1990), p. 83.

42. E. E. Berthold, "Recommendation of Gunner R. G. Manthei, U.S. Navy, for Temporary Promotion to Chief Gunner, U.S. Navy," 18 February 1942, NA, RG 181.

43. This unit would also be known as Advance Base Repair Units 1 and 2 and Repair and Salvage Units 1 and 2. Here it will called the Mobile Repair Unit.

44. H. N. Wallin, memorandum no. 8, "Report of the Situation on Various Ships as of 0900 This Date," 10 December 1941, NHC, Wallin Papers.

45. "How a Dead War Fleet Came Back to the Fight," *Washington Star*, 17 June 1945.

46. Manager's notice no. 171/41, 11 December 1941, NA, RG 181.

47. H. E. Kimmel, Pacific Fleet confidential memorandum no. 9CM-41, "Maintenance of Ships, Pacific Fleet," 16 December 1941, NA, RG 181.

48. *Pennsylvania* war damage report.
49. Log of *Vestal*, NA, RG 24.
50. BFSM 15 December 1941.

CHAPTER 3. GETTING DOWN TO WORK

1. Manager's notice no. 165, "Pearl Harbor Priority List," 9 December 1941, NHC, Wallin Papers.
2. Pacific Bridge Company salvage drawing no. PHS-E520, "Raising USS *California*. Miscellaneous Data from Notes by J. O. Foster," 13 March 1942, NA, RG 181.
3. Battle Force memorandum no. 7, 9 December 1941, NHC, Wallin Papers.
4. Log of *California*, NA, RG 24.
5. Ibid.
6. Battle Force memorandum no. 9, "Report of the Situation on Various Ships as of 0900 This Date," 10 December 1941, NHC, Wallin Papers.
7. "USS *Helena* Torpedo and Bomb Damage (War Damage Report)," 21 February 1942, NA, RG 181.
8. "USS *Oglala* Torpedo and Bomb Damage," war damage report no. 2, 14 February 1942, NA, RG 181.
9. E. C. Holtzworth, memorandum to planning superintendent, "Preliminary Salvage Operations of the *Shaw*," 13 December 1941, NA, RG 181.
10. Ibid.
11. "USS *Nevada*—Summary of Action Taken," undated, NA, RG 181.
12. Design superintendent, "USS *Nevada*—Buoyancy," 22 December 1941, NA, RG 181.
13. Ibid.
14. W. R. Furlong, "Diving Operations in Connection with Refloating Vessels Damaged by Enemy Action at Pearl Harbor, 7 December, 1941," 16 March 1944, NA, RG 181.
15. Norm Wallin to author, 11 November 2002.
16. W. C. G. Church, memorandum to H. F. Bruns, "Salvage Operations on USS *California*," 11 December 1941, NA, RG 181.
17. "USS *Tennessee* Bomb Damage," war damage report no. 22, 15 November 1942, NA, RG 181.
18. Ibid.
19. "Report of Damage, Battleships," 8 December.
20. Battle Force memorandum no. 7, 9 December 1941, NHC, Wallin Papers.
21. H. N. Wallin, memorandum no. 8, "Report of the Situation on Various Ships as of 0900 This Date," 10 December 1941, NHC, Wallin Papers.
22. "Activity of Ordnance Salvage Group (Material)," undated log of *Utah* ordnance personnel, NA, RG 181.
23. Commandant, Navy Yard Pearl Harbor, to Chief, BuOrd, "Salvaged Ordnance Material," 29 January 1942, NA, RG 181.
24. PHA, part 24, p. 1515.
25. CinCPac, "Salvage Work, Maintaining a Careful Record Of," 23 December 1941, NHC, Wallin Papers.
26. W. R. Furlong, "A Method of Manufacturing an Ice Barrier over Hull Openings to Expedite Salvage Operations," 2 February 1942, NA, RG 181.
27. H. N. Wallin, memorandum for file, "Progress of Work on Damaged Ships," 20 December 1941, NHC, Wallin Papers.
28. Design superintendent, USS *Oglala* salvage memorandum no. 1, "USS *Oglala*—Salvage—Removal of Weight," 15 December 1941, NHC, Wallin Papers.
29. Design superintendent, USS *Oglala* salvage memorandum no. 2, "USS *Oglala* (CM-4)—Salvage Of," 18 December, 1941, NHC, Wallin Papers.

30. BFSM 17 December 1941.

31. E. C. Holtzworth, memorandum to planning superintendent, "USS *Shaw*, Salvage Memorandum No. 3," 16 December 1941, NA, RG 181.

32. Commander, Battle Force, memorandum for flag secretary, 24 December 1941, NHC, Wallin Papers.

33. Homer Wallin, "Rejuvenation at Pearl Harbor," Naval Institute *Proceedings*, December 1946, p. 1530.

34. H. N. Wallin, memorandum no. 8, "Report of the Situation on Various Ships as of 0900 This Date," 10 December 1941, NHC, Wallin Papers.

35. BFSM 20 December 1941.

36. BFSM 17 December 1941.

37. BFSM 19–22 December 1941.

38. Commanding officer, USS *Perry*, "Japanese Air Raid on Pearl Harbor, December 7, 1941," 22 December 1941, http://www.history.navy.mil.

39. http://www.cruiserscout.com/navy4.html.

40. W. V. Hamilton, memorandum for H. N. Wallin, Force Material Officer, 19 December 1941, NHC, Wallin Papers.

41. PHA, "Report by the Secretary of the Navy to the President," exhibit 49.

CHAPTER 4. TRIAL AND ERROR

1. Senior surviving officer, USS *West Virginia*, "Action of December 7, 1941—Report Of," 11 December 1941, http://www.history.navy.mil.

2. Com14 to OpNav, serial 152225, undated, NHC, Wallin Papers.

3. Force material officer, "USS *Cassin*, USS *Downes*—Salvage Of," 15 December 1941, NHC, Wallin Papers.

4. It was the same bomb that had penetrated the upper and main decks, exited the ship at the second deck level causing the hole mentioned above, and detonated alongside between the first and second platforms. All of this was surmised later.

5. *Nevada* war damage report.

6. H. N. Wallin to Adm. W. A. Brockett, Chief of BuShips, 16 April 1964, courtesy of Norm Wallin.

7. Pacific Bridge Company drawing no. PHS-D502, "Raising USS *California*. Full Cell Cofferdam Scheme #1," 7 January 1942, NA, RG 181.

8. Pacific Bridge Company drawing no. PHS-D503, "Raising USS *California*. Partial Cell Cofferdam Scheme #2," 3 January 1942, NA, RG 181.

9. In descriptions of this process, the phrase "tremie concrete" denotes the method of delivering the mixture underwater rather than a particular kind of concrete. Some writers describing the salvage of the *West Virginia* erroneously refer to "tremic concrete," evidently mistaking the *e* in the original documents for a *c*.

10. Pacific Bridge Company drawing no. PHS-D504, "Raising USS *California*. Partial Single Wall Cofferdam Scheme #3," 2 January 1942, NA, RG 181.

11. F. I. Winant Jr. (USS *Medusa*), handwritten memo to F. C. Stelter Jr., 22 December 1941, NA, RG 181.

12. Subsequent investigation of the undamaged uptake gratings tended to discount the "bomb down the stack" theory.

13. Commanding officer, USS *Arizona*, "Material Damage Sustained in Attack on December 7, 1941," 28 January 1942, NHC, Wallin Papers.

14. Paul Stillwell, *Battleship Arizona* (Annapolis: Naval Institute Press, 1991), pp. 255–56.

15. BFSM 23 December 1941.

16. Commanding officer, "Salvage Operations, USS *Arizona*," 15 December 1941, NA, RG 181.

17. Diving officer, "Diving Operations in Connection with the Salvage of the USS *Arizona*," 15 November 1943, NA, RG 181.

18. CinCPac, "Summary of Damage Sustained by Ships of Pacific Fleet from Enemy Attacks at Pearl Harbor, 7 December 1941," 21 December 1941, NHC, Wallin Papers.

19. F. C. Stelter Jr., "Accessible Ordnance Material Remaining on the *Arizona*," 11 January 1942, NA, RG 181.

20. "Activity of Ordnance Salvage Group (Material)," undated log of *Utah* ordnance personnel, NA, RG 181.

21. Salvage Organization memorandum to Commander, Base Force, 27 December 1941, NA, RG 181.

22. Commanding officer, "USS *Utah*—Material Damage," 7 January 1942, NA, RG 181.

23. http://www.historyhall.com/Utah/utahpage.htm.

24. BFSM 21 December 1941.

25. Ship superintendent, USS *West Virginia*, "Examination of Underwater Damage of USS *West Virginia*," 3 January 1942, NA, RG 181.

26. Salvage officer, "USS *West Virginia*, Report of Salvage Of," 15 June 1942, NA, RG 181.

27. BFSM 3 January 1942.

28. http://www.usswestvirginia.org/stories.

29. Ship superintendent, USS *West Virginia*, "Daily Log of Repair and Salvage Operations. Report of Work on USS *West Virginia*," 31 December 1941, NA, RG 181.

30. Dale E. Cloutier, email to author, 16 August 2001.

31. BFSM 19 December 1941.

32. BFSM 21 December 1941.

33. BFSM 19 December 1941.

34. BFSM 27 December 1941.

35. BFSM 28 December 1941.

36. BFSM 31 December 1941.

37. BFSM 28 December 1941.

38. BFSM 24 December 1941.

39. PHA, part 24, pp. 1387–88.

40. Ibid., p. 1708.

41. Ibid., p. 1539.

42. Ibid., p. 1478.

43. H. N. Wallin to Adm. W. A. Brockett, Chief of BuShips, 16 April 1964, courtesy of Norm Wallin.

CHAPTER 5. THE NAVY YARD TAKES OVER

1. G. P. Steele to author, 7 November 2002.

2. H. N. Wallin, "Salvage Division—Comments Regarding, on Taking over January 9, 1942," 11 January 1942, NHC, Wallin Papers.

3. Log of *Shaw*, NHC, Wallin Papers.

4. BFSM 27 December 1941.

5. A. E. Graham, Pacific Bridge Company, "Contract Noy-5049—Salvage Operations—General," 16 February 1942, NA, RG 181.

6. "Activity of Ordnance Salvage Group (Material)," undated log of *Utah* ordnance personnel, NA, RG 181.

7. U.S. Mobile Salvage and Repair Unit 1, "Progress Report of Work on USS *Shaw*," 7–30 January 1942, NA, RG 181.

8. F. C. Stelter Jr., "USS *Utah* Ammunition—Salvage Of," 6 January 1942, NA, RG 181. This sec-

tion on the *Utah* ordnance salvage is based upon F. C. Stelter Jr., memorandum for H. C. Jones, "Resume of Salvage Operations Being Conducted on the USS *Utah*," 2 February 1942; the "Activity of Ordnance Salvage Group (Material)" memorandum; and the daily Salvage Division memorandum from Wallin to Furlong during that period (all NA, RG 181).

9. The Salvage Division daily memorandum and the *Utah*'s ordnance salvage group log differ as to the exact location of the holes that were cut.

10. F. C. Stelter Jr., memorandum for H. C. Jones, "Resume of Salvage Operations Being Conducted on the USS *Utah*," 2 February 1942, NA, RG 181.

11. Commandant, Navy Yard Pearl Harbor, dispatch 210131 to BuPers, September 1942, NA, RG 181.

12. "Activity of Ordnance Salvage Group (Material)," NA, RG 181.

13. BFSM 1 January 1942.

14. BFSM 4 January 1942.

15. Commandant, Navy Yard Pearl Harbor, "Salvaged Ordnance Material," 29 January 1942, NA, RG 181.

16. U.S. Mobile Salvage and Repair Unit 1, "Progress Report of Work on USS *Downes*," 4–9 January 1942, NA, RG 181.

17. U.S. Mobile Salvage and Repair Unit 1, "Progress Report of Work on USS *Cassin*," 4–9 January 1942, NA, RG 181.

18. W. L. Painter, memorandum for H. N. Wallin, "Daily Report," 26 January 1942, NA, RG 181.

19. H. N. Wallin, "Salvage of USS *California* and USS *West Virginia*—Delay on Account of Lack of Carpenters," 6 February 1942, NHC, Wallin Papers.

20. L. Curtis, "*Nevada*, Preparations for Unwatering," 30 December 1941, and H. L. Thompson, memorandum for all heads of departments, 31 December 1941, NA, RG 181.

21. *Nevada* war damage report, p. 24.

22. "Restoration of Unwatered Compartments, Damaged Machinery, and Disposition of Recovered Material, Scrap and Trash," salvage bulletin no. 14A, 14 March 1942, NHC, Wallin Papers.

23. "Recovered Material, Landing Of," salvage bulletin no. 6, 26 January 1942, NHC, Wallin Papers.

24. F. M. Earle, "USS *Oglala*—Salvage," 19 January 1942, NHC, Wallin Papers.

25. W. R. Furlong, "Organization for Handling Salvaged Material and Disposition of Material," 11 January 1942, NA, RG 181.

26. W. White, "Daily Salvage Record," 10 January 1942, NA, RG 181.

27. C. W. Nimitz, "Airplane Situation, Hawaiian Area," 7 January 1942, NA, RG 181.

28. H. N. Wallin, "Resume Report of Salvage Operations for Forwarding to Navy Yard," 20 January 1942, NA, RG 181.

29. Salvage bulletin no. 3, 21 January 1942; no. 2, 21 January 1942; and no. 11, 30 January 1942, NHC, Wallin Papers.

CHAPTER 6. THE SOUND OF HAMMERS AND SAWS

1. G. M. Ankers, "Report of Salvage Work," 18 January 1942, NHC, Wallin Papers.

2. G. M. Ankers, "Report of Salvage Work," 29 January 1942, and G. M. Ankers, "Report of Salvage Operations," 30 January 1942, NHC, Wallin Papers.

3. E. C. Holtzworth, memorandum for the planning superintendent, "Flotation of USS *Nevada*," 22 January 1942, NA, RG 181.

4. PHA, part 39, pp. 1–21.

5. "USS *Cassin* and USS *Downes* Bomb Damage," war damage report no. 13, 28 May 1942, NHC.

6. C. Gillette, "USS *Cassin* and USS *Downes*—Current Salvage and Ultimate Disposition," 5 January 1942, NHC, Wallin Papers.

7. W. L. Calhoun, "Maintenance of Ships—U.S. Pacific Fleet," 31 December 1941, NA, RG 181.

8. F. Earle, "USS *Downes*—Notes on Conference January 7," 7 January 1942, NHC, Wallin Papers.

9. U.S. Mobile Salvage and Repair Unit 1, "Report of Damage to Hull, USS *Downes*," undated, NA, RG 181.

10. G. M. Ankers, "Report of Salvage Operations," 5 February 1942, NHC, Wallin Papers.

11. C. M. Parker, "Report of the Department of Industrial Medicine from August 13, 1941 to June 30, 1942," 30 June 1942, NHC, Wallin Papers.

12. H. N. Wallin, "USS *Nevada* (BB36)—Time and Condition of Delivery to Navy Yard," 14 February 1942, NHC, Wallin Papers.

13. It was subsequently discovered that the blister plating above the torpedo hole had buckled outward slightly as a result of the hit, which prevented the upper bearing edge of the patch from seating properly against the shell.

14. M. L. McClung, "USS *Oglala*—Salvaging Of," 27 February 1942, NHC, Wallin Papers.

15. Pearl Harbor Repair and Salvage Unit, "Progress Report of Work on USS *Cassin*, 31 January 1942–13 February 1942" and "Progress Report of Work on USS *Downes*, 5 February 1942–6 February 1942," undated, NA, RG 181.

16. Log of *Shaw*, NHC, Wallin Papers.

17. F. C. Stelter Jr., "USS *Utah*—Report on Cessation of Ordnance Salvage Operations," 13 February 1942, NA, RG 181.

18. Salvage Division memorandum, 14 February 1942, NA, RG 181.

19. Taped interview with H. N. Wallin, 3 January 1979, courtesy of Norm Wallin.

20. E. C. Genereaux, "Daily Report on the USS *West Virginia*," 27 February 1942, NA, RG 181.

21. Emile Genereaux, *The Captain Loved the Sea* (Eureka, Calif.: Humbolt County Maritime Museum, 1985), p. 69.

22. Wallin interview, 3 January 1979.

23. Edward C. Raymer, *Descent into Darkness: Pearl Harbor, 1941: A Navy Diver's Memoir* (Novato, Calif.: Presidio Press, 1996), pp. 94–95.

24. H. N. Wallin, "Contract Noy-5049—Services of Contractors in Connection with Salvage Work," 24 February 1942, NA, RG 181.

25. Ibid.

26. C. Gillette, "Contract Noy-5049—Services of Contractors in Connection with Salvage Work," 25 February 1942, NA, RG 181.

27. A. E. Graham, Pacific Bridge Company, "Contract Noy-5049—Salvage Operations—General," 16 February 1942, NA, RG 181.

28. H. N. Wallin, "Contract Noy-5049—Services of Contractors in Connection with Salvage Work," 24 February 1942, NA, RG 181.

29. W. R. Furlong, "Salvage Operations on USS *Arizona*, USS *Oklahoma*, USS *Utah*—Decision as to Extent Of," 15 March 1942, NA, RG 181.

30. Analysis of the coral bottom would indicate that its porosity was such that the water level could not be reduced sufficiently within a cofferdam. Water would continue to seep in from the bottom, and the pumps would not be able to keep up.

31. Between 1924 and 1931, a British engineer named Ernest Cox had successfully raised thirty-two sunken battleships, cruisers, and destroyers that the Imperial German Fleet had scuttled at Scapa Flow on 21 June 1919 rather than surrender them to the British. Cox raised many with the use of compressed air, some of them upside down.

32. The *Hornet*'s destination was Alameda, not Pearl Harbor. She was to be loaded with a special squadron of Army Air Force B-25s under the command of Jimmy Doolittle for a hit-and-run raid on the Japanese mainland.

CHAPTER 7. NO TIME TO BE CONCERNED WITH PERSONAL COMFORT

1. *California* war damage report.

2. "Salvage Operations on the USS *California*, Preliminary Schedule For," salvage bulletin no. 22, 2 March 1942, NA, RG 181.

3. W. White, "Comment on Salvage Officer's Letter of March 16, 1942," 17 March 1942, and H. N. Wallin, "USS *West Virginia*, Schedule of Operations," 8 March 1942, NHC, Wallin Papers.

4. K. F. Horne, "Report of Work Accomplished by the Unit during Period January 10 to January 16, 1942, Inclusive," 18 January 1942, NA, RG 181.

5. C. A. Peterson, "USS *California* (BB44)—Salvage, Request for Clarification of Directives," 7 March 1942, NA, RG 181.

6. W. R. Furlong, "USS *California* (BB44)—Salvage, Request for Clarification of Directives Concerning," 12 March 1942, NA, RG 181.

7. This section on the *Oglala* is based on H. N. Wallin, "USS *Oglala*, Schedule of Operations for Righting," salvage bulletin no. 35, 9 April 1942; H. N. Wallin, "USS *Oglala*—Report of Salvage Of," 3 July 1942; and H. N. Wallin, "Status of Salvage Work as of Noon Today" (a daily report from Wallin to Gillette and the successor to the daily Base Force salvage memorandum), 24 March–10 April 1942 (all NA, RG 181).

8. H. N. Wallin, "Restoration of Unwatered Compartments, Damaged Machinery and Disposition of Recovered Material, Scrap and Trash," salvage bulletin no. 14, 13 February 1942, NHC, Wallin Papers.

9. The *California*, *Maryland*, and *West Virginia* had General Electric, the *Tennessee* and *Colorado* Westinghouse.

10. H. N. Wallin, "Dehumidifier Units Now Available for Salvage Purposes," salvage bulletin no. 19, 19 February 1942, NHC, Wallin Papers.

11. C. W. Nimitz, "USS *California* and USS *West Virginia*—Reconditioning of Main Propulsion Equipment Subsequent to Salvage of Vessels," 18 February 1942, NHC, Wallin Papers.

12. Pacific Bridge Company salvage drawing no. PHS-E520, "Raising USS *California*. Miscellaneous Data from Notes by J. O. Foster," 13 March 1942, NA, RG 181.

13. H. N. Wallin, "Status of Salvage Work as of Noon Today," 15 March 1942, NA, RG 181.

14. H. N. Wallin, "Salvage and Reconditioning Work—Speeding up Of," salvage bulletin no. 29, 16 March 1942, NHC, Wallin Papers.

15. H. N. Wallin to E. Cochrane, 5 March 1942, NHC, Wallin Papers.

16. Edward C. Raymer, *Descent into Darkness: Pearl Harbor, 1941: A Navy Diver's Memoir* (Novato, Calif.: Presidio Press, 1996), pp. 110–11.

17. Ibid., p. 119.

18. W. R. Furlong, "Diving Operations in Connection with Refloating Vessels Damaged by Enemy Action at Pearl Harbor, 7 December, 1941," 16 March 1944, NA, RG 181.

19. H. E. Haynes, "Diving Operations in Connection with the Salvage of the USS *Nevada*," 25 April 1942; "Diving Operations in Connection with the Salvage of the USS *California*," 5 May 1942; and "Diving Operations in Connection with the Salvage of the USS *West Virginia*," 23 June 1942, NA, RG 181.

20. W. R. Furlong, "Diving Operations in Connection with Refloating Vessels Damaged by Enemy Action at Pearl Harbor, 7 December, 1941," 16 March 1944, NA, RG 181.

21. C. Gillette, "The Commandant's Conference on the Status of Work on Vessels under Repair," 5 April 1942, NA, RG 181.

22. C. Gillette, "Conservation of Materials—Elimination of Waste," salvage bulletin no. 31, 3 April 1942, NHC, Wallin Papers.

23. H. N. Wallin, "USS *California*, General Schedule of Salvage," salvage bulletin no. 32, 4 April 1942, NA, RG 181.

24. H. N. Wallin, "USS *California*, Report of Salvage Of," 15 April 1942, NA, RG 181.

25. J. Warris, "Report on Explosion in USS *California*, Sunday, April 5, 1942," 6 April 1942, NHC, Wallin Papers.

26. John Anderson Miller, *Men and Volts at War: The Story of General Electric in World War II* (New York: McGraw-Hill, 1947), pp. 48–49.

27. Raymer, *Descent into Darkness*, pp. 82–85.

28. Emile Genereaux, *The Captain Loved the Sea* (Eureka, Calif.: Humbolt County Maritime Museum, 1985), pp. 68–69.

CHAPTER 8. A MONOTONOUS, BACKBREAKING JOB

1. J. A. McNally, memorandum for H. N. Wallin, "USS *Arizona* and USS *California*, Decision as to Extent of Salvage Operations to Be Undertaken," 10 March 1942, NHC, Wallin Papers.

2. M. L. McClung, memorandum to H. N. Wallin, "USS *Oglala*," 23 April 1942, NHC, Wallin Papers.

3. "Salvage Report of Captain William White USN (Ret)," http://www.wvculture.org/history/usswv/salvage.html; "USS *West Virginia*—Ship's Organization and Salvage Instructions," 5 May 1942, NHC, Wallin Papers.

4. H. N. Wallin, "Rigging for Services—Lighting, Water, Steam, Ventilation, Removing of Trash, and Compressed Air in Connection with Salvage Operations," salvage bulletin no. 21, 27 February 1942, NHC, Wallin Papers.

5. "Salvage Report of Captain William White USN (Ret)," http://www.wvculture.org/history/usswv/salvage.html; "USS *West Virginia*—Ship's Organization and Salvage Instructions," 5 May 1942, NHC, Wallin Papers.

6. W. White, "Directive for Salvage of Personal Effects from Lockers and Storerooms," 13 May 1942, NHC, Wallin Papers.

7. H. N. Wallin, "Status of Salvage Work as of Noon Today," 17 May 1942, NA, RG 181.

8. H. N. Wallin, "USS *Oglala*—Report of Salvage Of," 3 July 1942, NA, RG 181.

9. Daily survey and draft readings of the USS *West Virginia*, NHC, Wallin Papers.

10. E. R. Weaver, "Four Point Moor," 12 May 1942, NHC, Wallin Papers.

11. The Pearl Harbor Navy Yard Design Section's summary of the damage, "Structural Report of Damage to USS *West Virginia*," technical report no. R-BB48-11/1-15, NHC, Wallin Papers, concluded that as many as seven torpedoes and two dud bombs had hit the battleship. In recent years, as has been the case with the *Oklahoma*, others have concluded that she was struck by nine torpedoes.

12. "USS *West Virginia*—Salvage Operations Preparatory to Drydocking, Approximate Schedule Of," salvage bulletin no. 40, 30 May 1942, NA, RG 181.

13. "Salvage Report of Captain William White USN (Ret)," http://www.wvculture.org/history/usswv/salvage.html.

14. W. White, ship's order no. 6-42, "Air Raid Precautions," 31 May 1942, NHC, Wallin Papers.

15. "Precautions to Be Taken on USS *West Virginia* in Case of Air Raid," salvage bulletin no. 38, 26 May 1942, NHC, Wallin Papers.

16. Wallin later reported only sixty-six bodies recovered, yet the daily memoranda from the ship (which made up Wallin's own summary to Gillette) count sixty-seven.

17. H. N. Wallin, "USS *West Virginia*, Report of Salvage Of," 15 June 1942, NA, RG 181.

18. Edward C. Raymer, *Descent into Darkness: Pearl Harbor, 1941: A Navy Diver's Memoir* (Novato, Calif.: Presidio Press, 1996), pp. 125–26.

19. H. N. Wallin, "USS *West Virginia*, Report of Salvage Of," 15 June 1942, NA, RG 181.

20. E. C. Holtzworth, "USS *West Virginia* (BB48)—Undocking during Repairs," 3 June 1942, NHC, Wallin Papers.

21. "Salvage Report of Captain William White USN (Ret)," http://www.wvculture.org/history/usswv/salvage.html.

22. H. N. Wallin to E. Cochrane, 5 March 1942, NHC, Wallin Papers.

23. W. R. Furlong, "The Commandant's Conference on the Status of Work on Vessels under Repair," 4, 11, and 25 May 1942, NA, RG 181.

24. W. R. Furlong, "The Commandant's Conference on the Status of Work on Vessels under Repair," 14 September 1942, NA, RG 181.

25. John Alden, "Up from Ashes—The Saga of *Cassin* and *Downes*," Naval Institute *Proceedings*, January 1961.

26. H. N. Wallin, "USS *Oglala*—Report of Salvage Of," 3 July 1942, NA, RG 181.

27. H. N. Wallin, "USS *Oglala*—Request for Stability Studies," 16 May 1942, NHC, Wallin Papers.

28. H. N. Wallin, "USS *Oglala*—Report of Salvage Of," 3 July 1942, NA, RG 181.

29. Norm Wallin to author, 11 November 2002.

30. Homer Wallin, *Pearl Harbor: How, Why, Fleet Salvage, and Final Appraisal* (Washington, D.C.: Naval History Division, 1968), p. 249.

31. H. N. Wallin, "Status of Salvage Work as of Noon Today," 2 July 1942, NA, RG 181. Wallin's book (*Pearl Harbor: How, Why, Fleet Salvage, and Final Appraisal*) has the fire occurring on 2 July, but his own daily memoranda to Gillette list it as occurring between 1815 and 1830 on 1 July 1942.

32. J. A. Ginella, Pacific Bridge Company, memorandum to H. N. Wallin, 14 July 1942, NA, RG 181.

33. A. E. Graham, Pacific Bridge Company, memorandum to H. N. Wallin, 22 June 1942, NHC, Wallin Papers.

34. W. R. Furlong, "Report on Salvage," 19 July 1942, NA, RG 181.

35. W. R. Furlong, "Officer and Enlisted Personnel Qualified for Salvage Duty," 9 June 1942, NA, RG 181.

36. Tom Gillette to author, 27 February 2002.

37. W. L. Calhoun, "Damaged Ships—Preliminary Estimate of Problem of Salvage," undated, NHC, Wallin Papers.

38. H. N. Wallin, "Status of Salvage Work as of Noon Today," 12 July 1942, NA, RG 181.

39. Unless otherwise noted, information concerning the righting of the *Oklahoma* is from "Salvage of USS *Oklahoma*," Whitaker's 74-page article in vol. 52 of the *Transactions of the Society of Naval Architects and Marine Engineers* (1944).

40. H. N. Wallin, "USS *Oklahoma*—Progress Report on Salvage Of," 18 July 1942, NA, RG 181.

41. Ibid.

42. H. E. Haynes, "Diving Operations in Connection with the Salvage of the USS *Oklahoma*," 9 January 1944, NA, RG 181.

43. John Anderson Miller, *Men and Volts at War: The Story of General Electric in World War II* (New York: McGraw-Hill, 1947), p. 50.

44. J. J. Morton, "Contract Noy-5049, Project No. 13A, Further Salvage Operations—Working Area," 5 April 1943, NA, RG 181.

45. "USS *Oklahoma* Salvage Righting Operations, Salvage Section Personnel Details," 6 March 1943, NA, RG 181.

46. Report, "Inspection Trip of the Assistant Secretary of the Navy, the Honorable Ralph A. Bard, to the Fourteenth Naval District, April 1943," NA, RG 181.

47. Raymer, *Descent into Darkness*, pp. 189–90.

48. Mary E. Cary to C. P. Altland, 11 August 1943, NA, RG 181.

49. W. R. Furlong, "Diving Operations in Connection with Refloating Vessels Damaged by Enemy Action at Pearl Harbor, 7 December 1941," 16 March 1944, NA, RG 181.

50. F. H. Whitaker, "USS *Oklahoma*—Drydocking," salvage bulletin no. 119, 27 December 1943, NA, RG 181.

51. Wallin, among others, had written that the *Oklahoma* had been docked in Dry Dock 2, and subsequent photograph captions have perpetuated this error.

52. L. T. Haugen, "*Oklahoma*—Continuation of Work," 5 February 1944, NA, RG 181.

53. F. H. Whitaker, "Enlisted Personnel—Complement," 1 February 1944, NA, RG 181.

54. Personnel folder, Salvage Operations Unit, 1941–46, NA, RG 181.

55. R. Ghormley, "Righting the *Utah*," 7 February 1944, NA, RG 181.

56. W. R. Furlong, "USS *Utah*—Salvage—Estimate of Time for Completion of Work under Contract," 22 December 1943, and F. H. Whitaker, "Enlisted Personnel—Complement," 1 February 1944, NA, RG 181. Furlong expressed the optimistic view that the *Utah* could be dry-docked; Whitaker estimated that the salvage job would end once she was righted.

57. W. R. Furlong, "USS *Utah*—Salvage—Monthly Report," 15 March 1944, NA, RG 181.

58. Ibid.

59. C. W. Nimitz, "USS *Utah*—Disposal Of," 26 February 1944, NA, RG 181.

EPILOGUE

1. Mrs. Lela Norton to F. H. Whitaker, 10 January 1944, NA, RG 181.

Bibliography

With the exception of Adm. Homer Wallin's book *Pearl Harbor: Why, How, Fleet Salvage, and Final Appraisal,* there are few secondary sources covering the salvage operation in any detail. This work is based almost entirely on primary source material: salvage memoranda, salvage bulletins, daily reports, Bureau of Ships war damage reports, and ships' logs.

PRIMARY SOURCES

Hawaii War Records Depository. University of Hawaii at Manoa Library.

Naval Historical Center. http://www.history.navy.mil.

Papers of Vice Adm. Homer Wallin. Operational Archives. Naval Historical Center. Department of the Navy, Washington, D.C.

Pearl Harbor Naval Shipyard. Commandant's Conference on Repair of Vessels, 1942–43. Record Group 181. National Archives, Pacific Sierra Region, San Bruno, Calif.

———. Commandant's Office, General Correspondence, 1940–47. Record Group 181. National Archives, Pacific Sierra Region, San Bruno, Calif.

———. Pearl Harbor Salvage Unit Records, Ships' Drawings. Record Group 181. National Archives, Pacific Sierra Region, San Bruno, Calif.

———. Salvage Operations Unit, 1941–46. Record Group 181. National Archives, Pacific Sierra Region, San Bruno, Calif.

———. Salvage Work of Base Force, 1942–43. Record Group 181. National Archives, Pacific Sierra Region, San Bruno, Calif.

Ships' Logs. Record Group 24. National Archives, College Park, Md.

USS *Utah.* http://ussutah.org.

USS *West Virginia.* http://www.usswestvirginia.org.

Wallin, H. N. "Some Events in the Life-Time of Homer Norman Wallin." Unpublished autobiographical essay, April 1974. Courtesy of Norm Wallin.

West Virginia Division of Culture and History, State Archives. http://www.wvculture.org.

SECONDARY SOURCES

Alden, John. "Up from the Ashes—The Saga of *Cassin* and *Downes.*" Naval Institute *Proceedings,* January 1961.

Bartholomew, C. A. *Mud, Muscle, and Miracles: Marine Salvage in the United States Navy.* Washington, D.C.: Naval Historical Center and Naval Sea Systems Command, 1990.

Bibliography

Buell, Thomas. *The Quiet Warrior: A Biography of Admiral Raymond A. Spruance*. Boston: Little, Brown and Co., 1974.

Caren, Eric C. *Pearl Harbor Extra: A Newspaper Account of the United States Entry into World War II*. Edison, N.J.: Castle Books, 2001.

Friedman, Norman. *U.S. Battleships: An Illustrated Design History*. Annapolis: Naval Institute Press, 1985.

Friedman, Norman, Arthur Baker, Arnold Lott, and Robert Sumrall. *USS Arizona Ship's Data: A Photographic History*. Honolulu: Arizona Memorial Museum Assn., 1978.

Genereaux, Emile. *The Captain Loved the Sea*. Eureka, Calif.: Humbolt County Maritime Museum, 1985.

Goldstein, Donald, Katherine Dillon, and J. Michael Wenger. *The Way It Was: Pearl Harbor, the Original Photographs*. New York: Brassey's, 1991.

Gores, Joseph. *Marine Salvage: The Unforgiving Business of No Cure, No Pay*. Garden City, N.Y.: Doubleday and Co., 1971.

Halsey, William F., and J. Bryan III. *Admiral Halsey's Story*. New York: McGraw-Hill, 1947.

Hone, Thomas. "The Destruction of the Battle Line at Pearl Harbor." Naval Institute *Proceedings*, December 1977.

"How a Dead Fleet Came Back to Fight." *Washington Star*, 17 June 1945.

Hyde, A. P. *Pearl Harbor, Then and Now: After the Battle*. London: Battle of Britain Prints No. 38, 1982.

Kimmel, Husband E. *Admiral Kimmel's Story*. Chicago: Henry Regnery, 1955.

Landauer, Lyndall and Don. *Pearl: The History of the United States Navy in Pearl Harbor*. South Lake Tahoe, Calif.: Flying Cloud Press, 1999.

Lenihan, Daniel, ed. *Submerged Cultural Resources Study*. Sante Fa, N.M.: Southwest Cultural Resources Center Professional Papers, 1989.

Mason, Theodore. *Battleship Sailor*. Annapolis, Md.: Naval Institute Press, 1982.

Miller, John Anderson. *Men and Volts at War: The Story of General Electric in World War II*. New York: McGraw-Hill, 1947.

Morison, Samuel Eliot. *History of United States Naval Operations in World War II*. Vol. 3, *The Rising Sun in the Pacific*. Boston: Little, Brown and Co., 1948.

Potter, E. B. *Bull Halsey, a Biography*. Annapolis, Md.: Naval Institute Press, 1985.

——— *Nimitz*. Annapolis, Md.: Naval Institute Press, 1976.

Prange, Gordon W., with Donald Goldstein and Katherine V. Dillon. *Dec. 7, 1941: The Day the Japanese Attacked Pearl Harbor*. New York: McGraw-Hill, 1988.

——— *Miracle at Midway*. New York: McGraw-Hill, 1982.

Raymer, Edward C. *Descent into Darkness: Pearl Harbor, 1941: A Navy Diver's Memoir*. Novato, Calif.: Presidio Press, 1996.

Slackman, Michael. *Target: Pearl Harbor*. Honolulu: University of Hawaii Press, 1990.

Stillwell, Paul. *Air Raid Pearl Harbor!* Annapolis, Md.: Naval Institute Press, 1981.

——— *Battleship Arizona*. Annapolis, Md.: Naval Institute Press, 1991.

United States Congress. *Pearl Harbor Attack: Hearings before the Joint Committee on the Investigation of the Pearl Harbor Attack*. 39 vols. 79th Cong. Washington, D.C.: U.S. Government Printing Office, 1946.

Wallin, Homer. *Pearl Harbor: Why, How, Fleet Salvage, and Final Appraisal*. Washington, D.C.: Naval History Division, 1968.

——— "Rejuvenation at Pearl Harbor." Naval Institute *Proceedings*, December 1946.

——— "USS *Oglala*: A Proud and Cantankerous Old Lady." *Naval Engineers Journal*, April 1965.

Whitaker, Francis. "Salvage of USS *Oklahoma*." *Transactions of the Society of Naval Architects and Marine Engineers* 52 (1944).

Young, Stephen. *Trapped at Pearl Harbor: Escape from Battleship* Oklahoma. Annapolis: Naval Institute Press, 1991.

Index

About the Author

Daniel Madsen was born just north of San Francisco in Sausalito, California, where Liberty ships and tankers were built during World War II. His interest in the navy was sparked when, at the age of nine, he watched the USS *New Jersey* glide beneath the Golden Gate Bridge, home from her Vietnam tour. He earned a bachelor's degree in communications from California State University, Sacramento, in 1983. Madsen's first book is *Forgotten Fleet: The Mothball Navy*, published by the Naval Institute Press in 1999. He is currently writing a book about veterans returning to the United States after World War II, how they readjusted to civilian life, and how they affected society. He lives with his wife and two sons on a small farm in the wine country of Northern California.